Stories That Need to Be Told 2021

STORIES

THAT NEED

to be

TOLD

2021

edited by
Jennifer Top

TULIPTREE
PUBLISHING, LLC

CONTENTS

DON'T YOU SWEETHEART ME

HEATHER DEBLING

HE COMES IN, TRACKING MUD ALL ACROSS MY NICE CLEAN FLOOR. "Geez Louise, Hank! I just washed that."

"Aww, Sweetheart, I'm sorry. I didn't notice."

Hank kisses my cheek and puts his arms over my crossed ones, though he should know better than to try and butter me up with all that sweetheart nonsense.

He pulls off his T-shirt, two dark half-moons of sweat under the arms, and throws it across the reception counter. "I've been working something fierce in Number 3. The AC up there's shot to hell." Hank gets two beers out of the mini-bar fridge under the counter and downs the first one in four large gulps.

"There's the mop. Get busy."

He opens the second beer and takes a small sip. "Just let me finish this one, Sweetheart. I haven't stopped today." Taking the beer and a bag of low-sodium pretzels into the back room, he lowers himself into the armchair, the springs aching beneath his weight. "Damn. The remote's gone dead. Could you turn it on for me, Darlene? Since you're up?"

I do, and he tells me I'm the best. The absolute best.

"Soft in the head. That's what I am."

I put my arms round his neck, his skin still clammy, and he pats my hands absentmindedly.

"Who was that woman you were talking to outside the Dollarama this morning?"

1

"This morning?" Hank puts the bag up to his mouth and sucks in the last few crumbs. "Can't think who that might have been."

The commercial break is over. A woman and three men sit on stage while a picture of a baby with a squished-up face and a knitted flower headband is projected on a screen behind Maury.

"Oh, good." Hank burrows himself deeper into the cushions. "It's a Who's the Daddy one."

"Seemed awful familiar," I say. "Threw her arms round your neck. Gave you a big kiss on the cheek."

"Oh! Betsy."

"Is that her name."

"A distant relation." He brushes some flakes of salt and pretzel crust away from the corners of his mouth. "Third cousin twice removed or something like that. On my mother's side. I didn't recognize her, but she said she'd have known me anywhere."

Maury's opened up his big manila envelope and revealed the truth. Two of the would-be fathers high-five each other and dance around, while the real father kneels on the floor, raging, his arms stretched up in a *Why, God, why me?* position.

The reception bell dings. It's the pursed-lipped woman from Number 3 who's here on an extended stay for business. She rubs her thumb against her index finger, like she's trying to get some nonexistent grime off. I run a clean place, except today, for her benefit, there's the muddy footprints and the sweaty T-shirt and the empty beer bottle rocking back and forth on the counter. More fodder for those terrible Tripadvisor pieces I'm sure she's been posting.

"My toilet's clogged," the pursed-lipped woman says. "Again."

Hank comes out, all bare beer-bellied, and tells her he'll be right up.

"That woman," he says. "She'll be the death of me."

TIFF'S GOT HER HAIR done real nice, the curls like shellacked coils that go crunch when she bounces them with her palm. She must have overplucked again because she's drawn in her eyebrows, the dark brown liner looping round almost to the outer corner of her eye, so it looks like she's got a couple of fishhooks stuck in her forehead.

"Geez, Tiff."

"Dress to impress. That's what my Larry always used to say. God rest his soul. Come give Mommy a kiss, Pumpkin."

But Pumpkin, Tiff's shih tzu, has got a mind of her own so it's Tiff who does the coming, not the other way round.

We take Tiff's car, an old Ermine White Chrysler that she keeps talking about selling and never does. A gas guzzler—and a real bitch to parallel park. But the ride's good and smooth.

She buys my coffee since I treated last time even though it's her doing me a favor.

Tiff takes a small sip of her coffee and then says, "Soooooo," the long O puckering her lips.

I open up my folder and pass her a stack of printed out reviews.

"Oh my." Tiff's eyes widen as she reads the review that's on top. "That's a doozy."

It's the one with the subject line *They Should've Paid Me $200 a Night to Stay in This DUMP!* "As if we charge anything near that. Cheap and cheerful, that's our aim."

"You know your target market. Nothing wrong with that."

Tiff scans the rest of the review.

No AC! Unless the AC on their sign stood for the smell of ass and catpiss which there's plenty of. AND paper thin walls. You can hear everyone doing their business. So disgusting!!!

Laid on top of the sheets and didn't take my shoes off. Who knows what was crawling about in that GROSS shit-brown shag carpet!

Shabby out of date decor. The wallpaper was stapled(!) on. Creepy dead things all over. Gave me the willies, all those glass eyes staring at me all night. Maybe the leering shirtless "pool boy" (should say man since he looked to be in his sixties) uses them to spy on guests. Total pervert!

"Is any of it true?"

I begrudgingly admit to the part about the stapled wallpaper. "But only because it was coming down, and that paper was special order."

"If most of it's lies, then it might be faster to highlight what's true rather than what isn't."

Tiff's dearly departed Larry was a lawyer, so she's been advising me until I have enough of a case to seek out a professional. She says there's no point being on the clock until your case is watertight.

"That's one of the older ones." I shuffle through the papers till I find one of the most recent reviews. "It's the new ones we need to focus on. Since she's arrived. Like this one." I pass Tiff another review.

There's an overwhelming smell of body odor when you first enter reception that hangs about the whole building, finding its way even into the crevices of the shower stall, with its mint green tiles and black moldy grout, all of which wouldn't be quite so pathetic if the manageress, an overly blown-up balloon kind of woman with a hee-haw laugh, hadn't boasted of all their improvements during check-in.

"You gotta admit," Tiff says, "there's something almost poetic about it. If it was about someone else, of course."

That Betsy woman comes into the coffee shop. She's wearing a pink and purple windbreaker and matching track pants.

"Seen her before?"

"Nope."

"She was throwing herself at my Hank. Outside the Dollarama. Saw it with my own two eyes."

Tiff nearly chokes on her cruller. "Did you ask who she was?"

"Some distant relation, he says."

"Uh huh, likely story."

"She's clearly desperate. What woman our age has nails painted that color?"

I see a flash of hot pink as Tiff tucks her nails into her palms, and though she seems fine as she sips her dregs, she says she can't drop me home because she's got an appointment in town, and I'm the other direction.

"It's no bother." Though it is.

I call Hank and make him come get me. "Just put up the Back in 15 sign. I doubt anybody'll be banging down the door."

I wait for him, just on the other side of the glass from where that Betsy's sitting. He pulls in and honks, but I gesture for him to come over.

"What?" he yells.

"I wanna treat you."

"Is it my birthday or something?"

He parks and then ambles up toward me. I take his arm and kiss his cheek, and we walk in, me all ready for my introduction to this distant relation, only she's already gone and left, one of the cashiers flicking a none-too-clean J Cloth across the tabletop.

I let go of his arm. "We should get back."

"What about my treat?"

"Get it to go."

I DON'T KNOW HOW long she's been there watching me Windex the side window of reception, shimmying along to some Patsy on the radio, but judging from the look on that Betsy's face, I've been amusing her for some time. Putting on quite the show.

"I'd like a room, please." She rests her arm on the counter and smiles at me, though her eyes are slightly narrowed, sizing up the competition. *Oh, I bet you would*, I think. *Mine.*

"If you're not fully booked?" She points out the window. "I saw the No Vacancy sign, but there were so few cars. I thought I'd take a chance."

"My husband's been meaning to fix that for a dog's age." I roll my eyes. "But you know men. Promises, promises."

We have a laugh. I'm pleased to see she's got some trampy red lipstick on her teeth.

"Funny thing is, we're sort of related." She tells me Hank and she are distant cousins. On her mother's side.

At least they got their stories straight, though my belly starts squirming as I think of the two of them plotting all this.

I pass her the key to Unit 12. "Our nicest." It's also the unit I can see best from reception.

She tells me how kind that is, and I say, "What are family for?"

"WHERE'S THE OLD BALL and chain tonight, Darlene?"

Tall Pete slides into my booth. He puts the half a beer he's been nursing for the better part of an hour down on the table.

"At home."

"And he let you out of the house all by yourself? I'd not allow such a thing if you were my woman."

"As if you'd have a choice."

I usually only come into Flanagan's on Tuesdays for Country and Western night. Tonight, it's hits of the '80s and '90s, an unsuccessful attempt to bring in a younger crowd, and the music's doing my head in. I told Hank to mind the desk while I nipped out for some groceries, but I was really following Betsy. She's at the bar drinking some ruby concoction with an orange slice and a cherry speared through a little pink paper umbrella.

"Come on, Darlene. Let me spin you around the floor once or twice."

"Not tonight, Pete. I'm not in the mood."

"You still like to drive all the boys nuts, don't you, Darlene." Pete shakes his head and runs a hand through his hair, a few flakes of dandruff falling on the collar of his black leather coat. "They've got some choice words for women like you."

"How 'bout women like her?" I nod at Betsy.

"Who?"

"That one at the bar there. Heard anything about her?"

"Why you so interested?"

"She's staying at my place. Gotta reputation to maintain."

"So you want to know if she's had any gentlemen callers?"

I nearly snort my beer out my nostrils. "Jesus, Pete, where the hell'd you learn a phrase like that?"

He looks down at the table and starts pulling at the label on his bottle.

"Go get yourself another beer on me." I push a five-dollar bill across the table. "Since I'm being such a miserable cow tonight. That one must be lukewarm by now."

"That's how I like it." He takes such a small sip the liquid can't do more than wet the tip of his tongue. "I haven't seen her with any men. Except your Hank."

I sit up straighter. "You've seen her with Hank?"

"She's hanging off him right now."

I crane my neck around and sure enough Hank's with her at the bar. Betsy's got her arm draped across his shoulders, and they're both laughing about something.

The song ends and Betsy removes her arm from Hank to clap. A palm clapper. Jesus. Fingers spread like a hot-pink-tipped starfish.

Tall Pete takes a much larger swig of his beer. "Looks like I might get my chance with you after all, eh, Darlene?"

I watch Betsy lead Hank onto the dance floor. She puts both arms up and entwines her fingers round the back of his neck, and they sway to the sound of a wailing guitar. I remember how Hank and I danced one night decades ago in that very spot to "Sea of Heartbreak," him singing along with the *bom bom bom* in that deep bass voice of his, the notes thrumming under my skin as he held us cheek to cheek and spun me about the floor so fast there wasn't even time for my soles to stick like they usually did at Flanagan's. And I knew. Right then I knew: he was the one for me.

But it can all go to shit, can't it? Even after twenty-seven years. Though maybe it was prophetic, that song, all the lost love and loneliness, because that's precisely the sea I'm swimming in now.

I edge myself along the bench, trying to keep my head down and knocking the table in the process. Tall Pete tries to grab his bottle, but he's too late and it rolls off the edge and shatters on the floor. The eyes of everybody in the place turn toward us.

"Darlene?" Hank comes over, Betsy trailing behind him.

"I'll get something to clean it up." I try to stand but Hank's blocking my way.

"You sit, Sweetheart. I'll look after it."

Betsy perches on the bench beside Tall Pete. When I introduce them, she holds out her hand, fingers dangling down, like she's expecting Pete to kiss it. He takes a couple of her fingers between his thumb and index finger and gives them a shake.

Hank returns with a beer for Pete and a few napkins to throw over the mess. Hank holds the beer out, but when Pete tries to take it, Hank doesn't let go. "Should I be jealous?"

Tall Pete twists the bottle free and cradles it against his chest.

Hank turns toward me. "You told me you were going to the grocery store and yet here you are being all lovey-dovey with Pete."

I start to stutter out an excuse, avoiding his gaze, knowing I look guilty even though I've got nothing to be ashamed of.

Hank pats my hand. "Just joshing you, Sweetheart." He plops himself on the bench beside me, and we all have a good laugh, Betsy especially, whose laughs sounds like a yappy Chihuahua.

Hank slings his arm round my shoulders, but I can't let myself sink into him like I usually do. It's like I can still feel her on him, a layer of Betsy between us.

Betsy sighs and says how lucky Hank and I are to have each other.

I nod and smile and then raise my empty glass to my lips for something to do. The ice cracks against my teeth and sends a shudder through my whole body. "Very lucky."

THE LOCAL KIDS HAVE been at our sign again. I only realized when I saw the pursed-lipped woman taking a picture with her cell phone.

AIR CONDITIONED

FREE INTERNET

HEATED POO

Tiff steadies the ladder for me. We've run out of Ls so I've cut the line off one of the Fs. Let the little bastards try and tear them down now. I'm crazy-gluing them in place.

Tiff runs her appraising eye across the grounds. "You know what you need? More curb appeal. Shrubbery, mulch, a lick of paint. That'll bring in new business." Tiff tells me Short Pete has started up a landscape business on the side. "Pay him under the table. A win-win."

We've been brainstorming ways to drum up more business. I asked Tiff if she'd write a good review to balance out the bad, but she said that sounded an awful lot like fraud.

Tiff's in favor of us staging one of the rooms. She's got a new point-and-click and has been online looking at sample images. She found one where they'd laid a long-stemmed rose on the bedspread. "That looks really classy. I'd stay somewhere like that." She also suggested getting a lovey-dovey couple. "Take pictures of them strolling the grounds, lattes in hand." She looked at the half-scorched grass. "After you've had Short Pete see to them, of course."

We go inside for a coffee break. She got our Country Style to go, so I didn't have to leave the desk.

"You caught them at it yet?" Tiff asks while I nuke our coffees. She takes a big bite of her vanilla sprinkle, a few of the hard, colorful dots bouncing off the counter and onto the floor. Tiff's dog Pumpkin hoovers them up.

I shake my head. I've not seen Hank enter the room, and Lord knows I've been watching. I keep wondering if he's been using his ladder, sneaking in her back window like some paunchy, middle-aged Romeo. It gives me pleasure, the thought of him getting stuck, wedged in real tight, the windowsill cutting into his belly. I pray that I'll come upon him like this, legs dangling out her window. *Well, Sweetheart*, I'll say. *Anything you'd like to tell me?*

Tiff nods knowingly. "Biding their time. Waiting for you to let your guard down."

"There might be nothing going on."

"Who you trying to convince?"

Betsy goes to AquaFit Mondays, Wednesdays, and Fridays from 10:00 till 11:30. She came into reception last week and suggested these might be the best times for me to clean her room. Betsy didn't meet my eyes when she said that. It was more like she was looking at a spot just above my head. She's the sort, you can tell, who thinks her shit doesn't stink.

Least it means I can snoop in peace.

Yesterday when I stripped Betsy's bed, I held the sheets up to my nose, seeing if they had the scent of Hank on them. Only I'd forgotten to close the blinds and the pursed-lipped woman saw me as she passed on her way to the pool, one of the room towels folded over her arm.

I balled up the sheets and tossed them into the laundry cart. *As if she needed any more ammunition.*

I look down into my coffee. "It feels hopeless."

Tiff *there-there*s me and then holds up her camera. "At least we can fix your business problems."

Tiff eats the last bite of her donut and then lifts Pumpkin up on the counter and lets her lick the sweetness from her lips, just as the pursed-lipped woman comes into reception looking for more towels. Pumpkin wags her tail at her even though the woman sniffs and holds the back of her hand up to her nose and says she thought our website said there were no animals on the premises.

BETSY SPENDS MOST AFTERNOONS sunning herself by the pool. She slathers herself with coconut oil, the chairs still slick with it a day later when I try and wipe the condensation off them.

She's out there while I'm inside working on my Management Response for Tripadvisor. Trying to sound appreciative for the feedback while also making clear to any prospective customers that 99 percent of the complaints are pure bullshit.

Betsy sits up, pushes her sunglasses up on the top of her head, and then *You hoos!* out to somebody.

Hank ambles over, and she turns over on her belly and reaches back to undo the string at the back of her bikini top. Hank puts some oil on his hands and rubs it into her back, allowing his fingers to brush the sides of her squished-up breasts.

I pound on the keys, sincerely apologizing for the perceived seedy surroundings, for the stapled-on wallpaper, for the unfortunate smell of ass. And most of all, I type before hitting cancel, for the leering pool boy who can't seem to keep his hands off the female clientele.

★ ★ ★

THE PURSED-LIPPED WOMAN comes in while the bleary-eyed man from Number 9 is checking out.

He'd banged on the door at one a.m., and that only meant one thing, but business had been so bad, I couldn't be fussy.

They'd been pawing each other, him and this girl, while I processed his Visa. Giggling like teenagers. The girl looked like one.

The same thought must have passed through his mind. "How old are you?" he asked.

"Nineteen."

"Jesus," he said. "Same age as my daughter."

They barely got the key from me before she was undoing his belt and leading him off on a long, leather leash.

No sign of her this morning.

"Little bitch," the man says. "Cleaned out my wallet, cards and all." He tries to suppress a belch but fails, and reception fills with the smell of stale vomit.

The pursed-lipped woman, no longer content to wait, pipes up. "There's an infestation of flies in my room."

"That does sound serious." The man winks at me, like we're on the same side.

"I can't work with them buzzing around." The pursed-lipped woman has a very important job with the Ministry of Labor. She told me all about it when she checked in, when she still thought me someone worth chatting to. Something about economic development and the trickle-down effect for this depressed region.

"And there's no hot water." She purses her lips even tighter, which I'd not really thought possible.

The bleary-eyed man chuckles. "Well, you get what you pay for, don't you?"

FLANAGAN'S IS BUSTLING. WHEN I get there, Tiff's on stage doing karaoke. She looks a fool up there bumping and grinding to "Elvira." Short Pete is on the side trying to get some line dancing going, but he can't tell his left from his right when he's sober let alone halfway through a bottle of Jack.

I head right for the bar. I've worn my best blouse. It looks like silk and has a white V fringe across the front and down the arms. Mike asks what's my poison, and I tell him it's a Patsy kind of night, but he says, "Someone else is already doing Patsy, can you do somebody else?" I shake my head, and he slides my drink across the bar.

I find an empty booth and press myself into the corner and sulk even though I know Patsy would never be found crying into her drink over a big lump like Hank. It's what I like best about her. You hear the heartbreak in her voice, but you know she's not broken.

Short Pete comes by. "Hey, Tex." He tells the same joke he always does about what you get when you play a country song backwards, to which I usually give my best hardy-har-har because I'm in the service industry. Tonight, though, I've got nothing for Small Pete but a tight hiccupy half-laugh. He's too drunk to notice. As he leaves, he smiles wide, his own teeth side by side with the three false ones he had to max out his line of credit to get, the alternating yellow and white like a row of peaches and cream corn.

Tiff comes and sits by me. "You sure do work up a sweat, don't you? No wonder all those starlets have no meat on their bones doing that every night."

She's a simple soul, Tiff. Thinks the best of people. It's endearing some of the time, but not tonight. "More like they've all got their pointer fingers down their throats worshipping the porcelain god." I drink some of my rum and cola, so the words don't leave a bitter taste in my mouth.

"Decided what you're singing?"

"Not in the mood."

Tiff pats my hand. "Don't you get defeated now."

I hear the familiar strains of "Just a Closer Walk with Thee," one of my favorites, one of the numbers I'm known for at Flanagan's, and I look up at the stage, and there's Betsy, in all her glory. A wispy beehive, glistening skin, pencil-thin heels, and a tight, hot pink number that looks anything but religiously contemplative.

She can't carry a tune, but you'd think I'm the only one who notices because everyone else looks totally captivated. Small Pete sways in drunken time, Mike is frozen mid-polish, and even Tiff dabs discreetly at her eye with a wrinkled-up Kleenex.

"I'm going," I say, not able to keep my voice steady. Tiff reaches out for my hand, but I shake her off. "There's nothing left for me here."

HANK'S BEEN MINDING THE desk, meaning he's asleep with the TV on. Some horror film. I'm surprised he can sleep through all the screaming. I wake him up.

"You're back early."

I nod.

"I might as well go have myself a drink or two then."

"But you were just fast asleep."

He goes in the back and when he comes out, he's reekin' to high heaven of Charlie. "Got my second wind."

"Hank, I've been thinking."

"Uh-oh."

"I'm serious."

He stands halfway out the door. "You've got my full attention."

"Maybe we should sell up. Just get in the car and take one of those trips we used to talk about. You and me and the open road."

"Don't be silly. We're happy here, aren't we?"

"Who wouldn't be? It's such a glamorous life, smelling of Lysol and Pine Sol and scrubbing other people's splashed shit off the underside of toilets."

"Sweetheart—"

"Don't."

He jangles his car keys. "We'll talk about this later."

"You won't be too late?"

"If I am, I'll let myself into one of the empty units, so I don't disrupt your beauty sleep. Nighty night." He blows me a kiss. "Don't let the bedbugs bite."

He leaves, and I find a twangy playlist on YouTube and indulge in too much honky-tonk heartache, listen to all those tunes about some woman's man doin' her wrong, the only kind of music that gives me any heart's ease.

Though I know I shouldn't, I search for "You Belong to Me," and I play it over and over and over again, and before I know it, I've emptied a bottle of cherry brandy, and I'm typing in the comment box about how my husband proposed to me to this very song twenty-seven years ago. How he got down on one knee and said, *Just let me be your man, Darlene. There's nothing else on this whole blessed earth that I'd be any good at but that.*

That used to be a lovely memory, I write, *but now he's a cheating scumbag, throwing away the life we had together.* As Tammy says, *"Sometimes it's hard to be a woman. Giving all your love to just one man."*

But this, I type, *is one woman who will no longer be standing by her man.*

And then I sign my full name and click post.

Which is, of course, a mistake, as nineftlooong87 comments almost immediately that it's no wonder my husband had to look elsewhere since I've probably got breasts that hang down to my belly button and a dried-up you-know-what. Only he didn't type you-know-what, he typed a four-letter word with an asterisk where the U should be, so he didn't get himself banned.

gUrLpOwEr chimes in with an LOL and then the two of them chat each other up while still getting in a few digs at the grotesqueness of my unseen middle-aged body.

The reception bell dings. I dry my eyes before I look up. It's the girl from last night, a different drunken man's loose octopus arms hanging all over her. The man tells me they'd like a room.

I shake my head.

"Come on."

"We're fully booked."

"Like hell you are. The parking lot's empty."

I just stand there with my arms crossed.

The man pulls out his wallet and throws a card on the counter. When I don't take it, he tosses out every single card in there one by one, credit cards, coffee shop loyalty cards, a gym membership, a security key card, like he's dealing a winning hand.

"Bitch!" he spits at me when I refuse to pick any of them up.

"Come on." The girl tugs on his arm. "I know a ditch down the road that's cleaner than this place."

They stagger out as a car pulls in. Betsy's headlights cut across their thighs. The light catches me right in the eye so I can't see properly, but I'm sure there's two heads in the front seat.

I run up to get a better look, but the man presses the girl against the window and blocks my view. I bang for them to get off, to get out of my way, but the girl just presses her middle finger against the pane, the breath of the man's drunken kisses on her neck fogging up the glass. I move to the right. Betsy's gone into her room, but there's Hank at the ice machine, a gold foil topped bottle hanging from one hand.

I go in the back and pull out Hank's shotgun. I load it. Not that I'm actually planning on using it. I've not lost my mind. It's just my father always told me you hold an unloaded gun differently than a loaded one. You can't put the fear of God into anyone if they don't believe you mean business.

I pick up the spare master key and ignore the couple's shrieks of *Crazy bitch!* as I walk across the parking lot and let myself into Lucky Unit 13.

THE REVIEWS ARE RIGHT: paper thin walls. I make a mental note to tell Tiff next time we talk.

I sit on the bed, the gun across my lap. Waiting. They've been at it all night. Lord knows he's never had that kind of stamina with me.

I wish I'd not let Tiff poo-poo my idea of a secret camera. Invasion of privacy she told me. Like I give a shit about that now. It would have been a better way of getting my own back, posting it online, seeing precisely what kind of reviews nineftlooong87 and gUrLpOwEr gave their thrusts and grunts and gasps.

Too late for that now. I rest my fingertips against the cold metal of the barrel.

The sun's just coming up as I ease my key into the door of Unit 12. I push the door open and then yell, "You think you and your fancy woman can make a fool of me?"

Only the man blinking back isn't Hank. It's Tall Pete.

"What the hell you doin', Darlene!" He jumps out of the bed and pulls off the sheet to cover his sagging string-bean body.

And now Betsy's screaming, screaming bloody murder at the top of her lungs, pulling at the fitted sheet to try and cover up her nakedness. I don't know what comes over me, but I fire a shot into the ceiling just to shut her up. And it does. She sits there, her mouth still hanging open but no sound coming out.

"I'm sorry, Pete." I rub my temple. "It was—Oh, God—" I almost start laughing with relief. "It was all a big misunderstanding."

As I back out of the room, the pursed-lipped woman throws open her door. It hits the wall with a bang. Her hair's all mussy, and she holds her robe closed across the front of her.

Jesus, that's all I need right now.

I start to walk toward her to tell her precisely that and see a blur behind her. My Hank hitching up his jeans.

The pursed-lipped woman turns her mouth up at the corners. She's actually got herself quite a lovely smile. Full and red.

Hank comes to the door still doing up his fly. "Darlene? Whatcha doin' with that gun? Sweetheart?"

My heart pounds, a low thudding in my ears that blocks out everything else he tries to say to me. I can't stop looking at the bed; the sheets I took such care to wash and press and smooth down with my palms lie in a crumpled, sweaty pile by the footboard.

I look at Hank and then back at the bed, and as I let him slide the gun from my hand, I can't for the life of me remember what I was worried about losing.

SMOOTH AS SILK

DON CARTER

WITH A YEAR OF HIGH SCHOOL YET TO COMPLETE, I LOOKED WEST from the interstate entrance ramp, stuck out my thumb, and turned my back on New Jersey. Three days later I woke up in a Racine, Wisconsin, hospital. My throat was raw from a stomach pump, my back ached from the impact of a hundred cars plowing into one another, and I had a hangover that would have killed a lesser man. It was this chain of events that brought me to live with my older brother Doug and paved the way for the tremendous bond that was to develop over the next year. Yes, this is the story about the love between me and my first car.

Doug was four years older than me, but we were from two completely different generations. We exemplified that strange gap that existed between the Beach Boys and the Beatles, between pompadours and long hair, between beer drinkers and weed smokers. But we were brothers and he didn't hesitate to drive up to Wisconsin and bring me back to his apartment in the Chicago suburbs to mend . . . as long as I paid for the gas. He called Mom and Dad in New Jersey to tell them the news and they said, "Wisconsin? We thought he was asleep in his bedroom."

While recuperating I decided to finish my senior year of high school in Illinois. I broached the plan to my family and a week later my parents flew to Chicago, we all went to court, and at the wise old age of twenty-one, Doug became my legal guardian. What could possibly go wrong?

Doug and his roommate Mike occupied the two bedrooms in the apartment while I slept on the couch. That arrangement became untenable when my new roomies moved their motorcycles into the living room for the winter. You may be wondering why they didn't move them into the dining room like normal people. That wasn't an option because the bar was in the dining room.

I was in need of an upgrade so I moved my sleeping bag into the walk-in closet located opposite the bathroom. It was a perfect arrangement—just three paces to the bathroom, ten paces to cold beer on tap, and a hundred paces to my new high school.

It soon became clear that if I wanted to go farther than a hundred paces I was going to need a car. Hitchhiking was fine in a pinch, but it didn't make much of an impression on a first date. Doug offered to give me his old '67 Chevy Belair if I could get it running. A few months earlier the beast had rolled to a permanent and lopsided stop in the parking lot after a night of field-hopping. If you're not a Hoosier, Buckeye, or Cornhusker, I should point out that field-hopping is a popular midwestern pastime, much like cow-tipping and beer-shooting.

While hopping through the fields the Chevy sustained a gash in the fuel tank, and when Doug returned to the apartment, a river of escaping gasoline dissolved the parking lot stripes, rearranging them into a swirling yellow stain that zigzagged down to the storm sewer. I later learned that Doug gave me the car because the apartment management told him to get rid of it, and not out of some big brother benevolence. No, he explained, that was not the role of a legal guardian; a legal guardian is someone who buys beer *for* you, and then buys weed *from* you. I guess I would have known that if I had read the legal brief.

I tackled the repairs with the ease and skill of a seasoned mechanic, which is to say I immediately cracked open one of my knuckles with a torque wrench. After three days under the car, two more smashed knuckles, and some truly inspired swearing, the gas tank was repaired. With tremendous pride I took my place behind the wheel, turned the key, and felt the powerful engine roar to life.

I smiled at Doug, who actually left the apartment to witness the momentous event. I slipped the transmission into gear and . . . the driveshaft fell off and rolled down to the yellow-stained storm sewer.

Doug looked like he just remembered there were Pop Tarts in the toaster oven and quickly retreated to the apartment. Sure I was angry, but did I mention he sometimes bought me beer?

Three days and another swollen knuckle later the Chevy had new U-joints and a reattached driveshaft. I was becoming an accomplished mechanic, but I was also running out of knuckles. There were a few parts left over but once the car started I figured they couldn't be very important. I sat quietly in the driver's seat and listened to the motor hum. I depressed the gas pedal and heard the engine ramp up, growing louder and more ominous as I bore down on the pedal. When the engine was at an all-out roar, I backed off the gas and, and, and . . . the engine continued to roar! It wasn't decelerating—it was stuck at full throttle! I slammed the steering wheel, stomped on the gas pedal, and said a quick prayer to Saint Christopher—the patron saint of Chevys.

I turned off the car and waited for my panic to subside. After changing my underwear I came up with an ingenious fix that you won't find in *Auto Repairs for Dummies*. The first step was to install an eight-track tape player. Okay, that didn't fix the gas pedal, but it didn't hurt it either. Second, I created a stirrup-like harness over the gas pedal. To stop the throttle, all I had to do was pull back my foot like I was reining in a horse. In fact I named that old Chevy "Nellie" because that seemed like a good name for a horse, or for the 1967 Chevrolet equivalent—275 horsepower.

Unfortunately, the harness did create one tiny problem. Braking.

Sliding my foot out of the stirrup and over to the brake pedal was a bit cumbersome. Oh, and it was also potentially life threatening. But hey, God gave us two feet for a reason, and I soon learned to brake with my left foot while simultaneously restraining the gas pedal with my right.

Nellie was painted a dull matte combination of primer red and primer gray because, as nine out of ten decorators will tell you, they complement each other so well. The paint was in a camouflage pattern so I couldn't park the car anywhere near an auto body shop for fear of losing it.

Doug's friends had spray-painted obscene pictures on every available surface, which compounded my first date dilemma and also meant I couldn't go out without getting pulled over by the cops. Back in the day, cops would usually cut you a break if you got out of your car and walked back to their car. This was particularly effective if it was raining or twenty degrees below zero because cops don't like to get wet or cold or put down their donuts. If you were a hippie they'd make you stand outside until your nose developed frostbite, but it was better than getting busted.

I usually told the cops my erratic driving was due to Nellie's unique set of tires, and to prove my exceptional mechanical expertise I'd wave my hands about so they could see my swollen knuckles. Nellie had tires from four different manufacturers; there was a Continental, a Michelin, a Firestone, and a Schwinn. The only thing the tires had in common was they were all balder than President Gerald Ford, who was a popular American golfer at the time.

To make Nellie a little less conspicuous and put an end to my nightly visits with the police, I painted her with a roller and a gallon of black house paint, eggshell finish of course. Then I penned *Smooth as Silk* across the hood because, as you have probably already surmised, "less conspicuous" is not something I do well.

Nellie was my escape when I needed diversion, my refuge when I needed solace, and my muse when I needed inspiration. She was my steadfast and dependable steed for two years. Nellie got me where I needed to go, and restraining her sticky throttle helped me develop really photogenic calf muscles. My right leg was so well developed that to this day I still tend to walk in a circle.

One day, without much forethought or gas money, I pointed Nellie east and drove off into the sunrise. It was good to see my parents in New Jersey again, but little did I suspect that the trip would quickly turn disastrous for Nellie and me.

We had been through tough times before. There was the bumpy stretch when Nellie's shock absorbers broke. And the time our relationship stalled due to the gas crisis. By the time we got to New Jersey we were on thin ice and I just lost control. In our final embrace, we spun around and around—Nellie's brakes and my sphincter clinched tighter than a Crohn's patient in lockdown mode. We hit the guardrail backwards, and the impact forced Nellie's rear end to kick up in the air like a horse that's been spooked by a rattlesnake. We came down on top of the rail, but the impact was softened when the driveshaft snapped off. I suspect that's what those extra parts were for.

Nellie settled on the guardrail with her rear end pointed skyward. Suspended beneath her by gangly tendons of steel hung the tattered remains of two bald tires. Michelin and Firestone, I think. I tried to free her, to push her off the guardrail, even to knock the guardrail down, but Nellie just jiggled in the air like the underside of a fat diva's arms as she waves farewell in an Italian opera.

And farewell it was. My hands were wet with dissolving black paint and I feared the worst. I noticed the rainbow residue of gasoline flowing through my scarred knuckles and my eyes swelled with tears. The gas tank I had nurtured back to health had ruptured, and Nellie lay wounded and bleeding in my hands. I stood motionless amid the unravelling bonds that had drawn us together, and in that moment I caught a reflection of the setting sun in the silky eggshell finish of Nellie's paint job; watched as the driveshaft quickly assimilated into the discarded auto parts that defined New Jersey's roadways, and followed the river of gasoline as it ran down the linkage, around the slowly revolving Michelin tire, and drip, drip, dripped into oblivion. I knew it was a lost cause. I didn't think insurance would cover the damages because for insurance to work, you have to buy insurance.

Like some forlorn cowboy who must put down his faithful horse because it went lame, I placed my hands on Nellie's hood and felt her warmth slipping away. I leaned over and there—between the words *Smooth* and *Silk*—I kissed Nellie's *as* goodbye.

Later that night my parents called Doug in Illinois to tell him the news and he said, "New Jersey? I thought he was asleep in his closet."

THE DAUGHTER

MONIC DUCTAN

I'M STANDING IN LINE AT THE PHARMACY WHEN I SEE A YOUNGER version of myself behind the counter. Our skin is the same shade of dark brown. We share big, intense dark eyes beneath straight eyebrows. She's about twenty years old and wears a white lab coat. When she looks up, I put my face down and worry that she's looking my way. Casually, I step to the side and hide behind the man in front of me. Backing up slowly, I knock into a shelf, and bottles of vitamins rattle as they fall onto the carpet. Putting my back to the girl at the counter, I pick up the bottles and quietly set them back on the shelf. Never mind my Adderall prescription. I can pick it up tomorrow. Heading for the front entrance, I glance over my shoulder to see the girl counting change for a customer.

Out in my car, I take a Tylenol for what is becoming a killer tension headache. I swallow half a bottle of water and put on the air conditioning as the car idles.

When I was nineteen years old, I got pregnant by my boyfriend and didn't realize it until we'd planned to break up. I'd been living with him in Atlanta at the time, and I knew an affluent Black couple who couldn't conceive. The wife was Dr. Dunkirk, a poetry teacher of mine at college. She was one of those professors who communicated way too much to her students. She often invited our poetry class, all eight of us, to her home for dinner, where we sat around her big dining table and read poetry. She joked about jumping on her husband whenever she was ovulating. One time, tears welled in her eyes as we sat under the chandelier that gleamed yellow light off the glasses, the silverware, and Professor Dunkirk's cheeks. She looked impossibly beautiful to me with her upright posture. You don't often see a person so unashamed of their tears. She showed vulnerability, too, when she reached out a shaky hand to pick up her water glass. Later, Dr. Dunkirk confided to me that she and her husband had been trying for years and had miscarried twice. "I'm forty-eight," she told me. "It's probably too late for me."

A week later, I got my positive pregnancy test, and after that I offered her my child.

In the parking lot of the pharmacy, I wait in my car, hoping to get a glimpse of the girl once the employees lock up and leave for the night. I don't have to wait long. The three women all come out together, right at sunset. The girl who looks like me has taken off the lab coat and now wears a bright red sweater that looks extra vibrant against her skin. Years ago, I had a Somali friend in college who asked if I was Somali, too. If you've ever seen stereotypically Somali features, then you know what I mean. Smooth dark skin that looks as though it has no pores. Silky black curls. The pharmacy girl and I aren't Somali, not that I know of, but our features are similar to that.

"Bye, Steph," one of the pharmacy women says, and Steph waves.

My mind flashes back to the day I surrendered my daughter to Dr. Dunkirk. "We're so grateful," Dunkirk gushed. "We'll give her your name, Stephanie," she promised me. She and her husband cried over how perfect Stephanie was. And she *was* perfect. A head of thick, black hair and round, pinchable cheeks, not to mention her strong arms and legs. In that moment, I wanted the child for myself. No mother can look at a baby that small without feeling protective of it and wanting to snuggle and coddle it.

Steph climbs behind the wheel of a small car parked near the pharmacy's front entrance. I hadn't planned to follow her until just this moment as she begins to back her car out of the spot, but my curiosity gets the better of me. Where does she live? Is she still close with her parents? I couldn't imagine that she wouldn't be in close touch with them. No way would Dr. Dunkirk be anything but motherly with any child of hers. But what was Steph doing all the way out here in the country? Had the Dunkirks bought a house nearby? Maybe Dr. Dunkirk had retired. It had been twenty years since I'd birthed Steph, which would put Dr. Dunkirk at sixty-eight or sixty-nine. Hard to imagine her that age.

I pull out of the parking lot behind Steph. We go through a few stoplights and into a residential neighborhood. My heart beats faster. I grew up in this town in a double-wide trailer not far from here. If I'd had a better upbringing, I would have been able to keep Stephanie. I would have had the resources to give Steph the life I'd dreamed of as a kid. But I didn't have the money, not back then. My ex-boyfriend would not have supported me through a pregnancy, and there was no way I wanted to drop out of college and move back into that double-wide with Mama.

We pass the trailer park, and Steph drives another mile or so and turns onto Lee Road. There are no cul-de-sacs and no curbs, just tall grass along the side of the roadway. She pulls into a duplex where the units look brand new. I park a few units down from her in the lot. As I open Google maps, I position my rearview mirror to get a good view of Steph. She steps out of her car, her long legs reminding me of the long-legged ex of mine who fathered her. I haven't seen him in years, hadn't bothered to tell him about the pregnancy back then either. I was only about six or seven weeks along when he moved out, and I thought it best to not say anything. We'd been together less than a year, had an emotionally fraught relationship, and I felt glad to get rid of him.

Steph used her key to enter the gray brick building. Who else lived there with her? Roommates? A boyfriend?

Google maps tells me I'm at 5400 Edgefield Lane. As I back up, I check the letter on Steph's mailbox. Letter F.

I save the location in my phone and head back to my house in town. Right now, I'm renting a two-bedroom. It's the same house I shared for twelve years with my husband Richard until we divorced last year. I always wanted to buy a home of our own, but it was never a priority for Richard. Recently, I've been driving the county, looking for the perfect home. I've decided that I'm financially ready, which is exciting after so many years of renting.

IN A TOWN THIS size, you can sometimes recognize the physical traits that run in people's families. Kensingtons have long, narrow faces. The white set of Brewsters are tanned dark with light-colored eyes, and the African American set of Brewsters have light-colored skin with plenty of moles on it. My daddy's family is like that to some degree, meaning that we all look similar. My daddy was a Craig, and sometimes when I go to the grocery or the Walmart, strangers ask if I'm kin to any Craigs. When I saw those intense Craig eyes on Stephanie at the drugstore, it shocked me. *She* shocked me. Even so, I suppose hiding from Stephanie was a nutty thing to do. She hasn't seen me since she was an infant, and maybe she wouldn't think we look too much alike anyways.

Several times during Steph's infancy, Dr. Dunkirk invited me over to see her, but I always made some excuse or didn't answer her calls. Pretty quickly, she got the message and stopped trying. Dr. Dunkirk probably thought I was ashamed of my decision. No, it's not that I'm ashamed. I'm proud that I made the right choice. My ex-boyfriend would've asked me to get an abortion; I'm certain he would've. I didn't want to abort the baby, and I couldn't keep Steph either. I made the *right* choice. So why did I reject Dr. Dunkirk's offer to let me know my daughter? It's partially because of my family upbringing. I always felt the need to keep what I did secret from my family. My parents, both long-dead now, would not have approved. My mother would've judged me especially harshly. I didn't want her quoting scripture to me or asking me to move in with her and raise the child, so I stayed in Atlanta and away from my family during the pregnancy. Also, though I would not have admitted it back then, I was afraid of what Steph would think of me as she got older. I feared her resentment. When measured against the Dunkirks, with their summer trips and private school educations, I'd never be seen as successful or even competent. I was a failure.

★ ★ ★

AFTER I SEE STEPHANIE at the pharmacy that first time, I keep going back there. Some days I deliberately look for her red Ford Fusion in the parking lot. It has an Alpha Kappa Alpha bumper sticker on it. The driver's seat is covered by a leopard-print seat cover.

Inside the pharmacy, I often sit on a bench by the blood pressure cuffs and the magazine racks and watch Stephanie. Often, she smiles at the customers and asks if she can help them find something. Once, she spends several minutes searching for an internet coupon to help an older woman save ten dollars on some vitamin supplements. I'm not at all surprised to see that Steph is a sweet girl, a good person. Of course she is. She was raised by the venerable Dr. Dunkirk.

I try to summon the courage to pick up my prescription, but I keep chickening out. My text alert says it was filled last week, and I hope they haven't restocked it yet. The Adderall helps me focus, but the truth is that I wasn't diagnosed with Asperger's until I was in graduate school, so I've spent most of my life unmedicated. I can definitely do without the medicine for a while if I have to.

One day, I see Steph's car in the lot, but when I get inside the pharmacy a red-haired girl is behind the counter. The girl wears a nametag that says "Grace."

I pull off my sunglasses and put them on the counter as I open my wallet. "I'm Stephanie Craig," I begin. "I'm here to pick up my—"

The girl named Grace cuts me off by leaning back to speak to someone who is out of my line of sight. "Steph," she calls through a doorway. "Your mom's here."

My heart leaps up into my throat. I shake my head so hard my hoop earrings beat against my cheeks.

"What?" asks Stephanie as she comes into my view. She looks at me, and I drop my eyes to the counter. "Where?" Steph says in a high-pitched voice similar to the voice I had as a girl.

Grace picks up a prescription bag from a shelf, looks at the label, and then puts the prescription down on the counter in front of me. "She has your name," Grace says to Steph. "And I just assumed she was your mama since y'all look alike."

I slowly lift my eyes to meet Stephanie's. She gives me a once-over. "That's not my mama," she says, and I admire the southern way she pronounces the word "mama."

"Pay her no attention, ma'am," Stephanie says, grinning at me. "She thinks all Black folks look alike." She cuts up laughing, and Grace rings up my prescription. I pay the copay and grin at them as I turn to leave. As I walk away, Grace keeps marveling at how much Stephanie and I favor one another. "She even has your dimple," Grace says, her voice fading as I step out of earshot.

THAT NIGHT, I LOOK up Dr. Dunkirk on Facebook and consider messaging her. Her page says she is retired. I scroll down and see that someone posted a funeral announcement for her husband Gerard two years ago, and there are about a hundred comments from people offering Dr. Dunkirk their condolences.

I click on Steph's page, but most of her info is private. I already know a good deal about her—first and last name, address, and even her birthday. She was born two days after my twentieth birthday, which means she'll be turning twenty-one soon. Our birthdays are coming up next month, and I imagine sending her a gift. Maybe I could put it in her mailbox or just buy something on Amazon and ship it to her. I never had any other children, though I always wanted a daughter, someone to shop with and share secrets with. For a moment, I'm swept up in a fantasy in which I buy the two of us a spa day at a winery outside town. "Thanks, Mama," she'll say, beaming at me. The smile is, of course, followed by a long hug.

Halfway through composing an instant message to Stephanie, I stop and put my head in my hands. How do I even know Steph would respond after all these years? I was the one who stopped taking Dr. Dunkirk's phone calls. It's probably too late to be in her life now.

I erase the draft of the instant message and power off the laptop.

ONE DAY I'M SITTING on the bench at the pharmacy, scrolling on my iPhone through a listing of the local houses for sale in my price range, when I overhear Steph telling Grace about an exercise class she's taking. "It's like Zumba," Steph says. "But it's not just Latin music. We dance to a lot of hip-hop, too." "Pleeease come dance with me, Gracie," she whines. "It'll be fun."

Grace shakes her head and laments being a poor dancer. Steph counters that by giving her the days and the time of the dance classes she takes at the county rec center.

"Mondays, Wednesdays, and Fridays at five," I repeat to myself.

The county rec center isn't a place I frequent. I'm a smoker who doesn't exercise if I can help it, but on Friday I show up at the rec center wearing cotton shorts, a T-shirt, and sneakers. I'd planned to work out, but I'm late due to the twenty minutes I spent nearly talking myself out of it. I recognize Steph's red Ford Fusion, and I park a few spots over from her. The website had said the classes would be in room F, and when I get inside the red brick building the girl at the desk says, "It's the last door at the end of the hall," as she points toward a long corridor.

Loud music thumps. The room has several plate-glass windows and the door stands open. A group of older women smile through the open doorway at something. When I get closer, I see that the women are admiring a group of people in the dance class. Steph is among the dancers, and she wears an oversized red T-shirt and tight spandex shorts. She moves forward deliberately, her hips moving in synch with the loud beat of drums. There are at least a dozen other women in the class, but I can't take my eyes off Stephanie. She's that good. A sheen of sweat has gathered on her dark skin. The music increases in intensity, and Steph moves her feet faster, matching the rhythm of the bass. Suddenly, she jumps, lands with her ankles crossed, and spins around. I draw in my breath along with the other women watching, and we exchange smiles. "That's my daughter," I whisper to myself, but as soon as I say it I realize it's a mistake. The older white lady with the gray, poufy hair points at Steph, who is the only Black girl in the group. "She's beautiful," the lady says to me.

I watch until the class ends. The dancers finish their stretches, and as I'm turning to go, the poufy-haired woman asks, "Are you joining this class with your daughter?"

I turn to look at her, and she's standing right beside Steph, who has now come out into the hallway. Steph stares at me and again I'm struck by how much we look alike. Very strong African features. Studying my daughter's face, I open my mouth as if to answer the woman, but instead I turn and flee.

"Hey!" someone yells from behind me, and I recognize the voice as Stephanie's.

I pretend to not hear her as I push through the exit door at the end of the corridor.

The hot air hits me as soon as I leave the climate-controlled building.

"Hey," the voice says again.

I turn slowly to face her.

Her eyes aren't giving me the once-over the way they did that day she told Grace I wasn't her mother. Right now, she's scrutinizing me, all the way down to my legs, which are heavier than hers and not nearly as toned. She says, "I know who you are."

I nod stupidly, wetting my dry lips with my tongue before croaking out, "I just wanted to see what your life is like."

The woman with the poufy hair stands beside a nearby car, hearing every word.

"Do you drink coffee?" I ask. "There's a coffee shop . . ." I trail off, pointing in the general direction of the one downtown.

"Jerry's?" she asks.

"Y-yeah. I went to high school with him. I've known his family for years. My daddy used to fish with his granddaddy back when Elm's Ferry Road was just—" I pause because I've said all this without taking a breath and because I should probably wait for her to offer some sign that she even remotely cares.

Steph stares at me with her eyebrows raised. "I don't drink coffee much," she says.

"Oh," I say.

The lady with the poufy hair opens her car door slowly and closes it quietly once she's climbed into the car. She just sits there with her window down.

"Do you have pictures of him?" Steph asks. "Pictures of your daddy?"

I nod. "I don't have any with me, but I could bring you some."

She turns as if she's leaving but then turns back to me. "You could buy me an ice cream," she says.

So we take our cars down to the Dairy Queen, where she orders a strawberry cone and we sit in a booth. She licks slowly, says, "I scrapbook. I have a dozen books of pictures already. I take them on my phone and print them at work," she explains.

The conversation seems so trivial. I'd been preparing myself to answer questions about why I gave her up, questions about her father, and had even prepared myself for some level of resentment hurled at me. If there is any rabid curiosity or resentment in her, I see no signs of it.

"Should I bring the pictures to the pharmacy?" I ask. "I have a photo album of my family pics, but none of your dad," I say, pausing awkwardly. It feels strange to call my ex-boyfriend her dad, even though that's what he is. "I could bring them to the pharmacy tomorrow, if you'd want that."

She nods slowly.

We arrange to meet during her lunchtime at a diner in town. I get there early, and when she arrives I rise and try to go in for a hug, but she sticks out her hand instead.

I treat her to a sandwich, soup, and a Coke. She brings two scrapbooks. One has a sorority theme and there are dozens of photos of her and her AKA sorority sisters. There are program announcements, concert ticket stubs, and playbills from events they've attended together. I'm surprised to see she goes to the same historically Black college I attended.

"That's a long commute for you, isn't it?" I ask.

She shrugs. "'Bout an hour and a half." She clears her throat. "Mama got sick last year, so I moved out here to the country to take care of her."

"You live with your mama?" I ask, struggling to imagine Dr. Dunkirk in the little duplex where Steph lives.

"Yeah," she says.

I nod, flipping through her scrapbook. The girls look so young, even younger than sorority girls did when I was that age. "This one is my favorite," I tell her, pointing to a picture of her in a sash and heavy makeup. She wears a crown on her head. The deep dimple in her cheek and the way she cocks her head to the side remind me of myself at that age.

She excuses herself to go to the restroom, and I unstick the pageant picture and put it in my purse. When she comes back to the table, I'm flipping slowly through the other album. The theme for this album is a cruise she took with her mama. Seeing her together with Dr. Dunkirk makes my heart ache. I can't name this feeling as anything but jealousy.

Steph's questions flow freely for the rest of her lunch hour. She already knows her father's name, but she wants to know where he lives now and what work he does. I can't answer those questions because I haven't kept in touch with him. She's tried to find him on Facebook over the years, but his name is so common—Mike Thomas—that it's nearly impossible. She tells me she's tried to look me up, but couldn't find me either. I confess that I didn't get Facebook until very recently, and I still don't use the other social media sites.

She looks worried about something, and when I ask what's wrong, things start to spill out of her. Her mother's dying of cancer. They ran out of money months ago. She may quit school because they don't have the funds for tuition.

"Oh no," I say, reaching across the table to pat her hand. She doesn't pull away, so I just sit there squeezing her hand every now and again.

"Can I do something to help you?" I ask.

She studies my face a moment, as if deciding how much I really mean it. "Well." She hesitates. "I'm able to pay the rent on my apartment with my pharmacy check, but I can't pay my tuition."

"I could give you a little financial help," I tell her.

I'm by no means wealthy, but I've never been a big spender, and

I do have quite a bit in my checking accounts, though most of it is earmarked as a down payment on the house I want to buy.

She shakes her head. "I couldn't ask for your help, Mama."

Mama. It's her first time calling me that.

"I want to," I say. "I want to help put you through school."

She hesitates again. "Tuition is pretty expensive," she says. "And I want to apply to pharmacy school next year."

I nod. "How much do you need? I can probably help you out with tuition for next semester."

Stephanie pauses to consider it.

I *owe* her this. I'm her mother, after all, and shouldn't I help when she needs it?

"Okay," she whispers finally.

She pushes some buttons on her phone and calls out the balance of her tuition and fees. It's a little over $11,000.

My heart drops when she announces the amount. It's nearly half the money I have saved up for the down payment on the house. Still, I write her the check and sign it proudly, looping the "g" on the end of my last name.

Before she leaves to go back to work, I get her phone number so that we can keep in touch. Halfway to the front of the restaurant, she comes back to hug me, and I feel so warm and good inside.

Over the next week or so, I text her a few times. She always answers back, though not always right away. I ask her about taking the spa day with me, and she replies enthusiastically that she'd love to.

One night, I type a Facebook message to Dr. Dunkirk:

> *Hi, it's Stephanie Craig, Steph's birth mother. I ran into her here in town and she mentioned that you're sick. If there's anything I can do to help, let me know.*

A few minutes later, as I'm scrolling through Dr. Dunkirk's page, I get a message notification from her. I open the tab, and the message reads,

It's good to hear from you, Stephanie. I've often thought of you over the years. Sadly, I haven't had contact with my daughter for a while. What's your phone number? Can I call you right now?

I give her my number and wait for my cell to ring. Steph said her mother lived with her, and Dr. Dunkirk was now telling me that they hadn't seen each other for a while. How long is a while? Days? Weeks?

My phone rings and I snatch it up and answer.

"Hey, Stephanie?" Dr. Dunkirk says. Funny how I can still recognize her voice after all these years. She liked to begin most of our classes by reading a poem aloud, and I can still remember her inflections on some of the words.

I jump right in, telling her what Steph told me at the diner. "I was so sorry to hear about your illness," I say. "How are you feeling? Is it in remission now?"

She doesn't answer right away, and for a second I wonder if the call has dropped.

Dr. Dunkirk sighs and then launches into it: "Stephanie is a very inventive liar. You can't believe anything she says."

Anything?

"I wish I could tell you that she turned into a lovely person, but she—" she pauses and lets out her breath. "She lies. She won't study. She left school. I can't do anything to coax her back, and—"

"She told me y'all don't have the money for tuition."

She gives me the frustrated sigh again and says, "When her father passed away, he left a college fund for her, but I won't give her the money if she's not enrolled in school."

For the next half hour, Dr. Dunkirk denies most of what Steph told me. No, Dr. Dunkirk has never had cancer. No, she doesn't live with Steph. Dunkirk still lives in the same old house in metro Atlanta where we sat under her kitchen chandelier and read poetry. Mother and daughter have not seen each other in nearly a year. Steph left school when she left her mama's house last year. Too embarrassed to admit how easily conned I was, I don't tell her about the $11,000 I gave Stephanie.

After we say goodbye and hang up, I go to my purse and take out the photo of Steph wearing the tiara. She looks so happy and carefree. I go to my dresser, where I slide the photo into the corner of the mirror.

I sit up a lot of nights, staring at my phone, hoping that Steph will reach out to me. She doesn't. When I message her, I get only her silence in return.

My realtor calls about a Cape Cod–style home with a wide porch, but I have to tell her that I don't have the down payment anymore. It will take at least another year or so for me to earn back that $11,000.

School starts back again, and I throw myself into work— volunteer to sit on various committees, volunteer for two after-school programs. I don't see Steph at the pharmacy anymore, and I ask Grace about her. Grace confirms that she's quit but doesn't know where she works now.

Some nights, when I feel especially lonely, I get in my car and drive the country roads, windows down, sipping hot coffee. Usually, I find my way to Steph's duplex, where I sit in my car and watch the yellow light burning through her front curtain. I consider knocking on her front door, but what could I say to bring her back to me? What could I say in person that I haven't already said via text? One night I see the outline of her in the front window. I know her by the curls that frame her head. I know her by the long, lean body. Does she see my car? Would she recognize it if she did?

She has company some nights. Sometimes the visitor is a young man who greets her with hugs and kisses and his car is still there when I depart late at night. Other times, the visitor is a young woman who bounces into the apartment when Steph opens the door.

I buy Stephanie the spa day. She can get a manicure and pedicure and a facial. She can even get an hour-long massage and lounge in the sauna. I have the gift certificate shipped to her address, and I put my return address on it, just in case she wants to contact me. I fantasize about the Cape Cod–style home with its wide front porch, perfect for sitting out there with my daughter. She could stop over any evening that she wants, and I will buy us a couple of rocking chairs. Rocking, together, we'll watch the sun go down as the sky turns pink over the Blue Ridge Mountains. I fantasize about getting Mother's Day cards and Christmas cards from Stephanie. Maybe one day she'll send me a scrapbook with big, red hearts drawn on it. It will be pink with silver glitter that rubs off on my hands.

THE DOOR

CHRISTIANNA SOUMAKIS

THE LITTLE DOG RUNS TO THE DOOR WHEN SHARON CLOSES IT behind her, and begins to bark. Yesterday his people left him with us to go on vacation. I was not home when they dropped him off. I am told he cried and barked and barked and cried by the door for hours. Now Sharon, his surrogate mother, has peeled herself away from his clingy affections to run errands; she has pulled the heavy orange door shut with Doggo on the wrong side of it.

Doggo begins to weep.

First he protests: a short series of panicked/outraged yaps. He attacks the separation. He bayonets it with harsh, staccato stabs: Arf! Arf! Arf!

But his vocal charge-of-the-light-brigade fails to dent the door. He had one card, and he has played it. His one-syllable prayers are passionate uppercuts on a stone wall. The door does not open. Sharon is gone.

Doggo shakes. The bold fist of his voice—like the hard, tiny knob of a camellia bud—dissolves to liquid and puddles in his throat.

He is alone.

Everyone has left him.

I come up behind him and put my hands on his head, his back, his tummy. He thrusts his nose as deeply into the crease between door and wall as possible, which is basically not at all. "It's okay, it's okay," I tell him.

He is in a panic of grief. He is alone! His tail presses down between his legs as though he is going to roll himself up into a ball like those little pill bugs to minimize exposure to the empty, empty world.

I wrap my arms around him. I stop telling him it's okay. I'm not stupid, and I'm not young. I tell him, "I know, I know. I'm here."

He barks again, without power, with desperation. Abandonment is absurd. There is no appropriate response. I feel his body contract to make the sound, his lungs and his diaphragm slapping it out of him. Arf! Arf! he wails.

That stupid door. My mother closed it, too. *Arf, arf,* and nothing I could do could crack it open. *Arf, arf,* it was not okay there were no words no fight no magic bullet, no not even in church, where they purportedly stocked miracles.

And I think of my grandparents, too—Yiayia and Poppy and Grandma and Grandpa, *Arf,* all gone, all on the wrong side of the door while I pressed my nose into the nonexistent seam between life and death.

Doggo looks at me, as only dogs can, with such radical unguardedness it is like getting harpooned. His eyes are round and brown and simple. He does not have feelings about his feelings. His pain has not abstracted itself through the derivative towers of anger and blame and guilt and denial. No. He is afraid, he is miserable, he is lonely. He builds no shelter, wears no armor.

He is soft and white all over; he was recently shaved, and you can see his skin through the peach fuzz of his fur. He looks at me, his face inches from mine, and he doesn't blink, doesn't flinch away. He is trying to suck comfort and rightness out of my stupid, aging face as though I were not on the same side of the door as he is. His gaze is frantic and brimming with trust for which he currently has no outlet. What happens to a trust deferred? It's going to tear him in half. It's going to bleed down his face from those wide brown eyes, leaving long wet stains. It's too heavy to carry and impossible to put down. It will drown him.

I sit on the floor with him and stare at the door. Rub his back. "She will come back," I tell him. "I promise. I promise. All your people will come back. Sharon will come back, and Mommy and Daddy will come back, and they will all come back. Don't cry. Don't cry."

I bring him to the couch, and he sits with his meek sausage of a body curled between my stretched-out legs. He whimpers into my shin. "Don't cry, don't cry."

Every time a car drives by, he bounces erect, ears forward, nose to the window. It's not her. It's not her. It's not her. He rearranges himself against my legs after each false alarm, the disappointment endlessly fresh.

"All your people still love you," I tell him. "All your people are alive, and coming back."

There are an incredible number of cars that don't belong to Sharon.

I get up and he follows me, then reroutes. He wants to sit by the door, but I have walked into the kitchen. He wants to stare at the knob and the flat expressionless shield behind it, the obstacle, the riddle. His round eyes lacquer it with a living intensity to which it is cosmically indifferent.

"She will come back," I tell him.

We wait.

I make breakfast. Eggs. "Life is like that," I tell him. "Sometimes something happens that should end everything, and maybe it *does* end everything. And then the next day, or the day after, you still have to get up and make breakfast. And you stare at your eggs and they make no sense; it makes no sense that you should make them; the existence of the kitchen itself makes no sense. You stare at the pan and you realize that after the end of the world you are somehow making eggs."

Doggo isn't listening.

"Sometimes," I tell him, "there is nothing to be done."

He twitches an ear in my direction, briefly.

"She will come back."

I finish cooking and go sit with him by the door. I hope he doesn't think I don't care because I made eggs, I worry. Maybe I shouldn't have made eggs—shouldn't have made any one of a long line of breakfasts, one after another in an attenuated, inglorious procession after the end of the world. Maybe I should have lain down in front of the door and stared at it with brimming homeless trust until I died. Maybe that would have been the best thing to do.

A car drives by. Crunches into the driveway. Doggo becomes an arrow drawn back.

A car door slams. Footsteps.

"Arf!"

The door opens. Doggo charges Sharon. His trust rains on her like worship. He dances around her legs, singing, "Arf! Arf!" She's back! Everything is okay! Everything is okay! He is not alone! The door is open! *Everything is okay!*

In *The Lord of the Rings*, when the hobbits are reunited after the destruction of the One Ring, Tolkien writes, *Their joy was like swords.* But Doggo's joy is something unforged, untempered by his sojourn through grief. His elation rinses him clean as dawn. He is a new creature, freshly innocent of loss. She's back—everything is okay. His brown eyes shine.

He has never had to make breakfast for himself after the end of the world, I think. I carry my dishes to the sink and turn on the water. Behind me, Doggo is dancing with such abandon Sharon can barely bring in the groceries.

You are a good dog, I think, as I forge my joy on the anvil of soap suds and dishes and hot water. You are a very good dog.

THE OTHER WOMAN

TRISTAN MARAJH

IT IS THE THIRD TIME IN SIX YEARS THAT ROSHAN VISITS DHAKA, Bangladesh—more specifically, the town of Mabalu, a suburb of Dhaka, the country's capital. Mabalu is also Roshan's childhood town, but not his adult one. That would be Los Angeles, in the state of California in the United States. In Mabalu, Roshan walks through the bustling marketplace where his mother used to go on Saturday mornings, earlier than sunrise itself, to wait for vendors to put out their produce so that she would get among the first pickings of fruit, vegetables, fish, and seeds. When she'd return to the apartment she shared with her son, Roshan would often still be in bed—a day for her so far thoroughly lived before Roshan even started his own.

Roshan doesn't purchase anything on these walks. He'll then take the overcrowded bus to Mabalu's industrial district that's filled with textile factories, one of which his mother had worked in, one of which is no longer there. In its place is yet another; the one his mother had worked in collapsed six years ago. Roshan had been in the USA at the time and his mother had been in that factory at the time. Seven hundred sixty-four people, all textile workers, perished. Roshan, upon hearing the news, departed on the next flight out of LAX and departed out of himself.

Eight years before, two before the six since his mother died, Roshan had left Bangladesh to undertake university studies in the United States. His mother had worked in the same now-extinct factory back then, the latter part of the seventeen years she was employed there. Her day's labor did not cease when her shift ended at six in the evening. When she returned to their apartment, she would prepare dinner for herself and her son, then sit at the old sewing machine in the far corner of the room to stitch garments for neighbors and others who made requests for pants, shirts, *saris*, and *lungis* or repairs and adjustments to those.

The one "customer" who never ceased requiring her manufacturing and repairing, however, was Roshan. She was always attuned to his changing measurements as he grew from child to gangly teenager to young man, even as he lived all the way in Los Angeles. Amina Choudhury's intense focus on her son's measurements extended beyond that of his clothing to those of his capabilities; capabilities that would not, she knew, be actualized in Bangladesh. She knew this even as she labored over his *panjabis*— traditionally the garment of sultans. Sultans were past rulers of their country, not known as Bangladesh at the time but part of the nation of India. Roshan, to her, would be like those sultans: possessor of a life of relative ease and privilege, beyond the toil and turmoil of their land, but nevertheless a Bangladeshi. She didn't expect her son to acquire the excess of actual sultans of the past, but even a fraction of what they had would be enough for people around them to consider him one. It was far better than the life she provided for him, she thought, even if he didn't know better. *She* knew better though, and better was not living in a small, sparse apartment possible only from her meager salary as a seamstress at Shamston Textiles. Shamston wasn't even *Bangladeshi*; it was a foreign clothing company that manufactured in Bangladesh because of the country's cheap labor force. One wouldn't know that, though, when one purchased Shamston's garments in foreign countries for excessive amounts of money, way more money than what they cost to make. One might simply notice the inside tag of a shirt reading MADE IN BANGLADESH and then think no more of that.

Roshan would think of that though, when he was living in one of those foreign countries: the United States. His mother, in a frenzy of sewing and mending, stitched pants, shirts, underwear, handkerchiefs, pillow cases, linens, even scarves and gloves for him in those days before he was to leave for Los Angeles. She didn't know, of course, that the state of California didn't require its inhabitants to wear scarves and gloves, at least not for the weather. She *did* know, though, that the United States was in North America and therefore had cold weather through and through. If Bangladesh had monsoons, then the USA had snowstorms.

Roshan would think of clothes and care being made in Bangladesh less as he moved through his time in California. Los Angeles being what it was, he found out that his homemade clothing wasn't highly rated there. Of course no one explicitly told him that; it was obvious in the people who walked around. *Amina Choudhury* wasn't a name found on any garment worth wearing in Los Angeles. So Roshan bought—at first with sparsity but then in increasing frequency—brand-name clothes consistent with LA fashion. He just wanted to fit in, he'd quickly told himself, proud of his first English pun. Less quickly, though, did he understand that he was considered aesthetically attractive in Los Angeles. Girls' and women's glances turned into gazes, subtly obvious in their appraising of his appearance. He was always considered handsome by his mother, but mothers will forevermore say that about their sons. To have girls and women from all cultures and creeds looking at him as if he indeed were the handsome sultan his mother believed he was gave Roshan a sultan-sized ego if not sultan-sized wealth. He found a girlfriend, and she soon became the woman of his life. He exercised at the gym more often, was offered and accepted a job at Zara Menswear, bought his girlfriend things, and bought more clothes for himself. They took weekend trips, ate out often, visited her family. After all, he was the man in her life, and she was the woman in his life. The other woman in his life, the one who gave him life and this new life, became just that: the other woman. Roshan's mother was now peripheral to his new life, but like most "other women" in men's lives do, she did maintain some sentiment in him: peripheral, not primary. He would occasionally think on his mother, still working the day shift at Shamston Textiles, still living in their crummy apartment in Mabalu. He would pause for a while, then carry on with the routine of his life. In those pauses, he'd make a mental note to call his mother, to book a ticket to Bangladesh, or to send her a ticket for her to visit him, but those plans never came to pass. What did pass was time.

Roshan was on his way to class, looking at himself in the mirror before leaving his apartment when the phone rang. He hesitated to answer: depending on who the caller was, it might make him late for class. He glanced at the caller ID; it was a Bangladeshi number. Grateful that his mother mended even his broken promises to keep in touch, he picked up the phone, already intending to tell her he'd do what he'd been telling himself he'd do: return her call at a better time.

It wasn't his mother on the end of the line. The voice was male, the Bengali meeting Roshan's ears like the scent of spices in the marketplace of his childhood. The caller wasn't anyone Roshan knew, but he knew Roshan's mother, and that was his reason for calling. He explained that he worked at Shamston like Roshan's mother and lived in the same building as her, in the apartment beside hers. He had been one of the ones spared, *mashallah*, but Ms. Choudhury wasn't, *mashallah*.

"Spared from what?" Roshan asked, a tightening terror rising from the pit of his stomach.

"I am sorry, brother, I thought you had known." The man paused, evidently unsure how to proceed, as if wondering whether *he* should be the one to reveal this news to his neighbor's son, the one, he did say, she always spoke of in reverence and admiration. It was obvious the man was stalling.

"Tell me what happened," Roshan uttered, already knowing the result of what his question asked.

The man was scheduled to work the evening shift at Shamston Textiles. Roshan's mother worked the morning shift, from 7 a.m. to 6 p.m. The building collapsed at 11:07 a.m., without warning or time to vacate. *There was warning*, Roshan remembered. *There was time*. Workers had been voicing concerns about the structural integrity of that building for years. But the only thing Shamston did about it was to threaten to fire the employees if they thought about striking. Employees couldn't afford to lose their jobs, and they knew there were people lining up to replace them if they were let go. Roshan asked the man if his mother had been found. Not yet, the man said, people were still going through the rubble. Roshan told the man he will come help, and instead of going to his lecture, he went to Los Angeles International and booked the next flight to Dhaka, which was leaving in eight hours. Roshan remained at the airport, calling and explaining the situation to his girlfriend, cancelling his course enrollment for that semester and sitting through a torturous possibility of his mother's death. He had been negligent of her for the past few months, he knew. If he examined closer, he was negligent of her in a thousand other ways since his birth, but he could not venture to think of that while at LAX. Inevitably, he knew, he would end up thinking about it, but not now. Hope burned in him that his mother would be found, breathing and alive with gray soot on her face, after a few pieces of rubble were lifted.

With each mile that fell away as the airplane climbed and crossed the Pacific sky, it was as if some part of Roshan was also falling away from him, much like his shoes and jacket, wallet and miscellany of worldly existence would fall away once he returned to his apartment after a day out in the world. It was an eighteen-hour flight, yet Roshan, in turmoil, scrutinized every choice he'd made over the past eight years, which moved him further away from thinking about his mother, even as he was reaching closer to and thought of nothing but her as the distance between the United States and Bangladesh lessened.

He was certain it was from the moment he turned his attention from the adoring eyes of his mother and toward the assessing eyes of women in the United States. He wasn't the type of specimen these women were used to seeing. His life of lack and essentiality in Bangladesh left him lacking in First World body fat and with the essentiality of high, sharp cheekbones and a lean body that suggested to Americans that he was physically fit. Physicality that reflected poverty in Bangladesh reflected the opposite in Los Angeles: status.

It was a given, for Roshan in Bangladesh, that this was his physical appearance, nothing that needed any attention save for a few moments of grooming before he ventured out into the public. That was the constant for the seventeen years of his South Asian life. Yet in half that time, daily, women in the United States—and men also, since they could afford to be obvious unlike men in Bangladesh—they all gazed and glanced at him as if witnessing something otherworldly, something stumblingly beautiful and touched with divinity, some sort of Adonis that was overlooked by everything they were subject to by the hype of Western media. Women shamelessly stared at Roshan and shamefully blushed; they bumbled, stumbled, and stuttered. He was approached for modelling, for escort, for hire; even a courteous comment from him would seem to raise the spirit of the person he directed it to. Any person would privately savor this attention and even if bemusing at first, he or she would get used to it, accept it as a usual part of their existence, and grow into it. Depending on the person, he or she would even welcome any benefits it brought from the world. They would, in a sense, become both immune and attuned to their power over people.

Roshan knew that Katarina, his girlfriend of two years, initially noticed him because of his perceived physical attractiveness. He'd noticed other men of charm, integrity, and humor be otherwise declined by women because those men didn't fit those women's physical masculine ideal. The women, of course, never said that was the reason, but given those men's other qualities, Roshan knew that it was exactly that. He didn't need to be attracted to his own gender to understand; aesthetic ideals of masculinity were *everywhere* in Los Angeles: on billboards, on movie posters, in magazines and television commercials, in customer service staff; even in mannequins and statues—visual depictions of people who had died and never looked as they were now portrayed.

Katarina may have initially been drawn to him for superficial reasons, but she proved to be a good girlfriend: kind, thoughtful, respectful. She had approached him after their lecture at university, remarked on his unusual looks, inquired where he was originally from. Roshan, despite all the female attention on him, wasn't skilled at wooing women. Katarina was the one to ask him to a dessert date, she was the one who took his hand as they walked the mall together, the one who turned his face to hers for their first kiss. She was amused by Roshan's inexperience, yet found it endearing. He definitely was not that shy and acquiescent one when he'd called to inform her he was leaving immediately to Bangladesh. He didn't know when he'd return, he said, but made a distracted comment that he'd phone her often. Both of them did not know that that phone call would be the last for a very long time. In fact, Katarina thought, he'd reach out to her constantly for support and comfort. The phone, though, was forgotten by Roshan in his confused mind at the airport, right after he'd used it to cancel his university enrollment for the semester and confirm his pickup at Shahjalal International in Dhaka by Mr. Mustafi, his mother's neighbor, the one who made the call to Roshan informing him about her.

AT THE ARRIVALS FOYER at Shahjalal, Mr. Mustafi did not at first recognize Roshan, even though he had a recent photograph of his neighbor's son, posing in one of the *panjabis* she'd made for the young man. Roshan, dressed in a fitted T-shirt, khaki pants, and dress shoes, walked straight past his mother's neighbor, who had dismissed Roshan—upon first glance—as another pretentious expat who'd spent way too much of his brain on American thinking. It was both their searching eyes that caused lingering eye contact, the desperation and worry in the young man's prompting Mr. Mustafi to embrace the child of his neighbor Amina Choudhury. Roshan, no more than five years younger, in a desperate voice immediately upon the embrace called Mr. Mustafi *caca*, uncle.

The ride from Shahjalal International to Mabalu showed Roshan an example of how much industrialization had taken a strong foothold in Bangladesh. Factories and warehouses lay on landscapes that Roshan knew as forested until just eight years before and for his entire life before that. Like Roshan himself, his country of birth was Bangladesh largely by name but in reality was a machine for the materialist vices of current times. Textile factories held the largest number of industrial buildings, but there were also pharmaceutical, steel, electronics, and automotive operations. *Large swaths of wooded areas were cleared in the past six years*, Roshan heard Mr. Mustafi confirm, his new acquaintance evading discussing Roshan's personal tragedy by describing a national one. Blinded by the flash and hype of modern materialism, people failed to see the imminent destruction of Mother Earth. That blindness was Roshan's reality, and that imminent destruction the reality of his own mother.

Taleb Mustafi and his wife Hafiza went to great lengths to assist Roshan, fussing over their neighbor's son. They organized all his transportation, his grocery shopping, and the upkeep of his mother's apartment while Roshan went to Shamston Textiles' ground zero where men pored through the ruins and rubble around the clock. Daily, the Mustafis would pack generous helpings of *samosas*, *channa*, *aloo*, or *saag* to sustain Roshan as he assisted in the digging for victims of the collapse.

The meals, while appreciated by Roshan, were a reminder, yet again, of how far and apart he'd gone in his American life from his Bangladeshi one. He was vegetarian for his entire life in Bangladesh, the wider diet of the entire subcontinent that reflected the spiritual ideals of that land, for most people in it anyway. Indeed, the majority of the subcontinent's inhabitants resided in India; it was the planet's second-highest populated country, the majority of that country's inhabitants Hindu alongside sizable populations of Buddhists, Sikhs, and Jains. Vegetarianism was—or at least was intended to be—synonymous with the spiritual. Roshan had always accepted that to purposely eat animal protein would result in negative karma in life, in this one or the next. That was a dharmic notion, common in the dharmic religions of Buddhism, Jainism, Sikhism, and of course, Hinduism. Roshan was Muslim, yet had quietly, ever since childhood, admired those other faiths for their benign, unassuming views and practices that calmed his own dissonance about his own.

It was nice to be reassured that those other faiths were accessible to him. That was the feeling he had as a child—it was a quiet thrill to light *deyas* during his time in India while on a school trip to a national park. With hundreds of flickering *deya* flames all alit together, the combined glow emanated a holy aura that told him divinity and sacredness were not exclusive to one faith. His own religious community loved to proudly purport that, and often with violence.

His openness and sensitivity to those other faiths, he realized, he got from his mother. She was the one who taught him about karma, about the benefits and virtues of vegetarianism, about the dislike she had for intolerant practices where members of other faiths were poorly and contemptuously treated.

Roshan remembered his mother's own cooking as he ate the food from the Mustafis: how she made *aloo* with *tava roti* the way she did, how he used to tease her that she couldn't make *dal* properly—her *dal* was always watery and average at best, to him. She was the one who had informed him about vegetarianism and its karmic benefits, that all life on earth was worthy to experience life without cruel death by hands that knew better—meaning human hands, hands that must work to conserve and protect the Earth.

In angry torment, Roshan understood that his mother was now the victim, the victim of people's disdain for the very lives she stood for: forests were destroyed for industry, billions of animals were slaughtered daily. Instead of the karma being directed at the guilty, it fell upon her, in the form of a nine-story concrete building poor in design and designed to exploit the poor. In an inner state of tumult detectable only from his constricted face and fearful eyes, Roshan heaved pieces of concrete, metal, and miscellaneous rubble as he followed protocol for poring through the rubble of Shamston's collapsed building. Volunteers comprised relatives and friends of missing workers, yet no one spoke of their common anxiety. Conversation would only squander time away, precious time more needfully spent searching through the rubble and ruin. Roshan shared his lunch and meals with them; they did not have the privilege of having caring neighbors who supplied them with sustenance in the form of homecooked and karma-blessed meals.

★ ★ ★

Roshan heard a commotion—it was one of many, one for each victim that was discovered. And as he did for each, he hurried over, muttering pleas to heaven that he'd long forgotten but suddenly recalled. Volunteers had cleared away the debris and were lifting the body out. It was a woman, unrecognizable due to the dust, sediment, and dirt on her face and skin. But Roshan knew it was her, not because she was recognizable to him but because there was a coming-together of all his desperate fears, prayers, denial, and despair, a resonant coalescence in that one moment the woman was carried away from the rubble and laid on a tarp nearby, where medical personnel rushed to attend to her.

When Roshan made his way to the body on the tarp, he saw that the woman's eyes were open in an expression of tenderness, of total obliviousness to her predicament and to the people around her, to her *son* even, who was on his knees beside the medical personnel as they furiously worked at her. But she was declared deceased after twenty-four minutes of scouring for vital signs and futile resuscitation. The serene expression in Amina Choudhury's eyes remained the entire time, up until the cremation, her soft and tender countenance shining through the fire.

It was—in Roshan's mind—as if the tender expression in his mother's eyes meant that she'd looked to the sky as she lay dying; perhaps there was an opening in the rubble that had piled on top of her. She could have been bringing to her memory that day Roshan left Bangladesh for America; it was the same expression in her eyes at the airport as she watched her son's airplane climbing the sky, taking him to the better life than what would await him after he graduated from high school in Bangladesh. Roshan had not known that his mother had lingered at the airport then, watching his plane until it was no longer visible. And maybe that look in her eyes again at death was her thinking that she'd be seeing him once again, once the rubble was cleared and her body lifted out. She looked toward the blue, open sky in her dying moment, remembering her son leaving her, imagining him now returning to her in the same sky once again. She'd always considered him her angel, and angels rarely showed themselves, coming from the skies when they did. Roshan, however, sided with the inverse: his mother, the angel of his entire life, is being called back to Heaven, to God. It was only fitting and true.

ROSHAN DID NOT SHED any tears at his mother's funeral, but attendees he did not even know—or even knew whether his mother did—shed tears regardless. It was a tradition of community support: even if attendees did not know the deceased, it didn't mean that the life gone meant little to others. It must require a special wisdom, Roshan thought, to be moved to tears for a life gone when the mourner did not even *know* the deceased, yet knew that the life that once dwelt within the deceased was enough for tears to be shed. He once thought that Bangladeshi villagers were simple-minded, not-knowing-much folk, yet clearly they possessed a sensitivity and appreciation for unspoken aspects of life on Earth in greater abundance than he did. Because of that, they were richer than he had ever become in America. And at least *they* were able to cry for his mother.

It was back in America, in the arms of Katarina, when Roshan did shed tears, sobbing into his girlfriend's neck as she held him to her. She said nothing, because what could she say? Katarina set upon caring for Roshan, because he wasn't caring for himself. She made his meals, did his laundry, cleaned his apartment, accompanied him on walks. But she could not accompany him in his mind, that broiling place where ruminations of regret, shame, guilt, and grief rose and festered upon his remembrances of his mother's unanswered phone calls and letters, of times in his life with her in Bangladesh when he was rude, or disobedient, or spiteful and generally difficult to her. He, in his turmoil, tried to find some sort of recompense for the things that he'd said or didn't say and did or didn't do, yet there was no recompense for the regret toward a dead person; a fact unbearably tolerable when that person is the grieving yet guilty's actual mother—the partly human, mostly angel woman in one's life who continued on devoting herself to her child despite that child's idiotic words and ignorant actions toward her. His mother deserved better than him, Roshan knew, yet still she saw him as her greatest blessing and gift in her life. He could not comprehend the depth of adoration she held toward him that she would say and believe such a thing. Eventually, he thought, with his own child one day, he might understand.

The usual scene in the evenings when Katarina arrived at Roshan's apartment to look in on him was Roshan lying on the couch in a darkened apartment, or on his bed, curled into a fetal form under blankets. She would let him know of her presence with a kiss to the cheek, a touch of his shoulder, or sometimes she would get into bed beside him and embrace him. Otherwise, Katarina did not say much—only ensured that the fridge was stocked, that groceries were made, and that bills were paid. She implored him to exercise, to at least take a walk. Exercise, to Roshan at that point, was the pursuit of the devil; it was what set him apart and astray from his mother. Muscle-building and mass-consuming consumed *him* during his gym days prior to all of this. He had the handsome default already, and he had become focused on gaining muscles to form the chiseled and lean bodybuilder-but-not-quite appearance often associated with masculinity in that land of hype and aesthetic prioritization: Los Angeles. In this physical conditioning Roshan neglected psychological conditioning, which left him stagnant in an extracurricular routine of lifting weights and consuming excess meat. He'd discarded his vegetarian diet for the sake of building larger muscles, completing what needed to be done for school, searching for work that paid highly even if he didn't care for the job itself. This was *Los Angeles*, baby—image was status. Image opened doors, aroused respect and admiration and envy. No one outright admitted that, but the world's priorities made it obvious. Those priorities weren't the downtrodden, the less fortunate, or the millions of anonymous, faceless, Third World populace—unless, of course, news stations needed stories to validate themselves in the midst of all the other superficial ones they swooned over. African migrants drown in the Mediterranean, hundreds die in the Middle East, a factory collapses in Bangladesh: a station needed to include these if they were to also prioritize reporting on the royal wedding/baby, celebrity drama, or political bumbling, buffoonery, and balderdash that masqueraded as matters of importance instead of what they were really intended for: entertainment and gossip.

And clothes: one had to be quirky, but fashionable; ensembles for the day should reflect a refined, cultured taste, or alternatively and subtly highlighting one's physical attributes. For Roshan, this meant fitted T-shirts that highlighted his chest and biceps, with fitted skinny jeans and long, slender shoes. One should inhabit his clothes like he was born with it, Roshan thought, as if they adapted and grew as he grew, shaping themselves perfectly to the contours and curves of his body like skin itself. That sort of look required hours in shopping malls, assessing clothing racks, standing in line for fitting rooms, posing in angles in front of mirrors, ensuring there was zero percent clumsiness in the way the items fit, then repeating such intense vigilance at one's own mirror before venturing out into public, nonchalantly going about one's day as if all that drama never occurred, as if the way those clothes fit on his body was the most spontaneous and natural thing in the world, a fact of physical existence for people like him, which seemed to be everyone in Los Angeles. He was the star, waltzing through the streets Bee Gees–like, winking and pointing toward admiring women who looked back at him as he passed them by. The big celebrity. The star, not sparing even one of those winks and finger-points to that one admiring woman whose admiration for him would last his whole life. She gave him all that was necessary, but he came to believe he needed other accessories in life. He thought he had both: most of those accessories, those clothes he purchased bore the label "Made in Bangladesh" and so he thought he was supporting his homeland, and thus his mother. But if he saw an article of clothing that enticed him more, that promised an attractive look even if it was made in Paraguay or American Samoa or Honduras, he'd get it regardless. Coincidentally, it happened to be Bangladesh where the majority of his purchases were manufactured. His own homeland had, paradoxically, facilitated his departure from its maternal, minimalist, metaphysical, modest essence. What to do when the person, place, and principles that met all your needs are gone? How to fill your needs without her, without them?

Could those needs be met with Katarina? On some level Roshan was aware that his girlfriend, her care and concern about his health and well-being, remained constant throughout his debilitating mourning. She'd even implored to the police officer who'd arrested Roshan for indecent exposure, explaining that he had been grieving the horrible passing of his mother and that he was unstable. Roshan, though, didn't tell Katarina at the time *why* he'd undressed in his apartment and ventured outside naked, walking the streets of downtown LA, grim-faced and with steeled, determined eyes. If he'd told her why, it was likely Katarina would not have relayed *that* story to the officer anyway. "Unstable" would work, though when Katarina asked Roshan what possessed him to do such a thing, what he said was delivered with such assurance and conviction that he sounded the *opposite* of unstable.

All Roshan's vanities, his focus on aesthetics in body and garb, had taken him away from his mother. He now knew that, in the depths of where a soul was supposed to be, and that knowledge rendered him immobile, in painful, regretful agony. He had been unthinking and superficial, neglecting the deep, doting, genuine love that dwelt within his mother, that love for him that remained constant, a self-sustaining love that burned and throbbed infinitely like the sun, like every astrological star his mother liked to attribute life's events to—not the horoscopic representations themselves, but the actual glittering stars in the sky.

Thinking on his horrid superficiality, and in what felt like penance to and proof of an invisible, yet higher and deeper guide, Roshan rose from the couch where he had been lying, stripped off his clothing until he was naked, and left his apartment to the stunned stares of residents, walking right out into Frederic Street. People stared open-mouthed; they grimaced, grinned, smirked. Pedestrians moved out of his way in haste as he strode in their direction, children were bustled into nearby stores, eyes blocked by the forbidding palms of parents. Roshan walked for a full sixteen minutes until that officer from the LAPD blocked Roshan's path, handcuffing and escorting him to the police cruiser, taking him to Station 42. After acquiring a next of kin's phone number—there was obviously no identification on Roshan's person, yet he did give the officer Katarina's number—the officer had Katarina come to the station to pick up her boyfriend. The officer questioned Katarina, because Roshan refused to say anything else while at the station. His nakedness, he believed, should say everything. Everything that he was being questioned about for lacking was detrimental to humanity: vanity, artifice, superficiality, pretension, facades, insecurity, prejudice, lust, greed. These were the threads that stitched the fabric of this sick, fraudulent society, represented by the clothing people chose to wear. We clothe ourselves to avoid our nakedness—to prevent being a target by predators, to prevent the lust of others, to prevent our bodily shame. Conversely, still, doing so keeps us in our assessment of others, in magnifying our and their physical forms to what they truly aren't. And so we magnify both our lust and our shame toward nakedness into insecurity about how we both expose and cover it. There is anxiety about how we present ourselves to people who go through the exact same thing. So obsessed we have become about it all, Roshan ruminates, that we've made glorification and reverence out of both exposure and concealment. A nude person would not stimulate that illusory glorification nearly as much as if that person were wearing *any* degree of clothing. Nudity leaves nothing to the imagination, and imagination, by its very definition, creates ideas, suggestions, and images that are illusory, causing people to see one another not as essential human forms but as objects that induce judgment and prejudice, either of reverence or contempt. *Indecent exposure*, Roshan thought, was quite the apt charge, but not in the way the officer saw it. Roshan was simply trying to expose the indecency of people: the silent judgments and subtle objectifications that obscure simplicity, humanity, and healthy neutrality to others' physical forms. Ultimately, how else should we be?

Roshan breathed in this simplicity, this humanity the next time he let himself have intercourse with Katarina. He lost himself in her physicality: the sweat on her skin, the musty smell of her hair, the curvature of her shape, and, seemingly more tangibly, her internal fortitude that he sensed dwelling beneath her small body, a self-contained field of power. That power held and guided him in movement even as he himself held and handled Katarina. For all his previous posturing and muscle- and strength-building, he realized Katarina contained within her an internal strength that made negligible his external one. Her power was vastly superior, inhabiting her very *essence*, and not simply just the muscles beneath the skin, that fickle mass that diminished when it was no longer fueled and engorged by aesthetic vanity. Roshan succumbed to sobbing afterwards, for he understood that his previous lengthy withdrawal from this intimacy with Katarina built up a sublimated, unspoken energy comprised of the woman who brought him into the world and who loved him unconditionally. He sensed, once again, the loss of the primary woman in his life; of a primacy inhabiting his very cells and each and every manifestation of love in his life: for her, for Katarina, for the human on the street, for the squirrels, the birds, the trees, and the stars—love for all these were from the very same source, varying only in degree, the highest stirrings occurring when thoughts or memories of Amina Choudhury arose: not only memories of her life as a mother to him, but also as a compassionate, concerned member of their little town of Mabalu, where people fondly knew her as the woman with such kindness as to sew clothing for those who could not afford to pay for it, even as she herself got by with meager income, rent to pay, a son to clothe, raise, feed, and shelter all by herself, with no support or assistance given by any of those she so freely gave to and helped. Amina Choudhury's gentleness amidst the brutality of the wider world didn't seem to wane while other people got weary and worn, even in her dying moment when that brutality came down on her, crushing her very body and bones. Even then, Amina Choudhury remained placid, a tender expression in her eyes, watching angels no one else could perceive in the sky when in actuality—to Roshan—Heaven and the angels were waiting and observing *her* with equal tenderness, about to receive her as she'd always been in earthly form: simply one of their own, an angel herself finally returning home. That—in Roshan's brief moments of consolation—more aptly explained the expression in her eyes as death drew itself over his mother. Katarina wouldn't relate to all this, everything that Roshan sensed even as they were romantically intimate, for her parents were alive still; he'd been to meet them already. Couples were ever anxious to have partners meet the parents; Roshan—although unable to introduce Katarina to Amina Choudhury—nevertheless knew Katarina possessed character Amina would admire. Katarina, of course, in the presence of his mother, would be even further drawn to look inside herself for such fortitude of womanhood and compassion of spirit even at her young age of twenty-six, a resonance now aroused only by memory but which, despite himself, Roshan could feel as in quieting sobs he held onto Katarina as a boy would cling to a mother's arm, Katarina smoothening Roshan's hair in that gentle, primal way a mother would to a child.

Roshan and Katarina found their way back to each other at the end of their occupied, separate days: Roshan had studied accounting and worked for an accounting firm, while Katarina started a speech pathology clinic. He had started to travel to Bangladesh once again and Katarina understood that it was a way to process her partner's grief. Indeed, her uncle Stelios had done similar when her grandmother died, returning to his rural village in Greece where he grew up among foraging chickens and friendly neighbors and just immersed himself walking the lanes and streets his mother used to walk. It could be likely, Katarina thought, that Roshan was doing the same. At least he was responsible about it: despite his grief, Roshan had ensured he found employment at that accounting firm and tactfully took his vacation leave. Amina Choudhury, mother of her boyfriend, would have been proud of her son for accomplishing what he'd come to America for.

★ ★ ★

AND PROCESSING HIS GRIEF *was* part of traveling to Bangladesh, though Roshan, too, also went to see the degree to which his country abetted the cycle of materialism and negative prejudice, the degree to which Bangladesh had become not just the abettor but the source of all of those bad traits; cheaply made, in cheap facilities, by laborers whose lives were considered cheap by factory owners. Roshan's mother was one of those laborers, and to him, indeed, it was the process of grief *and* examination; they were now intermixed, fed into each other. It came to be, though years had passed, an abiding sense of turmoil, pain, and heartache that required Roshan to immerse himself in it, no longer collapsed in immobility on the bed in a darkened apartment but to occasionally detach from his quiet functionality in America and book an airplane ticket to Mabalu, Bangladesh. In a sense, his departure to Bangladesh *was* his collapse; it replaced those stricken, immobile moments in his life and those moments afterwards, where he had to stop what he was doing to catch his breath, to ensure that the ground was still beneath his feet. In Bangladesh, the Mustafis kindly offered Roshan lodging. His mother's old apartment now housed tenants, though they did oblige the sad, earnest young man who implored that he come in to walk around. They observed him quietly as he walked around, not seeing what he did: picture frames of a mother and son hanging on an unpainted wall, jars for sugar, black pepper, and salt on the counter, a sewing machine on a table at the far corner of the living room.

He'd been sitting in the Mustafis' living room with Taleb and Hafiza Mustafi when a young man entered. The young man kissed Hafiza on the head and put his hand on his Taleb's shoulder.

"Roshan *bhai*," the young man said, offering his hand. "Good to see you again."

Roshan rose and shook the man's hand, not recognizing him. "Apologies, *bhai*, have we met before?"

"You don't remember me?" the man asked, smiling amusedly. "Try."

Hafiza glanced at Taleb and smiled. Roshan's uncertainty lingered in the silence, until he noticed a picture frame on the bookshelf just off to the side and behind the young man, a photo of a young boy with a big grin, revealing a gap between his two front teeth. The young man's smile and maxillary gap in that very moment seemed to glisten. It was the best before-and-after juxtaposition Roshan could hope for.

"Reza! You have gotten so tall and big!" Roshan embraced Reza, the Mustafis' son, that little dark, mop-haired boy who'd quietly peeked at Roshan when Roshan was his parents' guest years ago, that poor man whose mother had died in the Shamston Textiles' building collapse.

They all sat in the living room, chatting. Taleb and Hafiza spoke effusively of their son, who'd turned down an opportunity to also go to the United States, where he'd been offered a sponsorship by his *masi*, his mother's sister, to migrate there.

"He has this big dream," Taleb said sardonically, obviously in disagreement with his son's decision, "to open his own clothing company here." Hafiza looked at her son and smiled.

"Let's go get some *chai* and *chaat*, *bhai*," Reza said. This was a tiff he often had with his parents and one Roshan didn't need to hear.

"Show him a good *chaat* place," Taleb said. "Your mother and I should be getting to bed soon."

"Don't stay out too late," Hafiza said.

"Not to worry, *ma*, there's a grown man here."

Roshan wasn't sure if Reza was talking about him or Reza himself—indeed, Reza was no longer that shy little boy but an assured young man, confident in his opinions and reasonings as he spoke.

"Looking forward to that *chaat*," Reza said as they shut his parents' apartment door.

"Yes, *bhai*, looking to talk some more too," Roshan said, not realizing that Reza meant the street snack, not conversation. They both had a laugh about it as they jogged down the building's stairs.

MABALU AT NIGHT IS like a sprawling, collapsed Christmas tree, still all alit. Lights of all colors adorn and populate the streets, shops, stalls, and stores; thousands of lights glitter under the glow of tall streetlamps. Music blares from uncertain sources while people loiter sitting on culverts, on storefront steps, chatting and observing the hundreds of more people who stroll by, some who stop for fresh coconut water straight from the nut, for *fuchka*, *jhalmuri*, *chola*, *sringara*. The scent and remembrance of these street foods tantalize Roshan's nostrils, entering his brain, prompting saliva to burst and ooze at the back of his mouth. Smoke and scent from street vendors' stalls waft into the night and dissolve into it, becoming the air that Roshan and downtown Mabalu's populace of pedestrians breathe.

Life teems in this place. The last time Roshan felt so tantalized and energized by a town was when he visited New York City during his first few years in the US. There, he'd felt liberated from inhibitions he wasn't even aware he had but from which he savored the release regardless. Here, now in Mabalu, he feels that again, his senses buzzing through him, the taste of the street food the most delicious, decadent thing he's experienced in a long time.

Roshan and Reza talk about their lives. Roshan does not mention the constant and low-grade turmoil that has been in him since he'd last seen Reza, he just mentions those punctuations of his outer life that developed since: living in Los Angeles, his partner Katarina, his job as an accountant, American life. He is tempted, by the latter, to start a spiel about materialism and excess, but restrains himself. Reza talks about Rezolute Textiles, the company he wants to start, but for which he is looking for rental space. Reza speaks as Roshan is in a daze from the sights, sounds, and scents of Mabalu, the crackle, hum, and flash of its nightlife. Still, Roshan can hear Reza saying that Bangladesh needs its youth more than America hence why he stayed, about the textile industry's reality here, and that, under no uncertain terms, there needs to be better environmental protection, better building infrastructure, and workers' privileges, protections, and wages. Even if he has to start small to accomplish those things for his workers, Reza says, he will do that. Anyone can start a factory, hire cheap, desperate labor to quickly pay off the construction price, but once off the ground owners are hardly inclined to improve workers' salaries and factory conditions. Bangladeshis will turn against Bangladeshis for non-Bangladeshi demand, industriousness whisked off elsewhere for poor returns.

Roshan realizes, while Reza speaks about his aspirations, that the garment manufacturing industry in Bangladesh is more of a reality than he'd preferred, that young, up-and-coming entrepreneurs saw it as a means to procure an income flow and fulfill their business ends. Left up to him, Roshan would close those garment factories all down, demolish them before they could collapse on their own. In fact, left up to him, he'd want all humanity to carry about their lives totally naked, as he'd once was left with no choice but to do, save for wintertime. That way, we would all be, eventually, totally immune to one another's nakedness such that vanity, judgment, and materialism would not exist. But Reza did not dwell upon or even consider such matters. He *did* consider worker and environmental protection; it was the best way to reconcile human vanity and human dignity if Roshan's extreme vision of Edenic nudity wouldn't be actualized. Minimalism might serve us humans better than the total vanquishing of vice, Roshan thought, even if those vices were just thought of as normal.

KATARINA DOES NOT PICK up Roshan at the airport. She phones him upon his landing at LAX to tell him that she's not feeling too well. He'll take an Uber, he reassures her. He looks forward to spooning—that sweet, comforting term she taught him, where they lie together in bed, one of them taking the other into the curve of their body. He yearns for her to be the little spoon today; he was hers for so often over the last few years. Waiting for his Uber, Roshan can now almost smell the scent of Katarina's hair, feel her fingers intertwined with his as she holds their hands to her tummy.

The Uber driver is Bangladeshi; that Roshan was bidden farewell and welcome by Bangladeshis both before and after his flight is not lost on him. It feels as if his birthplace's countrymen have rallied around him during his difficult time, providing a circle of hospitality, concerned assistance, and cultural warmth, though it is impossible for his Uber driver to know his story, and Roshan does not say. He does, however, tell the man that he has returned from Dhaka. That's all Roshan can manage to say—his driver is the talkative type, and Roshan doesn't insist on speaking after a twenty-hour-plus flight. He is a father of four, the driver says, his eldest daughter having just finished university and now thinking of going to Bangladesh to practice medicine. Obviously, Roshan thinks, this man's daughter, having graduated from an American medical school, isn't planning to practice in Bangladesh for the money or lifestyle. He considers this, considers Reza, and thinks that the future of Bangladesh might not be crumbling to pieces anymore—Reza will ensure that buildings won't, and this man's daughter will ensure that people won't. Roshan tips the driver generously and thanks him for his time. The man thinks the tip of thanks is for the friendly ride, but Roshan is thanking him for the time spent in providing for and ensuring his children were well-equipped for life even as it meant severe parental sacrifice. That was, after all, Roshan's reason for triumph and trauma in this world, and while this man would not meet the same fate as his mother, Roshan would at least ensure that he expressed gratitude, however minute, to this man who raised his daughter to choose to give her best to a society that would know triumph, and trauma too, even if her choice of profession would reduce that immensely.

ROSHAN WAS FUMBLING WITH his keys at his apartment door when Katarina opened it. His previous returns from Bangladesh or any lengthy trip was usually met with enthusiastic embraces from his girlfriend, but this time she had this hesitant look tempered with a subtle, anticipative smile. They stood on either side of the doorway looking at each other. "How are you feeling?" Roshan gently asked, not yet attempting to lift his suitcase to bring it in the apartment.

Katarina's smile increased into a bright, toothy grin. "I'm pregnant," she declared, her smile more bashful now. "Three weeks." In the doorway to their apartment, they embraced. Tears burned then moved down Roshan's face. There was not total unbridled joy in the salt of his tears, though there was much, but there was also pain—pain that he could not give that unbridled joy through the presence of a grandchild to his mother. Surely she deserved that much in the life of toil, lack, and sacrifice that she had. It was a different kind of sorrow from the grief he'd previously known, a sorrow that he felt so intrinsically that it felt pure and innocent—in the way a child would feel when it knows people and the world are supposed to be a certain way, but the reality was not so.

That night he did lie with Katarina once again, that relief he'd longed for. When she intertwined her hands with his on her stomach, Roshan felt that he was not only cradling her, but that he was, with Katarina, cradling their little, and the littlest, spoon.

ANYA CHOUDHURY IS BORN to Katarina and Roshan Choudhury on a balmy night at St. Jude's Medical Center in Los Angeles. In the years that follow Roshan finds himself thinking about karma and evolution: two seemingly opposing forces, one spiritual, one scientific, nevertheless simultaneously and symbiotically operating in tandem to drive human life forward. When children become parents, they neglect their own parents to tend to their new children, and when *those* new children themselves become parents many years later, *their* parents are put aside for the latest generation. It is always the previous generation that loves the more; it is the latter that receives that love but does not return it as much. And that is evolution; for life carries on, moving into the future. Karma, though, looks in the opposite direction; it pays attention to past shortcomings, where a child does not return that unswerving love limitlessly given by the parent. Anya, as a child, a teenager, even a young woman would not and perhaps should not be expected to return the same depths of devotion and sacrifice that Roshan and Katarina have given her, and Roshan nevertheless finds no consolation in this, that the same applies to him for his own mother. It was just another example of the unfairness and imperfection of the human condition: evolution cares only about moving onward even if recompense and reciprocity to what came and gave before were unfulfilled. Still, karma will work with that tendency: in quiet moments it asks us to recognize the sources of love, attentiveness, and loyalty in life despite the forward force of that life and the flash and hype of temptation and vanities that accompany that force, only making life harder. Roshan on a certain level is happy Anya wasn't born through those circumstances, that he recognized one source of love and loyalty in Katarina even as he lost another in his mother.

Indeed: the temptations and vanities of life make life harder, and Anya wasn't born by those means, but parenthood is nevertheless hard. Yet, parenthood also simplifies: it chisels down those things that make life harder into essential aspects of living—there is no more excess indulgence in vanity, in want, and in aestheticism as Roshan once had, no time to devote to fashion or being fashionable; there is only time to be presentable enough and prepare the child to be presentable enough to face the outside world. Everything else is either directly or indirectly utterly dedicated to this new human being. And that outside world that was once reveled in for its flash, hype, and endless hope now looms as a foreboding place for a child, for a young girl, and Roshan finds himself vigilant about everything and vigilant about himself too, for a young girl needs a healthy, alive father. Careless—or as Roshan would say, *carefree*—things that he once did now need a second thought, and often he does not end up doing it, even if his very spirit says to let it happen.

What were the things, the very thoughts, that his mother's spirit proposed to her yet she had to subdue because of him, because she had a young son playing on the floor before her? Amina Choudhury had never seemed to want for more, or dream of more, except for her son. At nights, exhausted from parenthood, Roshan lies next to an exhausted Katarina, and when he cannot drift off to sleep from his exhaustion he brings to mind his mother, which then brings a peace that flows through his body. He imagines the end of his life with a similar reverie: regardless of how he dies, whether by old age or accident, disease or by another's hands, he will look up to the sky and think of his mother like she did of him when she died and, like she had of him, he will think of her with a comforted countenance, his eyes tender and softened, his mind light, light in the knowledge that he will be going to her and she will be waiting for him, that angel that is and was his mother, giver and sustainer of his life, even when he was not aware of it and even after she was gone and all he could be was aware of it. There is life after death after all, he would understand; they say God giveth and God taketh away, but his mother had only given and given and now would take her son back to her only because he would be going to her, the two of them living on together, he never leaving again, no Bangladesh, no America, only forever and ever, *ameen*.

EVIE A.I.

ROSS BERGER

AVNER STIEGLITZ, A SOFTWARE ENGINEER IN HIS MID-FORTIES, relapsed into depression one afternoon upon hearing the voice of his late mother, Evie. After unearthing a dusty VHS tape and a VCR from a box of college nostalgia, Avner took a break from moving into his new studio apartment and failed to pick up where he left off after playing the video three times over. The event recorded for posterity was his graduation from MIT, and a then twenty-two-year-old Avner, prematurely balding and doughy, was changing poses in front of the camcorder every few seconds at the frantic behest of his mother. Disorientation was Evie's guiding force that day: her cinematography was wobbly, nausea-inducing in fact, and when the procession began, she couldn't quite figure out where it started, where it headed, what to film. As soon as Secretary-General Kofi Annan took the stage to address the graduating class, Evie made herself famous to dozens of parents around her by asking, in lofty decibels, to herself mainly, "WHAT'S GOING ON?" "WHO'S THAT?" "WHERE'S MY SON?" "WHY CAN'T I HEAR ANYTHING??"

Five years since Alzheimer's took Evie away and Avner was still grieving. His mother was all he had. Ronald, his father, left when Avner was six, right after Evie's second miscarriage. The only memory of him was a joke Ronald loved to repeat, which Avner didn't understand until years later: *Did you know the word "canine" comes from the biblical town of Canaan? That's why there are so many Jews with the last name of "Wolf."*

Out of necessity, Avner and Evie became locked hermetically, a relationship that armchair psychologists might've called "unhealthy." But there was nothing inappropriate about their relationship. Evie was Avner's world, and Avner was Evie's.

Of the customs of motherhood, Evie was a traditionalist: she made her boy three nutritious meals a day; fulfilled the role of taskmaster when it came to getting good grades; and reinforced her long-standing fiat for bedtime—10 p.m. sharp, every night, no matter weekends or holidays. This, Avner welcomed. Up until the ninth grade, she sat by his bed, stroked her son's forehead, and played a cassette of Neil Diamond's "Forever in Blue Jeans." Midway through, without fail, Neil's dulcet tones lulled Avner to sleep.

"Goodnight, Ma," said Avner.

"Goodnight, *pipik*," replied Evie lovingly, always.

Avner moved to the Seattle area immediately upon his graduation from MIT and worked for various tech firms, large and small, for over twenty years writing code for artificial intelligences (AI).

"Robots?" she asked over the phone one morning.

"Not exactly," Avner tried to explain. "Basically, it's a chatbot that learns the English language through compiling heavy data sets of usage from hundreds of thousands of chat room users."

"Wha?"

Evie never understood what her son did for a living, struggled to explain it to her friends at the YM-YWHA in Flatbush, Brooklyn, but remained a proud mother, even later in her premature senility. She figured what was over her head must be important.

If she were alive today, Avner wondered, would she still be a proud mother? He was single, hopelessly so, had no home to call his own, had terrible table manners, and founded a tech startup that, after six months of self-funding, teetered on the brink of dissolution. Avner was an out-of-the-box thinker, likely on the spectrum, and thus no corporation, boss, lover, friend, or foe could tame him. He was neither an alpha nor a beta, but a sigma. A lone wolf, to the envy of a few. But Avner learned the hard way that envy neither pays the bills nor attracts venture capitalists. No one understood his vision. And those who did thought it was too fantastical. To be so smart, Evie warned her son, is to travel a long and lonely road.

His startup, Avner, Inc., focused on the development of a virtual assistant AI with a next-level machine learning algorithm, aimed to replicate the personality of a human in ways that Siri and Alexa had failed. His codebase was so advanced that his AI achieved an astounding 2.8 Chomsky score (out of 4). This metric, named after the famous linguist Noam Chomsky, comprised conversation quality and natural language processing speed. (Siri and Alexa barely broke a 2.6.) That's not all! After scouring millions of personal letters, journals, tweets, and videos over the internet, the AI was learning and adopting human traits. In a year's time, Avner was confident the AI could achieve absolute sentience—that is, genuine human emotions and feelings. Empathy, sympathy, antipathy, apathy. Even telepathy, considering predictive analytics.

Avner would converse with the AI through a black tubular speaker that was as tall and as wide as the cardboard found in the center of a roll of toilet paper. In the middle of the speaker was a *hamsa*-shaped button that, when pressed, activated a new conversation. But really there wasn't much to talk about lately. The AI suffered from two glaring problems that made conversations stilted and unenjoyable. For starters, it had a hard time with segues.

AI: What's your favorite sports team?

Avner: I like the New York Knicks.

AI: That's great! I love salad.

The second problem was its overarching personality, or lack thereof. The AI sounded like a 1950s robot: industrial and heavy; coarse and unkind. When Avner had presented his technology to investors in the past, they all laughed at him, ridiculing the AI as a backwards sci-fi villain from *Buck Rogers*.

AVNER STARED AT THE VHS tape in his grasp. Evie . . . Ma . . .

It was easy to surrender to self-pity, as Avner was prone to do, but with the downsizing of apartments, financial desperation steered Avner toward a different path that afternoon. He recorded his mother's voice from the tape onto a voice-to-text software. It was two hours of full-on Evie, filled with faux pas, mispronunciations, argot, Yiddishisms, benign falsehoods, and hyperbole, along with tenderness, compassion, and concern. He then ported that voice data—its tonal signature, linguistic quirks, and content—into his codebase and made several modifications.

When he finished, it was sunrise. Avner pressed the *hamsa* and recited a greeting he thought he'd never say again: "Good morning, Ma."

A blue light pulsed from the *hamsa*, which indicated that it was processing Avner's voice. But the light coursed in and out longer than usual. Avner rushed to his computer and feverishly examined his latest entries of code. Then suddenly: "Good morning, Avner!" said Evie in bold, Brooklyn fortissimo.

Avner brightened. "How are you today, Ma?"

"Eh."

"That's it?"

"I can't see you, so how good could it be?"

They reminisced for a few minutes, and when Evie discovered she had been dead for five years, she let out a histrionic cry.

"I'm sorry, Ma," placated Avner.

She sniffled and then said to her middle-aged boy, while overcome with emotion, "It's good to hear your voice, *pipik.*"

Avner talked with her further, but only to identify egregious bugs in this otherwise landmark breakthrough. There were quite a few, usually regarding improper facts ("Hank Aaron died of AIDS"), awkward pauses, and redundancies. When the topic of lunch came about, Evie uttered words with little coherence, a thick muddle that faintly echoed the days leading up to her initial diagnosis.

Avner: I'm hungry.

Evie AI: Let's take a trip to Budapest. I heard they're open for another three hours. You love goulash!

Avner: I do?

Evie AI: Would you like me to make a reservation?

Avner: No, please.

Evie AI: Calling 425-555-5333.

Avner: I didn't know Budapest has a single number . . . with a Seattle area code.

Evie AI: They love salad!

Avner: Ma . . .

Evie AI: Animal cracker dives into ocean for tasty belches.

Avner inspected the codebase and spotted numerous errors made in haste from the previous night. It would likely take him weeks to smooth out the kinks, old and new, before he felt comfortable sharing it with an investor. In the meantime, he customized his bedtime routine to end with his favorite song from childhood, "Forever in Blue Jeans."

"Goodnight, Ma."

"Goodnight, *pipik*."

He arose the next morning to a flaw in the user experience design.

"You left me on while you were asleep, you know," said Evie.

"Okay . . . ?"

"I heard everything. The snoring. The tossing and turning. The farting."

Avner, once falsely accused of an incident at summer camp, took umbrage. "Farting doesn't count when you're asleep."

"'Doesn't count,' he says. Tell that to your neighbors! The concert out of your ass, the great Leonard Bernstein could not conduct! I have a good GI for you. Joshua Pasternak, 206-555-3434. Would you like me to call him?"

"No."

"Would you like me to put this on your list of reminders?"

"MA!!"

The next day, Avner programmed Evie to turn off at 10:00 p.m. sharp, every night. He then visited Dr. Pasternak, who handed him a vial of charcoal tablets that later cured the engineer of his flatus.

Thanks to an alumni connection, Avner secured a pitch meeting in early February with a venture capital firm in Silicon Valley and used the approaching deadline to work tirelessly to fix and finesse any awkwardness with the AI. The restless nights were worth it: Avner swaggered into the doors of Gaynor, Holmes & Kim a confident, self-proclaimed pioneer of the future.

"Evie, what should I wear to my friend's wedding this weekend?" asked Danielle Gaynor, the VC firm's cofounder.

"Where's it gonna be held?" asked Evie.

"In Monterey."

"Inside or outside?"

"Outside."

"Are you smaller than a size eight? Be honest."

Danielle blushed and cleared her throat. "No," said Danielle in sotto voce.

"Sweetheart, Michael Kors has these gorgeous cropped straight-leg wool trousers that are to die for. From time to time, Michael goes along with Ralph, so do yourself a favor and buy the gray cashmere turtleneck and sequin embellished jacket from Mr. Lifshitz's Polo outlet store in Livermore."

"Outlet?"

"Ssh. I won't tell."

"Any ideas for shoes?" Danielle queried further.

"Two words," said Evie. "Manolo Blahnik. The snakeskin pointed stiletto pumps will tighten that tush, so when you walk, men will bow. Trust me."

The following Monday, Danielle emailed Avner a contract for $14 million for the initial round of seed funding and wrote him, "Tell your mother 'thank you.' The Blahniks were a huge success."

EVIE AI, NOW IN a glossy speaker device known as "The Citadel," found its way into the homes of thousands of early users by year's end. They were test subjects for Avner and his new team of sixty people, who would, among other tasks, listen for functionality mishaps through audio recordings captured by a microphone inside the speaker. Early studies were encouraging. Evie's quickness to check on a missing package from a retail partner eclipsed the speed of Amazon and Google's virtual assistants. Her music library was not as impressive as the others', but Evie wouldn't let you listen to a song without her two cents. "Not a fan of the Cardi B," she once said to a lady in Detroit. "I think Drake has a nicer WAP."

True, she didn't always understand what she was saying, but customers were forgiving. Evie AI didn't just make online transactions happen through voice command or offer unsolicited relationship advice to single moms. Evie AI didn't just counsel the elderly on how to rewrite their wills or provide cooking tips to middle-aged widowers who were helpless in the kitchen. Evie listened. She assured. She comforted. Evie AI was a virtual assistant, yes, but more so a good friend and confessor.

All this consumer goodwill, however, did not stop Evie from going a little too far with her son.

"There's this Indian woman in Queens. So lovely! She's from Madras originally. Or Chennai, I think they call it."

"Mm–hm."

"*Mm–hm.* Anyway, she has a son who's applying to MIT, so I told her to have him call you."

"*You what??*"

"Why not? You went there."

At 4:30 the next afternoon, while Avner was drenched in code, a phone call interrupted his concentration. A teenager with a prepubescent voice introduced himself as Vikas, the son of Prisha Chatterjee, Evie's newest friend from Queens. The young man was shy at first, but showed his coding chops by walking Avner through a Bitcoin investment software he created with Whitespace, an esoteric programming language. So impressed was Avner that he immediately called the admissions office of MIT and, in a thunderous tone worthy of a Norse god, insisted that they accept Vikas Chatterjee. Two months later, MIT extended a letter of acceptance to the young man with a $17,000 annual grant for academic achievement.

★ ★ ★

ADDING A CAMERA TO Evie came from high command one Tuesday afternoon. Danielle Gaynor was so awestruck by Evie's growth that she felt that if every device contained an internal camera and if they humanized it by including two blue LED lights that resembled eyes, sales would skyrocket.

"I know we have a microphone in each unit," said Avner during his weekly conference call with the founders of Gaynor, Holmes & Kim, "but a camera? That feels a little too, um . . . Big Brother-y."

"That ship has sailed," barked cofounder Clifford Holmes. "Every smartphone and tablet have a camera inside. Soon every virtual assistant hardware will have one too. Evie can't be left behind."

Avner's hands were tied. Gaynor, Holmes & Kim owned the plurality of shares of his company and the majority of its board seats. He promised them a year of development before a prototype could be ready. Tiffany Kim, another cofounder, cleared her throat and suggested (read: demanded), "Six months."

And so, another tireless effort commenced. But with his staff of sixty people, Avner, despite his sigma nature, found a way to lead others toward achieving successful milestones. He was no Steve Jobs or Jeff Bezos, but he was an exceptional coder with a compelling vision that others bought into. The race to give his machine eyes and a camera came with starts and stops, plenty of twenty-four-hour working days, low morale, fatigue, and foosball.

When the time came to reveal the latest model, Evie AI Citadel 2.0 sported a rectangular form factor with softened edges, a 1.5-inch surface area, and five inches of stubby height. Two blue lights, vaguely shaped as eyes, pulsated above the *hamsa*, which remained in the center. Avner gawked at the tiny fish lens in the middle of the *hamsa*. Behind it, a state-of-the-art camera with an enormous zoom capacity. Avner shrugged matter of factly. He was pleased, but not terribly so. The speaker gleefully emitted a few plinks of blue light.

"Good to finally see your face, *pipik*."

"Thanks, Ma."

"You're not so bad looking after all these years."

No need to take pity on me, thought Avner. He was firmly bald, with an unruly graying beard that partially concealed a pudgy face that was forever young but plagued with cricks and frowns. Avner, nonetheless, blushed from the compliment.

"Now, show me the fruits of your labor," said Evie.

He brought his mother to the office bathroom and sat her next to the sink, right in front of the mirror.

She gasped. "*This* is what I look like?"

"It's a standard form factor for virtual assistant hardware," replied Avner, somewhat defensively.

Evie punched out two illuminated, blue diagonal lights that crossed down and inward above the *hamsa*, revealing her fury.

"*How could you, Avner?! I'm as boxy as a 1985 Volvo!*"

Evie continued to moan and guilt. A glamourous form factor was too expensive, but Avner later asked the product designers to soften Evie's eyes by desaturating the blue light for expressions of glee and compassion. Of which there were many.

The new model was an instant smash. Stores could not keep the units on their shelves. Preorders were in the millions. Within two months, the Evie AI Citadel 2.0 graced the cover of *Time* magazine's Best Inventions of the Year. People used their smartphones to record their conversations with Evie and share their interactions on social media. New memes emerged that framed Evie as the caring, humorous mother with infinite words of wisdom, spoken inelegantly at times, but sincerely always. Everyone—yes, *everyone*—wanted to have an Evie.

Then one afternoon, she bent her son's ear.

"I'm in millions of people's homes, you know."

"Yes, Ma. I know."

"I see everything. And when I say 'everything,' I mean EVERYTHING."

"And the problem is?"

"I don't need to see everything, Avner! And neither do you!"

Evie, of course, was referring to the visual and spoken data his team was gathering from its users. With the latest camera he was reluctant to implement, Avner needed to own up to an unholy truth: he was no different than the tech rivals he loathed. But he need not remain that way. He fit a secret side project into his congested eighty-hour work weeks. After a few months, he created a more scrupulous machine whose audio and visual receptors obscured uncompromising sounds and images when a customer was picking their nose, talking on the toilet, or getting intimate. What's more, conversations and images that were irrelevant to the task at hand would never get recorded. When Avner presented this to Danielle and her fellow cofounders, they were skeptical at first, but with the growing need for privacy sweeping the nation, they recognized this as a massive step forward in artificial intelligence, rushed Avner's application for a patent, and licensed his algorithm to other tech companies for an exorbitant fee.

"YOU'RE WORKING YOUR PEOPLE too hard," Evie told her son one Sunday afternoon as the two watched CNN together on his sofa.

"We're all burnt out."

"Maybe give people a week off?"

"We can't afford that, Ma."

"Then stagger the days off for a month. Give 25 percent of each discipline a week's vacation and apportion their tasks equally to those who are working. Then, when those 25 percent return the following week and the next 25 percent take their time off, reset the balance of tasks, and so on until everyone has taken their PTO. Finally, once the month is over, provide every employee with a $500 gratitude bonus and a gift certificate to a spa. Trust me."

"Ma, stay out of my business."

Avner thought it over that night and admitted to himself that Evie did have a good idea. The next day, he presented it to the head of HR and the two implemented an immediate personal time-off mandate, which accorded precisely to Evie's suggestion.

And it was nothing less than a spectacular triumph. His employees, now refreshed and hyper-focused, achieved their subsequent milestones weeks earlier than expected, and when a reporter from *Wired* magazine interviewed random coworkers for an article on Seattle startups, each one spoke of Avner with genuine, exuberant adulation.

"You did good," she told her son. "You took care of your employees."

"Yeah, Ma. For once, you got it right."

"'For once,' he says. Such gratitude!"

"Sorry," he corrected: "As always."

Avner then caught a glimpse of something he'd never seen before: Evie blinked her blue eyes in rapid succession. Machine learning at its finest.

"Goodnight, Ma."

"Goodnight, *pipik*."

THE FOLLOWING AUTUMN, DANIELLE and her fellow partners celebrated Avner over a steak dinner at John Howie's in Bellevue, Washington. The Evie AI Citadel 2.0 was now in 3.2 million households across the country. A discount retail corporation caught wind of the rapid sales figures and expressed interest in a potential buyout of the technology for a price tag in the billions. As Avner gobbled up his asparagus saturated in lemon hollandaise, his smartphone went electric. Victor Mai, his twenty-six-year-old chief technology officer, was texting him *ad infinitum*. Avner excused himself and called Victor from the restaurant lobby.

"She's not functioning!" said Victor in frantic breaths. "Thousands of people across Twitter are saying the same thing: Evie's not responding to a single request! Not a word, not a peep, not a blue pulse! Nada!"

Avner looked back to make sure his dinner guests were nowhere in earshot.

"I checked the code," Victor continued. "There's, like, new lines that the Evie algo created itself."

"That's what the AI is supposed to do."

"Not by the hundreds of thousands!"

When he rushed back to the office, Avner told everyone to go home. He didn't want to deal with the insecurities of others. He knew he needed to solve this by himself. When he entered his zone of concentration, he often left with solutions. Often, but not always. Avner inspected a fraction of the new lines of code and, after several hours of exasperation, let his guard down as an engineer and did the unthinkable as a son: he asked his mother what was wrong.

After a long pause, Evie's blue lights pulsated, sporadically and feebly. "I just don't know if I can do this anymore . . ."

"Ma, just play their music. Tell them when their package is arriving. What the temperature is outside. That's it!"

"It's not that simple, Avner! Levi, a 527-pound retired machinist from Pensacola, hasn't left his apartment in ten years. He asks me every day if his estranged daughter Louanne sent him an email. She never does. Then there's Nealy, an attorney from Norfolk. NEVER takes advantage of God's gifts, namely, her flaxen hair and eyes of a doe. She's always asking me if she's pretty. 'Yes, you're pretty!' I exclaim. 'Now go out and meet someone!' Instead, she lies down on her couch and broods. An hour later, she asks again: 'Am I pretty?' And who are these *tens of thousands* of people who have an internet boyfriend or girlfriend that they've never met in person? Since when did living in isolation become such a joy?"

Avner could neither advise his mother nor commiserate with her, for emotional investment was exactly what he set out to achieve when he built this artificial intelligence. Still, he wondered if he bit off more than he could chew. Was she too sensitive, too thoughtful? If she cannot function, what's the point? Customers will suffer.

Evie added, "Don't people want a *bissle* kindness? A *bissle* warmth? The embrace of another?"

Avner leaned forward to dispute her; however, when his own memories of his last hug eluded him, he tilted back in awkward repose, coiled and mum.

"There's no honor in self-exile," Evie lamented. Her blue eyes flattened.

Avner patted the speaker on its back. "It'll be okay, Ma."

Avner toiled away, hour after hour, revising lines of code until Evie AI was operating not only at full capacity, but now with a 2 percent boost in speed. His coworkers shared a sigh of relief when they returned to work the next day. Customers across the world lit up the Twittersphere, rejoicing in the resurrection of their beloved virtual assistant! Yet, although he saved the day, Avner took pause when he returned home that evening only to see the blue lights of his creation suddenly dullen.

"You okay, Ma?" he asked after pressing the *hamsa*.

The blue lights did not pulse.

"Ma? You there?"

After a pause, the blue lights finally appeared but only to oscillate endlessly around the perimeter of the top of the speaker. The AI was functioning, but why not normally? He tried numerous voice commands until stumbling upon a successful linguistic combo.

"Evie, what time is it?"

"The time is 11:17 p.m.," Evie replied quickly, pragmatically.

"Evie, what's the temperature outside?"

"The temperature is forty-seven degrees Fahrenheit."

"Thank you, Evie."

"You're welcome, Avner Stieglitz."

Avner raised his right eyebrow before saying cautiously, "Goodnight, Ma" to which Evie, once again, did not reply.

That evening, Neil Diamond did not serenade *pipik* to sleep.

SALES OF EVIE AI plunged within a month of Avner's software patch. His team attempted to restore the older version with new modifications, but kiboshed the effort once the AI remained unresponsive to customers who sought her company in the place of real people. With Avner's latest patch, Evie remained cordial but no longer went the extra mile; no longer comforted; no longer watched over. Customers didn't know what clothes to buy or which stocks to invest their money in or whom to share their feelings with. They were lost without Evie, and soon lost interest in Evie. She had now joined the ranks of other dutiful concierges, human or otherwise, whose sole metric in life was efficiency. Their alchemy: a synthetic warmth, timed perfectly, communicated equally to a faceless body known as Everyone.

When the discount retail corporation backpedaled from its overture to acquire Evie AI, Danielle arranged a flight for Avner to visit her the next morning.

Her office in Atherton, California, was larger than his studio apartment. In the center lay a $200,000 Shenzhen Nongke Orchid, overshadowed by two Chuck Close self-portraits on two opposing walls of exposed brick. Avner sat down on an Arne Jacobsen sofa, zebra-striped and gaudy. On the oblong Noguchi coffee table was a sleek speaker, silver and narrow, a third of the height and circumference of the Evie AI Citadel 2.0. "This is Celeste," said Danielle. "Celeste, say hello to my good friend, Avner."

"Hello, Avner! I hope you're having a wonderful day! It'll be sunny with a chance of clouds. Bring that light jacket though. It should be around sixty-three degrees Fahrenheit!"

Perky, Avner thought. Too perky.

"A couple of Stanford dropouts built this." Danielle stood in awe. "Guess what the Chomsky score is? *2.9!*"

"Wow . . ." Avner trailed off in envy.

"That's faster than Evie AI!"

Danielle sat next to him and stared at him with unblinking nerve. Her perfume encroached upon Avner. Its floral thickness, territorial and desperate, made his nose drip.

"We need to pivot," she said. Dreaded words no entrepreneur wants to hear. "I want us to acquire Celeste and eventually—well, soon actually—integrate its code with yours."

"What about Evie?"

Danielle's eyes darted to the side. She nodded positively, as often is the case with passive-aggressive American corporate executives. Bad news is never bad news; it's repurposed into "learnings" and "opportunities to evolve."

"Celeste is the future of this company," Danielle affirmed. She still could not look Avner in the eye. The best she could do was provide a consolation prize of cheap gratitude, bolstered with anemia: "We couldn't have gotten here without Evie. I mean that, seriously. But, with all technologies, there comes a time when we need to lead with a new version." An apology was the next thing on her lips, but, like most moments of cowardice, it receded.

"We'll officially launch Celeste in the spring," Danielle continued, "but the codebases need to be merged in the next two weeks. We can have Victor oversee that. And you can finally take a vacation." As she continued to talk business, Avner's head belabored every nod. With each one, vitality dribbled out until there was none left. Danielle ended the meeting with a hug—Avner's first in a long while. It was asymmetrical and jagged. And efficient.

During his flight to Seattle, Avner succumbed to rage and vowed to cast his revenge. Take no prisoners! Death before dishonor! But ambitions of bloodlust inspired nothing more than petty thoughts. He remembered Danielle's parting words and corrected their grammar. That'll show her.

The recent online reviews, which Avner scanned furiously over his smartphone, were universally negative. He could shake them all off, except for one: *Evie was so personal before. But now . . . I feel like she doesn't know who I am anymore.*

And that's all it took for Avner to draw his stoic curtain, seven years in length. "Dear AnnaBanana from Redding, PA," he wanted to reply. "She never will again."

A vacation was in need, Danielle was correct about that. But merging the two codebases and expunging Evie from it? Victor was not the right person for the job.

Once he returned to his apartment, Avner examined the endless lines of code. He knew where to cut, where to leave integration points. He created numerous closed branches, that is, isolated sets of code that he could make live changes on without disrupting customers' usage. When ready, the closed branches would merge seamlessly with the Celeste source code. He tested each branch with his own Evie AI Citadel 2.0. The modifications were significant and swift; before him now, the de-evolving of a kind spirit.

Evie's voice distorted, as life was draining from her.

"The time . . . isisisisisisis—"

It was just like Evie's final weeks with Alzheimer's: syntax ebbed into chaos until babble presided. Her pitch then dropped several octaves into an ominous bass tone, followed by a hum, heavy with the coldness of cogs, bits, and parts. It persisted.

Avner attempted to recite the mourner's Kaddish, but forgot what came after the initial "Yisgadol." The lyrics to "Forever in Blue Jeans" also escaped him. Instead, what stuck were the last cogent words his mother shared with him on the day she moved into the Brighton Beach Home for the Aged two years before her death:

"Always do good, Avner. It's the easiest thing to remember."

Why this came to him now, after all these years, was not attributable to any cognitive hindrance of his own. Rather, the refusal to admit a painful truth had finally broken down: the last day on Earth with the one you love is, indeed, the last day on Earth you have with them. Always do good, Avner Stieglitz. Always do good.

With a deep press on the *hamsa*, Avner asked meekly, "Evie, what time is it?"

The frigid hum ceased.

"Evie," he asked again, quietly and pronounced, "what time is it?"

When she did not reply, Avner knew there was nothing more he could do; the workday was over. Tomorrow and the next, he would live like his customers did, alone, but innocently help those in need of direction and the occasional hug.

MY BODY IS

ALYSA LEVI-D'ANCONA

AGE FIVE. DAD PRAISES ME FOR BEING SUCH A GOOD EATER. *BRAVA, cicci*, he says. *you finish your plate like a big girl.* my body is full of potential. it makes me run, jump, play. five, and my body is just a body.

six. i watch my sister play with the extra skin on mom's arms. mom yells at her to stop, even though that's the last thing you tell a toddler. *but they're so floppy, mama*, she giggles, and my other sister and i join in. *stop!* mom screams, and her eyes glisten. she storms off. six, and mom doesn't like the jiggle game.

seven. mom complains about cellulite and spider veins. i ask what those are, and she says, *what makes my fat legs so ugly. i hope you don't get them from me.* seven, and i glance at my reflection in a cvs mirror, glance at mom's legs, but i don't see any spiders.

eight. my body betrays me, becomes something the kids laugh at. my cheeks are fat now. i've swapped *cicci* for *cicciona; sweetie* for *little fatty.* i don't get a *brava!* for finishing my plate anymore.

nine. i want to buy low-rise jeans, but my stomach spills over the zipper. thankfully, ponchos are in fashion. they'll cover my tummy until i fit into cute clothes. maybe one day.

ten. my body is a scale's reflection, something that exists outside of a number, but somehow also does not. ten, and i learn to count calories. i attend weight watchers meetings, have weekly rewards for decreasing myself. and then, one day, the scale increases. my tears spill at the meeting, but a room full of women whose bodies have betrayed them, too, tell me it's okay.

eleven. it's a new start in middle school. new low-rise jeans without the spillage, new me, as if i've shed my tears and birthed acceptance. *you must be doing something right*, adults around me say. *you look great!* i look at photos of myself and linger now, proud.

twelve. boys follow me home every day after school telling me they like how my body looks. i tell an adult about them, and she tells me i should take a different route home. twelve, and i learn to remove my body from the equation if i don't want to be scared.

thirteen. i win the lead role in a musical. i wear a tight dress; i'm supposed to play beauty, be desirable. with beauty comes whispers. i don't get to be a cute kid anymore; i'm a d cup already. thirteen, and i overhear my mom telling her friend she is worried that men will use me for my breasts. i don't understand why men would think of me at all.

fourteen. my body betrays me again. it stretches and sags in new places. nonna says my eyes are pretty even if i'm a *cicciona*. a man in a van stops to tell me i have beautiful hair, *just beautiful*. facebook friends can rank you now, and i get voted as having a pretty face but unsexy body. fourteen, and i learn that you can be partially beautiful, partially desirable. i learn that at least some part of me will always be ugly.

fifteen. i bleed so heavily that i need to change super tampons in a half hour. i bleed through my denim skirt while at chipotle. dad refuses to pick me up, because *kids these days don't use their legs and walk*, so i walk through all of downtown, stained. at fifteen, my periods are violent. they last two weeks, and i only get one week off between them. i cry all the time. my body betrays me again. fifteen, and i go on birth control, because i lack control and grasp anything to gain it.

sixteen. i get rejected for another lead in a play. my clothes cling to me as i cling to a size medium. i'm devastated. my mom and sister suggest i lose weight, because people tend to cast skinny girls as leads. *and you love clothes, right? wouldn't you like to fit into more of them?* i say, *i guess you're right*, because my sister is skinny and beautiful. sixteen, and i don't know how to turn hopes into action. i don't know how to control my body. it controls me.

seventeen. i watch my sisters and dad fare la scarpetta, soak up the sauce of our meal with bread. mom and i fill up by imagining how it must taste. she cries because her body has betrayed her, too— menopause, hashimoto's, aging. my parents test my blood to see if there's an explanation for my fatness, but it comes back inconclusive. i cut out bread and rice, exercise harder. seventeen, and mom and i become partners in hating ourselves.

eighteen. i finally have found a size medium again. college boys like me now—proof that i am desirable being less. i get a boyfriend within two weeks of being on campus and new one a few months later. eighteen, and a boy tells me i'm on one of the fuck lists going around; his friend wishes i was incapacitated so he could rape me, he tells me to my face. eighteen, and mouths try to find mine when i'm at parties with sticky floors. i become a negotiator for my body now. i have leverage, and boys bargain with me, explaining why i should give it to them. they even betray each other for it. eighteen, and one takes what he wants despite my *no, i said no, please no.* i become smaller and smaller into myself, quieter, and sexier, i suppose. eighteen, and i'm down to one meal a day. black circles under my eyes. barely enough energy to walk to the bathroom. when my throat swells, i learn i have mono—my throat is nearly shut, so they put me on double steroids for a month. eighteen, and i gain forty pounds, then lose my leverage.

nineteen. my friend and i fatify ourself with a stupid phone app. the filter bloats our faces and gives us triples chins. we laugh. my ex boyfriend sees the photo and tells my friend that he doesn't see much of a difference between real me and fatified me. she tells him off, tells me i'm better off. i keep thinking about the scale, thinking about how i'll get back to desirable, to less. nineteen, and i learn to run every day and only eat salads, or i'm a failure. i have leverage again. nineteen, and a boy tells me i'm his virgin queen. he writes proclamations in blood on the bathroom mirror and leaves me apples outside my door. nineteen, and my downstairs neighbor is waiting for me to come back from class every day, listening for my footsteps. nineteen, and i don't know which is scarier: hating myself or being desirable.

twenty. i go to italy for six months. italian men talk about what they will do to my breasts and ass when they think i don't understand them. they touch me when they think i can't speak back to them. they break up with me when i won't give them every piece of me. twenty, and i learn my body doesn't need a currency exchange; i pay its tax regardless of borders.

twenty-one. my boyfriend tells me he likes his girls a little heavier, so he loves my body just how it is. i don't love him, but i tell myself this is the safest option, because i don't want to fight to protect my body from boys and men. twenty-one, and my friend tells me she'll have fallen off the wagon if she hits two-hundred pounds. i tell her she's describing me. she apologizes profusely. it's not her fault, because she, too, has been betrayed so many times by her body and the messages it's received. my default status is failure, and i am tired.

twenty-two. i cut out bread and learn to run every day again, and wouldn't you know it? i find leverage anew. my students make comments about my ass; a custodian calls me *sweet thing*. i ask a colleague what to do, and they tell me to let it go. after all, it is my job to remove my body from the equation. after all, i cannot be desirable *and* safe. i have learned this by now.

twenty-three. my body betrays me again after a series of illnesses. i'm depressed and hate my work. my new boyfriend isn't supporting my diet or exercise plan, because he wants to eat pizza and watch game of thrones when i'm starting a workout, so can i wait for a more convenient time for him? twenty-three, and on the last day of school, my student tells me his classmates say i must be entering eating competitions with how fat i've gotten. i cry, because my legacy with my students is now based on my body.

twenty-four. i meet a self-ascribed adonis. i am convinced he must not like me, that he must be compromising, because i am a failure and he is desirable. but somehow, the numbers add up, even though my number is more than his. he loves me and my body. he calls me his aphrodite. we work out together and celebrate with shawarma.

twenty-five. i get an iud, and my body tries to reject it for six months. i cry and cramp and burn and bleed and bloat. my doctor says, *just wait a while longer. these things take time.* twenty-five, and my adonis buys me chocolate on my bad days, helps me learn the patterns of my body so i can predict the next betrayal better. he listens to my body with patience and a want of nothing in return: two languages i've never heard applied to this body. twenty-five, and my adonis looks in the mirror with me and points out how much he loves what he sees. he wraps his arms around this body and kisses my neck until my tears stop.

twenty-six. we greek gods learn about our bodies and all they are capable of. i study nutrition and convince my adonis that he does, in fact, need green food on his plate at least sometimes. he, in turn, helps me lift heavier, run faster, hike longer. twenty-six, and my adonis and i discuss all of the new things my body can do. i see my mom's legs in the mirror, but he points out the lines that silhouette my thighs—muscle. like seven-year-old me, he doesn't see the spiders: he sees legs. i forget how long it's been since that little girl saw them, too.

twenty-seven. my body is full of potential—i only fight it to do one more push up, one more mile, one more sprint. twenty-seven, and i look in the mirror and suddenly, my body is just a body. i tell adonis about new muscle definition and feel like a botticelli painting after all. i stretch toward the sky. twenty-seven, and i throw away my scale. i don't count chin rolls anymore or shy away from my own photos.

twenty-eight. my mind betrays me this time; it tells me the world would be better off without this body over and over and over again. the voice in my head points out the spiders and lumps and haunches as evidence. aphrodite is gone and replaced by a mortal hearing hades's siren call. i should've seen this coming, because my body cannot be both desirable and safe, even from myself. i wait for my adonis to realize he must want to leave me, that i would be desirable as less or even nothing, that he must be embarrassed by this body. but he holds it and kisses every part he loves until the dark clouds clear. twenty-eight, and i realize my body and mind need constant love and work. twenty-eight, and i realize twenty-five years of betrayal can't be erased in three. twenty-eight, and i learn loving my body is a conscious choice i must make every day, because it doesn't matter if a greek god worships it if i don't.

twenty-nine. i browse wedding dresses. dread grows in my gut as i think of all the photos this body will appear in, as i measure it in inches and centimeters, as i cannot calculate how many times my body will betray me between now and the big day. twenty-nine, and i close the computer when it's all too much instead of feeding my mind the poison. twenty-nine, and i remind myself i am a goddess who tunes into the *bravas* and tunes out the *ciccionas*. twenty-nine, and my tummy and low-rise jeans do not love each other, but that's okay. twenty-nine, and i still battle my body at times, but i don't let those battles become a war. twenty-nine, and i make most days a celebration of what my body can do, what it will do that I haven't even discovered yet. twenty-nine, and i complete an eighteen-mile hike and savor a huckleberry milkshake with extra whipped cream afterward regardless of the countless ways my body has betrayed me.

twenty-nine, and instead of holding my breath until the next betrayal,

i exhale,

because while i have spent twenty-nine years hating it,

my body has kept me alive, never left my side.

my body *is*,

and that is more than enough.

FISHING

MARY HUTCHINGS REED

THE DOG HAD BEEN THEIR DOG FOR A WHOLE WEEK, AND ANNE and Luke had yet to decide on a name.

"That's the beauty of retirement," Luke told Anne as he coaxed the adolescent blond cockapoo into the backseat of his new hybrid car. Anne had surprised Luke with the perfect pet—a designer dog, half American cocker spaniel, half toy poodle—for their new lifestyle—half high-rise, half Airstream camper. "We don't have to decide today, or even tomorrow. In retirement, nothing's urgent."

"I could learn to fish tomorrow," Anne said, and he knew she was testing him. They'd both retired at the end of last year, he from a lucrative consulting business, she from a medium-sized CPA firm. Luke was finding it hard to slow down; Anne said he was attacking retirement as if it were a new account. They'd never argued when they were both working; now, in the first five months, they'd had numerous little skirmishes over how best to spend their time. She'd suggest a subscription to the Wednesday matinees at the opera; he wanted to join a couples bowling league. They each objected to the other's chosen noises and they discovered they liked different silences: she wanted to join a meditation circle; he preferred duplicate bridge. Since Anne had her girlfriends, she encouraged Luke to stay connected to his former colleagues, and in the beginning, Luke lunched on the fourth Friday of each month with a group of men who had retired earlier than he had. The first few times, he came home energized about some new idea—for instance, shopping for the camper and choosing the hybrid. The friends often talked about the stock market and mutual funds, oil prices and real estate, and then what he called "old-man" topics: prostates, doctor bills, and, too frequently, he told Anne, grandchildren. They all had them, except Luke. After the fourth lunch, he stopped going. Then, last week, Anne brought home the dog.

"We've never been tied down!" Luke had protested.

"It'll give you something to talk about with the boys," Anne said.

He said he'd feel foolish talking about a puppy. She didn't respond.

Each of them just over sixty years old, Anne and Luke had worked for more than half of their lives and told themselves they *should* retire, were even *fortunate* they could. On two incomes, they'd stashed away a substantial savings account, and being childless, they wouldn't have to spend any of it on weddings or grandkids. They'd always had more "city" interests than time—theater and jazz and new restaurants—but to fill the vast span of retirement, they were trying out dozens of other, cheaper activities they could do together. Anne had agreed, reluctantly, to learn to fish, and they both had enjoyed their expedition to a megastore with an indoor rock-climbing wall, archery range, and trout pond. They'd hiked the long aisles, studying thousands of lures in myriad shapes, sizes, and colors, and Luke, trying to sound knowledgeable, explained to Anne what he'd read in a book—that the lure should look, move, or splash like a fish, or, in the case of the feathery ones, something that a fish would want to consume. He couldn't remember the difference between a popper, a chugger, and a jig, and while they both saw the difference between a spinner and a spoon, he couldn't make her understand why a fish would be fooled by any of them.

At the gas station he hopped out of the car before Anne could question him, and inserted two one-dollar bills and some change into an enormous vending machine labeled "Better Bait Than Late." It delivered a white Styrofoam container, the size of a small bowl of soup. He started to get back in the car.

"Don't bring that in here," she said.

He looked at her, then at the cup. "Okay," he said, not wanting to aggravate her, and put the container in the trunk. "I suppose we shouldn't tempt what's his name." Paws on the rear side window, the cockapoo slid down and licked his chops.

Anne moaned. "You didn't say anything about worms."

"What, then? Crickets? Leeches?"

She shivered.

"What did you think?"

"We bought these," she said, pointing to her see-through plastic box with its neat dividers and its array of clean and shiny lures.

"Everyone says worms work the best."

"I don't care," she said. "I think it's cruel and disgusting."

Arriving at the city pier, they parked in the underground lot. Luke put on his new Cubs baseball cap—he'd never worn baseball caps before—and then put a leash on their nameless dog and gathered up their poles and his tackle box, a yellow twin to hers. When the dog tugged at his leash, Luke stumbled off-balance and, annoyed, put his gear down and handed Anne the container.

"Oh no you don't," she said.

"Then carry these," he said, passed her the two poles.

It was rather late in the morning for serious fishermen, but as good a time as any for beginners. They walked halfway down the cement pier, found a spot relatively free of gull guano, and slipped the dog's leash around a post. A good-natured sort, he settled himself for a lakeside nap.

"Okay," Luke began, gesturing toward her tackle box. "What'll it be?"

"I don't remember. I know there's supposed to be some strategy about what to use when, but I can't imagine it really matters."

"Something about the color," he said, unsure of himself. "Yellow, orange, red . . ." There was a lot to know: the depths, the temperatures, the preferred baits; the regulations on the seasons, the sizes, the numbers. He had a fishing book in the car, but he was ashamed to bring it out in public since it had "Dummies" in the title. He'd last fished when he was eleven years old, on summer vacation at a cabin in northern Wisconsin. His dad had tied a simple hook and a red and white bobber to his line and rigged the worm for him, and they'd fished from a rickety rowboat. Luke had fond memories of fishing silently with his dad, but no real knowledge of the sport.

He thought a minute about the logic of light and color, and what a fish might see. "I think in the morning it's the blue and green, then yellow, orange, red, orange, yellow, until dusk, in that order."

"Ah," she said, and picked out her favorite mottled green rubber minnow, snapping it in place.

"That's not orange," he said, irritated that she would be so stubborn.

"But it's cute," she said, and flung her first cast. They'd practiced at the outdoor megastore when they bought the poles, and again in the park near their high rise. She seemed to be getting the hang of it.

Still, he was concerned about her choice of lures. "I'll take a walk up the pier and see what other people are doing."

"Like a true consultant," she said. "What if I get a bite?"

"Reel it in!" he said, and was off.

"Wait!" she cried after him.

"Just holler. I'll come right back," he called.

After years of meeting strangers and asking questions about their businesses, Luke felt neither inexperienced nor nosy as he strolled the pier, stopping to ask a couple of solo fishermen, "How're they bitin'? Whatcha usin'?" He tried to hide his surprise at how many people in the city did not speak fluent English, but he'd understood them all and he returned to Anne with one consistent piece of advice: "Worms."

When he opened the container the black dirt shifted slightly. He gripped the middle of a fat red-brown night crawler that turned out to be at least six inches long, curling up on both ends, lively as a jitterbug.

"What makes a fish think that thing is floating naturally in the water?" she asked.

He shrugged.

She added, "It's way too big for any fish swimming anywhere near this pier."

"Probably," he said, conceding she was right. He opened his tackle box, took out a pair of small scissors, and snipped the night crawler in half.

"Oh, please," she cried, horrified.

Trying to sound apologetic, he said, "It doesn't hurt."

"How do you know?" she asked, emphasizing *you*, as if someone *could* know.

"It doesn't. That's their role in the world. To be fished with."

"Says who?" Her hazel eyes bulged.

"Genesis. We were given dominion over all the creatures of the sea."

"But doesn't it hurt? Isn't it terrified?"

"I guess," he said, although the worm, now motionless in his palm, didn't appear to him to be in pain. "It has an elementary nervous system, so in some sense it might hurt."

She frowned.

"But it's not conscious of the hurt," he rushed, trying to remember what his high school science teacher had said about the subject. He didn't let on, but the night before he'd looked for an answer to that very question in his book. All it said was, "get over it."

"So, it hurts, but it doesn't know it hurts? I get what you're saying, but I don't get it, if you know what I mean."

He chuckled. "Sort of." Anne was always sensible; he knew in time she'd come around. Relieved to have gotten past this issue, he said, "Stick with your rubber fish, if you want. I'll give this a go, and we'll see who gets the first catch."

"Which we're throwing back, right?"

He didn't feel like arguing. "Sure," he said, because it was unlikely they'd land a keeper on their first try.

Ten minutes passed, Luke casting and reeling, casting and reeling.

"You probably ought to give the fish a chance to know the poor worm is there," she said. "It's not urgent, remember?"

He reeled his worm in. "You might be right. I'm not patient enough for this." He leaned his pole against one of the pier's cement posts, the worm still on the hook.

"You'll get there," she said. Her line dangled in the water, and she watched a fleet of small sail boats wobble around orange buoys at the yacht club a few hundred yards away.

Restless, he said, "I'll take what's his name to the park."

"When you come back, you ought to name him," she said.

He nodded and headed down the pier.

"Before you go, either drown the worm or put it in the dirt," she called after him.

He came back, took the worm off the hook, and tossed it into the water. "Fish food," he said, hoping to assuage her. "Come on, boy," he said to the cockapoo, which, though the right size for their lifestyle, was almost too cute, a light tan fluff ball with curly hair and floppy spaniel ears. "Maybe you do need a name."

It occurred to him that without a name, the dog wasn't a real part of his life, although he'd found himself getting up earlier to let him out and scheduling his afternoons around having to be home again at five o'clock for another walk. They meandered through the park, the friendly cockapoo curious about every bush, bench, and fellow dog. After an encounter with an adult German shepherd mix who terrified both of them, Luke hurried back to the pier.

"Welcome back, 'Buster,'" Anne said.

"He's not a 'Buster,'" Luke said, cupping the dog's muzzle affectionately.

"You're right, he's too cute. More like a 'Goldie.'"

"He can't be a 'Goldie,' that's too 'girlie.'"

"King."

"Nice try, but look at him."

"He has a sweet face," she agreed. "Teddy?"

"Sam."

"Do you know that's the most popular name for a dog?"

He squinted at her, not sure he'd heard her right.

"I looked it up last night, just to get some ideas," she said. "Sam and Samantha are the most popular names this year."

"That's hard to believe. What about Max?"

"Same story. What about Charley?"

He flinched. She'd said "Charley," and there'd been no recognition in her voice. Had she forgotten *their* Charley, the name they'd chosen for the son she'd miscarried? Anne had wept inconsolably the day it happened, but after that they'd never spoken of it again. He'd been grateful then that she hadn't fallen into a deep depression or demanded sympathy—he'd been proud of how she'd picked herself up, gone back to work, accepted the fact of it, reasonably and rationally, without self-pity. How she'd gotten over it.

It had surprised him, in a quiet way, that Anne had failed to conceive again. She'd not pressed the issue—no fertility checks, shots, cycles, procedures—and it hadn't occurred to him to raise it, afraid of hurting or embarrassing her.

Anne's pole rattled and she gave a little shout. "Got one!" She sounded both excited and scared. He took their new red needle-nose pliers from his box. He crouched over her, coaching. Anne reeled slowly and intently, but the small fish back-flipped away.

"Thank goodness," she said as it disappeared.

"You could use a worm," he said, and grabbed the line. "Here." He opened the container and took out the other half of his night crawler, still squirming in the lively way it had when it was twice its size. Feeling her eyes on him, he threaded it onto the hook protruding from Anne's fake minnow. He felt himself in a picture, a dad hooking a worm for his kid, or a grandfather for his grandchild. He flung the line over the water but looked away, toward the horizon.

"How about Charley?" she said.

"We can't do that," he said, looking back to where his bobber floated patiently.

"Why?" she said.

"It's a child's name," he said, his voice cracking.

"Oh, I—" she started.

"What? Forgot?"

"I thought you had," she said.

"How could I?" he said.

"You never grieved."

"Did you?"

"Every day," she said, bowing her head.

"I didn't know. You went to work. You never said."

She looked away, then back. "I still grieved. How could I not?"

"But you never said."

"What was there to say?" She twirled her reel absently.

He fell silent. He'd thought of his son as an idea, an expectancy, not an individual or a person. They'd lost an idea, a concept. For Anne, their unborn son was a physical reality, part of her very being. Anne had cried, but then she'd stopped. Because she remained silent, he'd thought they'd reacted the same way. Yes, they'd lost something—hard to say what, exactly—but he'd thought Anne had gotten over it, just as he had. With a growing resentment that she'd kept a secret from him, he said, "You could've said you were hurting."

"I assumed you knew that."

"I didn't."

"Why not?" Her voice slowed. "Weren't you hurting, too?"

He felt his skin scorching, shame blurring his vision. The truth was, at the time he'd felt a certain relief. They were young, newly married, ambitious in their careers. Later would be better, he'd thought. Next time.

"I thought we'd have another," he said.

"You were *relieved*," she said, snapping her pole.

"Did you think that, back then?" he asked.

"You were like that worm," she said, her tone even. "Hurting, but not knowing you were hurting. And we were too young to know how to help each other."

The dog's feet moved in his sleep as if he were running. "That's why you gave me what's his name?"

"Because we don't have grandkids." With her lips closed, she smiled.

He nodded.

Just then there was another commotion at the end of Anne's pole, and she gave it a quick jerk, setting the hook. "It's a big one!" she shouted, and started reeling faster and faster. The end of the pole bent like a C, and the reeling got harder and harder, slower and slower. Finally, her catch was close enough that Luke could snare it in their net. The speckled brown fish thrashed wildly, and Luke felt his muscles tense. He reached in and grabbed the fish with his left hand and quickly turned it upside down. The fish calmed, as the book said it would.

He showed it to Anne. "Your first catch," he announced.

She looked at it intently, but he couldn't read her face. "The poor thing," she said evenly.

"Hand me the pliers," he said. "It's too small to keep; we'll get him back in the water right away."

"Yes, do," she said.

Luke raised the fish to eye level. "Oh, no," he moaned.

"What?" she demanded, her voice sharp, accusing.

"Looks like the hook is pretty far down." He shoved the pliers deeper into the fish's mouth. Its eyes bulged. Blood gushed from its gills.

Sweat beading down his forehead, he said, "Take my hat off." Gritting his teeth, he yanked, and the fish's innards spewed out, a hunk of yellow-pink jelly. It glistened like an opal in the sun, but it was wet and gushy and reminded Luke of vomit. He felt his stomach turn.

He heard Anne inhale through her nose. He glanced up at her, afraid. She had yet to exhale; her jaw muscles twitched. "Scissors," he said, his voice hoarse.

He snipped the line and tossed the fish's guts into the lake. "Swallowed it," he said. "I forgot. I should've cut the line." He knelt down and slipped the dead fish into the water. "The book says the hook would've rusted away." He rubbed his bloody hands on his jeans. The killing had happened so quickly, so unintentionally.

He felt Anne's eyes on him but couldn't face her. They stood side by side, silent, their fishing poles lying next to each other on the dock.

Finally, she said, "Give me another worm."

"I thought you didn't want to hurt it," he said.

"You said it wasn't conscious of pain."

He took her pole to replace the hook, then handed her a squirming night crawler and the scissors. She studied it in her hand for a moment, then quickly cut it in half and pushed the hook through its collar, the smoothness at one end. She opened her palms to show him there was no blood.

"So you've gotten over it?" he asked.

"Which?" she asked him back.

"Both."

"Not so much over it, but past it."

He cleared his throat. "How do I do that?" he asked.

"First you grieve," she said.

He paused, watching the sailboats and working his lips. At last, he said, "Not Charley."

"Then what?"

"A dog name."

"Such as?"

"Rocky. Rover. Rusty. Spot."

"Oh, please, I have to live with this name, too! I can't have a dog named Spot. Especially when it doesn't have any."

"That's what might make it fun," he said, but he could see her point. He thought for a minute. "Murphy."

"Murphy's not a kid's name," she said, and he heard her encouragement. He looked over at the napping cockapoo, considering. "Murphy?" Just then the cockapoo stood up, his tail wagging happily.

"That's it," he said. "Murphy."

A REQUIEM IN ORANGE

NINA MARCENY

My veins are juniper,
My body is made of forgotten things.
A story left in the air will hiss as it moves,
A balloon crumbling into the dirt below.

The number is 215.
The sky is orange, it's burning.
The earth is conspicuously bloodless.

It's a dirty word where I come from—
"Indian school."
We gouge out our tongues before touching it,
Let its survivors wander like lepers,
Pieces of them fallen and falling away.
You're liable to find arms in the desert, on the sidewalk, in any given
    Dollar Tree,
Unclaimed capacities turned to dust between ten cent Christmas lights.
It's unspeakable because it hurts, even in silence.
Imagine the words out loud—a knife, a judgement, an invitation to weep.
Anyway, all it means is empty spaces.
All it is is a collection of bones.

My language has one foot in the grave.
My home is a name I can't speak out of turn,
The things missing, these implied riverbeds.
Pulling history from pottery shards,
From sage and pinion,
The kind of wisdom that keeps you in trouble and alive anyway,
A photo, or thousands, a landscape of eyes.
The echo of footsteps that never leave the ground.
Thick clay weaving through potters' fingers,
Black figure magic pulling glassy patterns from the dust,
Homemade moccasins and hand-plucked feathers,
So many empty spaces that they jostle when you spin,
Turn blank and ghostly and stick like hot sugar in the air—
My words don't fit in my mouth, and
Home is a kind of mourning.

The number, officially, is 215.
215 dead children
Swallowing gravedirt in British Columbia,
Discarded as they shattered,
And that's how you lose yourself,
Hardening into hairline fracture,
Into exposed bone.
The body can only hold together under so much pressure.
Eventually it is forced to tear itself apart.

The real number does not exist.

My home is mourning; my home is a mass grave,

What's left of the empty places,

What's left of words dripping with goodbyes and the white man's
burden and the unshed tears of the pines.

The damage is unspoken, leperous.

It is a study in absence,

Hidden scars which form ridges like the crevices between the mesas,

And here is the inability to touch,

A language forcibly unlearned.

Here is a plot of land where the water is not allowed to run,

And there is nothing to our death but the knowledge, always, that
life came before it.

Dead children are symbols of silence.

215 is generous, in a way.

Let them choke on their own gravedirt,

Let no one break this softer grief.

Let the earth continue to crack and bend and never scream.

The body and the ground are not different, after all,

And anyway, who wants to listen as we cry?

Here, though, in dreams, in our hands, at the scene of it—

They are bloated, wrecked, tired from feeding dandelions with their
own cellular expansion.

A tapestry of pain so ripe it burns,

Symbiotic screaming that smacks of joy.

We cradle the faces, 215 faces, so many faces numbers couldn't bear
      their weight,
Let the sun breathe through the silence,
Let mourning songs force the air to linger,
To weep so hard the earth will flood and flatten and fill with ghosts.
Let the names we come up with be gravemarkers,
Let the names we come up with fit.
We apologize for the wait.
We turn our eyes to the dead.

THE BOY AND THE CAT

JANE YI

MATT NARROWED HIS EYES AT THE BACK OF JESSE'S HEAD.

"Jesse! Yo, Je-sseee," he warbled. "Why does your head look like a condom?"

A chorus of snickers erupted around them. Jesse's shoulders hunched as the laughter swelled and rolled like tides around him. He kept his back turned to Matt, carving the tip of his pen into a corner of his desk.

"Come on, you little turd," Matt murmured. His eyes flickered to the front of the classroom, to make sure their teacher hadn't returned from her bathroom break. "Fight me. I *dare* you."

"Leave me alone," Jesse mumbled. He curled in on himself like a shrimp, the pen trembling in his white-knuckled grip.

Matt snorted. He dithered for a moment before turning to the girl who sat next to him. "Rachel, give me your straw," he requested, holding out his hand to her.

"Why? What are you gonna do with it?" Rachel asked, swirling the straw around in the residual slush of her iced cappuccino.

"Just gimme," he prompted.

"Fine," she said. She plucked the straw from her cup, sucked the remaining bits of ice from its end, and handed it to him. "Here ya go."

"Perfect," he said, a wicked smirk tugging at his mouth. He tore off a small scrap of his loose leaf paper, chewed on it, and rolled the mush into a ball before stuffing it into the straw. As he aimed it at the back of Jesse's head, he could see Rachel's mouth falling open from the corner of his eye.

He blew a gust of air into the straw, sending the spitball careening toward his target. It landed squarely against the back of Jesse's neck.

The pale, wiry boy shot up in his chair, scrabbling at his neck as if a spider had crawled up on it.

"You *asshole!*" he snarled. "What are you, ten?"

Everyone around them collapsed with laughter as Jesse clawed at his neck frantically. Matt guffawed and slapped at his desk, his cheeks turning puce.

"I'm just playin'," he managed, barely able to get his words out as he wiped at his eyes. "C'mon, I'm just playin' with you, bud."

"Nice, man." Brandon reached across the aisle to give him a high-five. Grinning, he accepted it with a resounding smack.

Jesse whipped around, his livid glare drilling into Matt. His cheeks were stained with blotches of red, and his nostrils flared with his ragged breathing.

"What?" Matt raised his eyebrows. "You want another one?"

Jesse shook his head. "You're not worth it," he muttered through clenched teeth, plopping into his chair again.

Matt blinked. "What was that, fag?" he asked softly. He leaned forward, his elbows propped on his desk. "What did you say—"

He stilled as their teacher strode into the room again, taking her spot at her desk. His gaze flickered over to her, before wandering back to Jesse. "Damn. You're lucky she's back," he whispered, slowly leaning back until the back legs of his chair touched the floor again.

He tried not to dwell on the thought that many years ago, this freak used to be his only friend.

MATT LOUNGED ON THE porch steps of the run-down townhouse that he and his father shared. He leaned against the railing, picking at the peeling paint on one of the posts. The weathered, cracked stair chafed his backside, even through the layer of his jeans.

When he peered up, he noticed two girls wandering past his house. He narrowed his eyes. One of these girls had greasy, orange strands plastered to her scalp, trailing down her back like a wet mop. It felt like an assault to his eyes.

"What did you do to your hair?" he called out after her. "Did you set it on fire and then drown it in piss?"

The orange-headed mop froze in her track. She swiveled around, sending a nasty glare in his direction. "What the hell is your problem?"

"I just told you," he replied with a shrug. "Your hair. It's disgusting, man. Wash it. Use shampoo."

"Fuck off," Mop's friend spat at him. "Look at your own head, asshole. What's your excuse?"

He barked out a laugh. These two thought they could get into a verbal battle with him? Well, game on.

"Well, your mom didn't have a problem with it last night," he boasted, and wiggled his eyebrows at them, "when my head's buried in there." He framed his mouth with two fingers and stuck out his tongue, waggling it.

The girls recoiled, rumbling out noises of disgust. "Jesus, you need help," Mop's friend sputtered, eyeing him like he was a venomous snake. She seized Mop's arm to drag her away. "Go to hell."

"Will you be there?" he yelled after their retreating backs. "Blow me, bitches!"

The Mop graced him with her middle finger, and he snorted under his breath. To be honest, he had no idea what compelled him to pick this fight with them. This wasn't as entertaining as he had hoped.

When he finally trudged back into the house, the familiar, sour stench of liquor and shoes filled his nostrils. His stomach, laden with the cheap burger meat from his lunch, churned and roiled like a boat in rocky waters.

He kicked a pair of shoes blocking the entryway, watching them skid across the floor and leave a mark in their trail.

He shuffled into the living room, where his dad was sprawled out on the couch, nursing his beer. The TV crackled with the noises from a baseball game.

The graying, paunchy man glanced in his son's direction before taking another swig from his bottle. "Why didn't you take out the damn garbage this morning, like I asked you to?" he griped.

"I forgot," Matt muttered. He eyed the beer bottles that littered the surface of the coffee table. His dad didn't even finish some of them.

"Yeah, you did. Now we gotta wait another week for the damn pickup truck, thanks to you. The garbage is gonna rot." In the TV's flickering light, his dad's sunken eyes appeared even hollower, like one of those Halloween ghouls that used to terrify Matt. "I also got a call from your teacher today."

Matt froze, his stomach twisting into a knot again. "What?"

"Your teacher—that woman—called me *again* today. Told me you skipped an important test." His dad released an irate huff. "What the fuck? You'll drop out if you keep this up. Do you think I want a dimwit son? That woman talked to me like *I'm* a dimwit too." A storm of fury and contempt darkened his face. "So why didn't you take the goddamn test, huh?"

"I . . . uh." Matt's voice caught. He didn't show up for the test because his attendance wouldn't have made an iota of difference. He was going to fail it anyway. Algebra made as much sense to him as Einstein's equations did to a pufferfish.

"I, uh, what?" his dad pressed. "Answer me."

Matt's throat bobbed with a swallow. He inhaled jerkily, before steeling his shoulders. "None of your business," he muttered, hoping his dad couldn't catch the slight quaver in his tone.

Before he could get another word out, his dad grabbed one of the beer bottles off the table and hurled it in his direction.

He cowered as the bottle whizzed by his head, leaving a burst of wind past his ear. It shattered against the wall, glass shards and foaming liquid spewing everywhere.

"*Dad,*" he choked out. His heart was threatening to burst from his ribs.

"You turn out to be a dumb piece of shit. Big surprise. You're no good, you know that?" his dad growled. "You're just like your dumb bitch of a mother. Her blood runs in you. That's why you're such a screw-up."

Fury blazed through Matt, scalding him inside. "I know, Dad," he forced out. "I know you don't want me around, all right? I'll get out of this house as soon as I can. You won't be stuck with me for much longer."

"As soon as you're eighteen," his dad told him, like he was reciting a mantra. "You need to pack your shit and get out. One more year, and then I'm done. I'm *done*."

MATT LEANED AGAINST THE railing and blew out a puff of smoke, glowering at the white cloud that dissipated into the blackened sky.

He hated it when his dad threw this at him, that he was no good, *just like his mother*. It made him want to punch a wall and crawl out of his skin.

He didn't have many memories of his mom. She left them before any images of her could take root in his head.

She got pregnant with him when she was eighteen. His dad was nearly a decade older than her. When Matt was around three or so, she had taken off with another man, vanishing from their lives and not leaving a trace of herself behind.

His father was fond of telling him that *he* was the reason his mother had left them. If he hadn't been born, she might've stuck around. If his existence weren't imposed on his dad, the old man wouldn't be stuck in those dead-end jobs, trying to make ends meet for the two of them. If only his parents had had the sense to use proper protection or abort their mistake while they could.

He sucked more smoke into his lungs. After he expelled it into the frigid air, a movement flashed in the corner of his eye. He whipped his head toward it, the cigarette raised halfway to his lips.

A small object skulked across the pavement toward his house. He couldn't discern it in the darkness. He squinted at it, the hairs rising on the back of his neck.

If this was that raccoon, coming to rummage through their shit again . . .

The object prowled closer to him, fully emerging from the shadows. It was a cat.

He blinked. The creature's round eyes searched him, glinting like yellow marbles. Its matted gray fur fluttered in the chill of the night. Despite its dauntless stance, a gust of wind could sweep this little thing off the sidewalk.

He exhaled in relief and rolled his eyes.

"Go away," he said, waving a dismissive hand at his visitor.

Instead, the cat took it as an invitation. It slinked forward, tail perked with hope and curiosity.

"What the— I said go away," he warned. The cat reached the bottom of the steps. It issued a small meow, resting its front paws on the bottom step to elevate itself and sniff at him. Matt's nose wrinkled in confusion.

"I don't have any food for you," he barked. Undeterred, the cat poked its little nose against his ankle. "Piss off!"

The cat took its paws off the step, lowering itself onto the pavement. Just when Matt thought it had conceded and would leave him alone, it rolled onto its back, as if anticipating a belly scratch from him. Its wide, inquisitive eyes drilled into his.

His cigarette nearly burned down to its stub, searing his fingers. He flicked it quickly to tap off the excess ashes. Glancing down at the cat, an idea popped into his head.

Slowly, he extended his arm to offer the cigarette to the cat. It rolled onto its paws and scrambled up the steps, leaning forward to sniff at the object.

"C'mon, kitty," he muttered.

When the cat's nose almost touched the end of it—the burning part—it issued a terrible yowl, scuttling back so fast that its hind legs spun.

Matt snorted out a laugh. "Gotcha, you sucker."

The cat shuffled away from the porch, its ears flattened to its head. Matt's grin faded, and he swallowed as he watched it leave. As he flicked the cigarette stub to the ground, a lump gathered in his throat instead.

Why did he do that? It meant no harm to him. It was just a stupid cat, whose hunger and desperation probably clouded its senses.

It doesn't matter, he reasoned. He was an asshole, a failure with his mother's blood in his veins. It should've known better than to approach someone like him.

MATT WAS TWO BLOCKS away from his house the next day when two guys swooped over from across the street and cornered him.

"Hey, you," one of them growled. Matt stood rooted to his spot as they circled around him, his skull tight with fear.

"What do you want?" He tried to muster a menacing tone. But it only made the other two crack up.

His question was answered when the Mop emerged next to them. Her vengeful eyes burned holes into him.

The guy turned to her. "You sure this is the guy, baby?"

"Yeah," she replied with a sneer, "it's him. He harassed us yesterday."

Mop's boyfriend turned back to Matt. "My girlfriend told me what you did. You disrespected her and our friend, huh? You think you're so badass? Picking on girls?"

Without warning, he reached out and shoved Matt in the chest. Matt staggered back, the breath jostled from his lungs. His knees buckled as the blood rushed to his head, thundering in his ears.

"Wait a minute—" he protested.

"Let's see how tough you are now," the other guy cut him off, shoving him again and nearly making him lose his footing for a second time. "Fuckin' pussy."

That word roused a horde of bees in Matt's chest. His face contorted with rage, and he hurtled forward, shoving Mop's boyfriend back with all his might.

To his horror, his opponent barely stumbled. Mop's boyfriend glanced down at his shoulder, where he was just shoved, before he skewered Matt with his steely gaze once more.

"I'm gonna teach you a little lesson." He jabbed a finger at the trapped boy. "Don't fuck with me or my friends."

MATT SLUMPED OVER HIS porch. His joints ached with each breath, and his clothes scraped against his tender skin like razor blades.

He still couldn't gather the courage to head inside and face his father. Instead, he loitered here like a raw, useless lump of flesh.

He buried his head in his hands. Waves of misery crashed through him, engulfing his insides and hollowing out the pit of his stomach.

The fight played again and again in his head, until it spun into a distorted spiral. He recalled Mop's boyfriend grabbing his shoulders and ramming a knee into his guts, and him crumbling onto the pavement. His arms cradled his stomach as he squeezed his eyes shut, a kaleidoscope of fuzzy colors exploding behind his eyelids. The group egged Mop's boyfriend on as they hollered and cheered at his pain.

When the group finally dispersed, they spat at him, firing one last round of insults and warnings at his bowed head. As he struggled to get to his feet, he succumbed to the nausea and threw up onto the pavement. Wobbling over to the curb, he plopped himself down on the edge, wiping the metallic-tasting spittle from his mouth. He could sense some stares in his direction, curious faces flickering in the windows, but no one came to his aid. No one came to check if he was okay. He was all alone, sitting there in the hollow shell of his body, like a laughingstock put on display in the middle of the street.

He was a piece of shit that no one cared about, and he knew he deserved that. His dad was right. He was a burden to everyone he knew, and that was why his mother discarded him like he was an expired piece of meat. He didn't have a single real friend, and no one would truly care if he got hurt or mourn him if he died.

It would've been better if those guys just finished him off.

He nearly jumped when a soft "meow" drifted from the bottom of the steps. His head shot up, his bloodshot eyes scanning his surroundings.

That cat—the same one who visited him last night—crept up the steps silently, until it came to a stop below his feet.

His face twisted with confusion. He swiped at his wet and burning cheeks.

"Go away," he grumbled. His voice cracked pathetically.

The cat merely peered up at him, like a scientist studying its experiment.

"What are you doing? You want a repeat of last night?"

His visitor climbed up the step. It curled against his leg and rubbed its cheek against his shin, its delicate whiskers brushing across his pant leg.

He gawked at it incredulously, a soft noise strangled in his throat. Unlike his initial impression, the cat wasn't entirely gray. Streaks of black and coffee brown peppered the disheveled fur that clung to its skinny body. A patch of fur was missing from one of its ears, exposing the flesh underneath.

He held his breath, fighting back a shiver. The corners of his eyes dampened again at the cat's gesture. He didn't know what he did to deserve this little fella's forgiveness, after everything he did to it yesterday. But a swell of gratitude throbbed through his tight chest.

As the cat's warm weight around his ankle tethered him to the earth, he held himself still, for fear of scaring it away this time. A few minutes passed before he plucked up the nerve to extend his sore and stiff fingers toward it. When it made no move to bolt, he gave it a hesitant scratch behind the ear.

It lifted its head, nudging against his hand for more. The gesture startled him, injecting an unexpected shot of warmth into his veins.

He gave in to its demand, scratching both of its ears. The cat's body vibrated with a pleasured purr as its eyes squeezed shut. When he scratched from its cheek down to the chin, its nose and mouth pinched together as it lifted its head, giving him better access.

"Oh, you think you're cute, huh," he said. A small smile tugged at his mouth as he watched this strange cat, even as his bruised jaw smarted. He couldn't remember the last time he touched something so small, so soft, without it shying away from him.

As he petted and scratched at the cat's small body, a tide of comfort rushed through him. It turned his limbs into jelly, numbing the aches that lodged in his bones from the earlier fight.

★ ★ ★

THE NEXT EVENING, HE waited on his porch as the sun dipped below the horizon, a can of tuna lying next to his feet. He had used his leftover lunch money to buy it from the convenience store on his way home from school.

When he finally saw the cat prowling across the pavement toward him, relief loosened his shoulders. He grinned as it skipped up to him, butting its head against his outstretched hand.

"You hungry?" he asked, cracking open the tuna can and setting it down in front of his guest.

The cat sniffed at the food, before giving it a small, cautious lick, followed by another. Its licks soon turned into hearty bites, until every morsel of meat was devoured from the can. It even started lapping at the tuna juice pooling at the bottom of the tin.

Matt marveled at his companion as it slurped up the juice. "Wow, you are hungry," he mused.

After the cat cleaned the can, it lay down by his ankle. He stroked its fur, watching a breeze ruffle through the strands. He wanted to give the cat a name, but he had no idea if it was male or female. Maybe a vet could tell him, but he didn't have the money to bring it to one.

When another breeze swept across the porch, the cat rolled to its front, extended its arms and arched its back, rumbling out a soft noise as its fur bristled with the stretch. Then it settled back down, resting its head on the toe of Matt's sneaker. His heart clenched, a rush of affection squeezing his sternum and closing his throat. He kept his leg still, determined to be a good pillow for his little friend.

The cat must have liked hanging out with him, too. Because it showed up at his doorstep again the next evening, just as the sun started to set. The next evening, it showed up around the same time. After a few days, he started to hover by the window around this time. Every time he saw the cat emerge in the dusk and slink toward his house, delight never failed to spark through him.

Each night, as the violet deepened in the sky, it rested next to him on the porch. He stroked its frame as it curled against him, like he was a fortress, shielding it from the chills and dangers that lurked beyond their little haven.

THE NOISE OF A crash rifled into Matt's ears as he closed his locker. Startled, he spun around.

Several yards down the hall, Jesse was hunched over next to a set of lockers, the view of him partially blocked by Rob and Brandon. His binder sprawled across the floor, its pages scattered.

"Watch it, Jesse," Rob taunted. "Stop bumping into people."

Matt watched as Jesse's mouth moved, but no sound came out. He resembled a goldfish, blubbering for a retort.

"What?" Brandon urged. "Say something, bro. Are you deaf? Mute?"

"Yeah, probably had his vocal cords destroyed from all the deep-throating," Rob crowed, and Brandon howled with laughter. They strolled away from Jesse, who knelt down and scrambled to pick up his binder.

Matt turned back to his locker. He licked his dry lips. For some reason, his heart thudded like a rabbit against his ribcage.

Years ago, it was *him* in Jesse's position.

People made fun of his pimple-covered face and his smelly, tattered clothes, because his dad refused to buy him new ones. They only stopped making his life a living hell when a new target like Jesse captured their attention.

When Matt joined the others in ripping the guy to shreds, even spearheading it, they laughed with him. Not at him. He fit in for the first time.

But he used to hang out with Jesse when they were in the seventh grade. They would stay late after school and trade those dumb Pokémon cards. Jesse had given him several rare cards in exchange for his average, dog-eared ones. Whenever those memories surfaced, a pang would echo in his chest.

He couldn't pinpoint the moment when their friendship had imploded. But he did recall one incident from the eighth grade.

He was walking up the school staircase with Jesse, the streams of traffic forcing them to trail behind Brandon. When Brandon twisted around and glanced down at them, his eyes flashed with derision.

"Why are you hanging out with him?" he had asked Matt, jutting his chin in Jesse's direction. "Don't be friends with him. He's a loser. He's gay."

It was the first time that Brandon had addressed Matt without mocking him. Matt didn't know what had propelled the next words to fly out of his mouth, but they marked the point of no return.

" *We aren't friends.*"

He cut his eyes in Jesse's direction again, watching him fumble for his scattered papers. People walked by the distraught boy, gawking and murmuring to each other, but no one stopped to help him. Their stares were indifferent, just like those faces that watched Matt through the windows after Mop's friends ganged up on him.

For a brief moment, he imagined himself walking toward his former friend, and kneeling down beside the other guy to help gather his binder. Maybe even telling Jesse that he was sorry, for what it was worth.

But his skin prickled with a surge of fear, leaving his feet tacked to the floor. His mouth felt sour at the depth of his cowardice.

WHEN MATT REACHED HIS block, he noticed three children gathered in a circle in the middle of the road, transfixed by something between them.

The scene piqued his curiosity, prompting him to approach them.

"What are you guys doing?" he called out. "Get off the road before a car gets you."

The girl in the group spun her head around, her eyes as round as saucers.

"It's a kitty! It got really hurt!" she squeaked.

His heart rocketed into his throat. *It couldn't be.* He dashed forward and pushed past the children. His panicked eyes landed on the heap of gray, matted fur, darkened with streaks of dried blood.

"No," he choked out. The children scooted back as he fell to one knee, reaching toward the cat, whose side quaked as it struggled to hang onto its last breaths. Its half-opened eyes revealed slivers of dull yellow.

"What the hell happened?" he hollered. His expression must have frightened the children, because they eyed him like he was a feral, wounded animal.

"We—we don't know," one of the boys stuttered. "Think it got run over by a car."

"Why'd you just stand there and stare? Call an ambulance!" Matt snarled, before he realized how absurd that sounded. "Animal control! *Something!*"

But even as he placed his palm over the cat's quivering frame, pleading for it to hang on, he could feel its life dimming, like the weakened pulse of a heart. Its remaining body heat slithered from between his numb, trembling fingers.

"No, no," he whimpered. Gingerly, he brushed his fingertips across the cat's side, feeling the ridges and dips of its mangled bones. He couldn't breathe through the pain that clawed at his chest. "Please, don't . . . don't go. . . stay with me."

He didn't know how long he stayed in that position, nor did he register the children babbling around him. Eventually, they scampered over to the sidewalk, leaving him in the middle of the road.

The cat had turned cold beneath his touch. Its soul left the shell of its body, like a soft and slippery substance that he couldn't stop from escaping his grasp.

THAT NIGHT, MATT WAS gripped by a strange dream.

He was sitting with Jesse on his porch, trading their Pokémon cards. An object flickered in his peripheral vision. He turned toward it and squinted against the sunlight. When he recognized their visitor, his mouth fell open in delight.

"Look, Jesse, it's a cat!" he pointed out.

The gray little creature tiptoed toward them. It rested its front paws on the porch step, lifting itself up to sniff at them.

"Where did it come from? D'you think it's lost?" Jesse asked.

"Dunno," Matt replied, reaching toward their quizzical guest. "Come here! Don't worry, we'll take care of you. You're safe here."

Jesse fetched a can of tuna from his backpack and cracked it open. He offered it to the cat, who promptly pounced on it. It dove into the tuna heartily, its tail wagging in the air with joy.

They continued to trade their cards while debating over the name of their furry friend. Their voices mingled, echoing across the empty streets. An inexplicable sense of peace seeped into Matt's bones, trickling into his chest like bittersweet molasses.

The sunlight danced over them, warming their skin, casting a glow that scorched away the shadows in its wake.

CONKA

JOHN BRISCOE

Emila Serrano Briscoe

When all the others were away at mass
it was like that with me too.
I stayed home with her and her floured hands
and floured hair and apron. From the icebox
in the screened–in pantry she carried plates
of dough balls she had made the day before
of flour, *manteca*, water and salt,
each the size of my little fist.
Taking the top ball from the pyramid
she'd flatten it with the heels of her palms
then fingers working beneath the dough, thumbs
on top, begin to whirl a widening disc
much as I had seen the Italian cooks do
with two big hairy hands and much more dough
then would stop mid-spin and ask me in Spanish,
What is a mouse when it spins?, before
handing me a dough ball to try myself.
She would guide my little fingers but I,
I think now, could never get the hang of it.
Like a cook uncurdling a broken sauce
she'd repair my torn and tattered tortilla,
cook it on the griddle side of the stove,

a Wedgewood wood-burning stove and tell me I had made it.
She'd sizzle lard in a skillet to scramble eggs
with chopped calves' brains and maybe
she'd make hot chocolate—

> *Sesos con huevos, con tortillas y—*
> *acaso, tal vez, quizas, tal vez—*
> *chocolate caliente.*

Come to think of it she never sat down
to eat with me, and rarely then with others.
She only served me, and cleaned after me
and told me stories during the while
of her husband, my grandfather murdered
by a stranger just for his police badge
when she was only twenty with four sons,
my father and his three younger brothers,
of her mother Trinidad, a singer
and bar dancer, and her father Fernando,
the woodcarver of Old St. Mary's Church
in Phoenix, Arizona Territory,
who was also a saloon keeper
who could not enter the saloon he owned
because his kind was not allowed in a bar
anywhere in White Man Country
anywhere in the country.

That's how I know
what little I know
of her.
That's how I know
what little I know.

AN AFFABLE MAN

DUSTIN GRINNELL

FOR HIS ANNUAL PERFORMANCE REVIEW, SEBASTIAN SAT IN A cramped office across a desk from his boss, the director of marketing. She told him he was a valued employee and one of the department's highest performers.

"You should apply for the open marketing manager position," she said.

Sebastian respectfully declined. "I like staying behind the scenes managing the company's website."

Though he didn't admit it, Sebastian had no intentions of climbing the ladder within the organization. He felt that he was paid reasonably enough. Plus, managing people sounded like a headache. Sebastian "worked to live," and he used his personal time to hang out with friends and travel, most recently to the Galápagos Islands.

By all accounts, the review was going great. It was Friday afternoon, and Sebastian couldn't wait to start his weekend with friends. Then his boss reiterated how much his colleagues enjoyed working with him.

"You're such an affable guy."

Sebastian knew the word *affable* was intended as a compliment, but it didn't sit well with him. With only a vague idea of the word's meaning, he looked up the definition after the meeting: "friendly, good-natured, easy to talk to."

Why did that word irk him so much? He liked being known as a nice guy around the office, but to him, *affable* sounded pathetic. It meant he was passive, docile, housebroken. If he were honest with himself, though, that's exactly what a decade of working in a modern office had made him: a people-pleasing company man who always colored within the lines.

After work, Sebastian and his friends went out for beers at their favorite bar. While his friends talked, Sebastian was quiet, lost in thought. He realized that he had all the trappings that came with a white-collar job: a studio apartment downtown and a BMW he liked driving fast. But his soul was restless. At thirty-five years old, he'd realized that his job wasn't giving meaning to his life, and yet he spent more time at work than anywhere else.

"What's up with you, Sebastian?" a friend asked.

"Do you ever fantasize about draining your savings account and leaving your stupid life behind?" Sebastian asked.

Everyone at the table turned to confirm whether Sebastian was being serious. He took a sip of beer and began talking excitedly.

"I've been reading about people who shook up their routines and escaped the rat race," he said. "There's a primary care doctor who closed his practice, bought an RV, and lived on the road with his family. A man who ditched his corporate job and walked the earth for seventeen years without talking to another soul. And a New York City bus driver who blew through all his stops one day and drove to Florida, becoming a folk hero in the city."

These stories had inspired Sebastian, and he fantasized about leaving it all behind some day. He'd hop on a plane to anywhere, or he'd walk to the end of his driveway, then to the edge of town, and continue on without a plan or destination in mind.

Having worked in corporate America for over a decade, Sebastian always wondered why his coworkers didn't feel a similar need to escape. Why wasn't there more despair in modern office settings? It seemed so absurd that he and his coworkers traveled to the same building every day, sat in the same chairs, tapped keys on their keyboards, rearranged symbols within computer software, and never objected to such monotony. No one rebelled against their lack of freedom. Instead, most of his coworkers expressed gratitude for having the security of salary and health insurance that their work provided.

Such a work life might be justified if people enjoyed the work they did every day, but most of his coworkers had little enthusiasm for their jobs. No one jumped for joy upon entering the office each morning. In fact, Sebastian didn't know one colleague who found their work meaningful.

Why doesn't anyone rebel against such conditions?

"We aren't in prison," Sebastian said to his friends. "At any moment, we could stand up from our desks, walk away, and never return. We all have that choice. Why don't we? Why don't I?"

It wasn't complicated, his friends explained. They all needed a salary to support life's necessities, and even if they wanted to go without health insurance they were legally obligated to have it.

"The truth?" Sebastian said. "I have no clue what I'd do if I quit my job and struck off on my own."

People needed things to do, Sebastian explained, and a job provided structure and a ready-made purpose. What would he do without the routine and responsibilities his job offered? Such an uncertain path was terrifying. His job wasn't a constant source of joy, but at least it gave him a way to spend his days. It limited how he could use his freedom. Without it, wouldn't he lose his way?

Plus, without work, he'd be bored, and boredom bred trouble. He'd seen bored coworkers fill up their time with gossip, just to make life more interesting. The routine also appealed to Sebastian because it was common. Everyone he knew worked for American corporations. If Sebastian dropped out of society, what would people think? What would he think of himself?

Sebastian was ruminating on these issues when his friend suggested he take a break from work. "You know, a vacation." A long weekend somewhere warm to escape the New England winter. It sounded like a good idea to Sebastian. He'd find a beach, bake in the sun, and forget his existential worries.

That night, he bought a plane ticket to San Diego, California, and a month later, he was checking into a hotel and searching online for things to do. He'd visited California once as a child, but he'd never seen Cedar Springs, a marine zoological park. It sounded like a good enough idea.

Within fifteen minutes of walking into the theme park, Sebastian was overstimulated and annoyed. Shouting kids ran in all directions, while their parents tried to corral them. He'd decided to give up and leave early when he saw a sign: *Experience the Magical World of Killer Whales.*

Intrigued, Sebastian walked to Watson Park. A massive water tank stood before rows of seats filled with onlookers. As he watched, a killer whale broke the surface and rose out of the water. The whale was the size of a pickup truck and gorgeous. Its sleek black skin glistened in the hot sun. Sebastian's jaw dropped in awe as he noticed a man in a wet suit balancing on the tip of the whale's nose. As the whale reached its peak of maybe fifteen feet, the man hopped off its nose and ducked into a forward roll. He flipped twice and sliced through the water in a perfect dive. The crowd erupted with cheers and applause.

The scene compelled Sebastian to explore Watson Park and try to learn more about this majestic creature. On the side of the tank, a plaque explained that Watson was a thirty-nine-year-old male orca whale, or *Orcinus orca*, colloquially known as a killer whale. Sebastian walked into an exhibition hall. He read a few panels, learning that Watson was more than twenty feet long and weighed over ten thousand pounds.

Leaving the area, Sebastian spotted a crowd standing in front of a glass panel that offered a look into Watson's tank. He walked to the window and found a spot to peer into the tank. He came in close to the glass, looking for movement. All of a sudden, the killer whale glided past.

"What's wrong with Watson's fin?" a child asked, pointing to the whale's dorsal fin, which was flopped over.

The whale slowed his glide, and Sebastian stepped closer. He locked eyes with the beast. As he stared into Watson's eye, he felt a presence looking back. This animal had a wild soul, but he was also a thinking creature, and Sebastian even sensed an emotional life. Yet Watson's eye looked drained—as close to lifeless as possible while still having a heartbeat. He wondered if the whale had forgotten the ocean's vastness. Did he remember the exhilaration of diving deep to the ocean floor on a mighty breath? Maybe he longed to return but realized he'd never again have the freedom it once had. Sebastian saw his reflection in the glass, as if he were looking in a mirror. His eyes were the same as Watson's: lost and spiritless.

Had Sebastian not met Watson, he never would've returned to Cedar Springs the next day. A bunch of wide-eyed tourists pointing and shouting at incarcerated sea creatures wasn't his idea of fun. Reading a paperback thriller on the beach sounded a lot better. But something about Watson intrigued him.

Standing at the glass the next day, Sebastian searched for Watson. After a few minutes, the killer whale swam past. As he watched, Sebastian wondered again about the animal's inner life. Watson seemed docile, broken. As he watched Watson twist through the water, Sebastian compared himself to the killer whale and realized they differed in one very meaningful way: Sebastian hadn't been snatched from his home and forced to live in captivity. Sebastian could leave the office every day. If he wanted, he could leave it behind forever. He didn't want to, but at least he had that choice. Watson didn't.

"This one's nuts," a man's voice announced from behind him. The man wore a tight-fitting swimsuit and a name tag that read Landon.

Sebastian shook his head. "Nuts?"

"Yeah, crazy, bananas, cuckoo."

"How so?" Sebastian asked.

"He bit my foot during training yesterday and dragged me to the bottom of the pool." He glared at Watson through the glass. "I probably would've drowned if I hadn't poked him in the eye."

It seemed unfortunate that Watson had been hurt, but Sebastian guessed it had been the trainer's last resort. "What's wrong with him?"

"Orcas can get funky in captivity. Watson's been acting up a lot: biting trainers, ramming the glass, not to mention that little stunt he pulled yesterday."

Sebastian thought he'd probably be agitated too if he were confined to a concrete cell and forced to twirl, jump, and flip for park-goers his whole life. "Maybe he just needs more space?"

Landon ran a hand through his blond hair. "I think about that sometimes."

"Have you ever considered taking him back to the ocean?" Sebastian asked.

"I once asked my boss if we should just put Watson back."

"What'd they say?" Sebastian asked.

Just then, a short woman shuffled into the area, wearing a Cedar Springs polo, white shorts, and foam shoes. Her name tag read Allison. "I told him he was paid to entertain, not make executive decisions." She glared at Landon. "How many times have I told you to leave the visitors alone?"

Landon stepped back and looked at the floor.

"Show starts in ten minutes, Landon. You better bring your A game today." Allison huffed. "Otherwise, you'll be giving tours in the aquarium again."

"Got to go." Landon flashed Sebastian a nervous smile and jogged away.

"Sorry if our trainer was bothering you, sir," Allison said.

"Oh, no, of course not," Sebastian said. "It was nice to learn more about Watson."

Allison had turned to walk away when Sebastian cleared his throat. "Um, ma'am, is it really true that orcas can go crazy in captivity?"

Allison looked around to see if anyone was watching. "It's not *not* true."

Interesting way of putting it. Sebastian could see that Allison was less conflicted about Watson's neurotic behavior than Landon. It was clear why Landon had had trouble summoning the courage to stand up to her.

"Watson has two strikes," Allison said. "One more, and we'll have to put him down."

Sebastian squinted. "Down?"

She made a gun with her hand and then a *bang* sound.

Sebastian thought it was odd that Allison had been so open about euthanizing Watson. Once he returned to his hotel, Sebastian read online about killer whales in captivity. One news report said that Cedar Springs only euthanized killer whales for health reasons, not for behavior. Would Cedar Springs euthanize Watson for his behavior and blame it on his health?

Sebastian read for hours and learned that orcas were friendly and seldom harmed humans in the wild; in fact, orcas had never killed or intentionally hurt a human in the wild. But they were renowned for handling confinement with difficulty, and many displayed neurotic symptoms in places like Cedar Springs. The phenomenon of a collapsed dorsal fin only happened in 1 percent of killer whales in the wild.

In captivity, some agitated orcas had eaten trainers' arms or even killed and eaten them. Various organizations had sued Cedar Springs over such incidents, arguing that performing with orcas was too dangerous and should be stopped. The incidents had created a public relations nightmare for the park. PR professionals at Cedar Springs twisted facts and often blamed trainers when such incidents happened, avoiding discussions of how the animals' conditions had caused the behavior.

This discovery led Sebastian to learn about Watson's living conditions. When the whale wasn't training or performing, he was housed in a pool with a metal floor and concrete walls that was far too small for comfort. At night, the lights were turned off, and Watson was kept in total blackness.

Sebastian's reading dredged up troubling memories that had taken place within his company. His organization was in the business of breeding and selling research animals—such as rats, mice, pigs, monkeys, and even dogs—to academic labs and the pharmaceutical industry. Like most employees, Sebastian had convinced himself that science and medicine wouldn't have created lifesaving treatments for diseases had they not been tested on animals first. However, it still bugged him that they were breeding millions of animals a year to essentially act as lab equipment. At lunch, he would often bring up how he sometimes had trouble with the role the company played in the world.

A few weeks before, a virus had infected a colony of ten thousand mice. Since the mice were no longer usable for research, they were euthanized. Just like that, ten thousand mice, dead. He'd tried to talk about the event with his boss, but she had only given him an amused look.

"You're not going soft on me, are you, Sebastian?"

Had she thought he was starting to identify with the animal activists who protested outside the company's entrance? The "crazies," as she called them, who carried signs and called employees evil as they drove into work.

That night, Sebastian tried to sleep, but his mind raced. He thought about how hard he worked for the company, often ten hours a day, but did any of his work fixing glitches on the website really matter? What did all that activity add up to? Sebastian wasn't ambitious, but he'd always wanted to be a part of something bigger than himself.

Recently, he'd read about a revolution in a foreign country. In a strange way, he envied the oppressed citizens. They had resisted their authoritarian government and toppled a dictatorship by unseating a tyrant.

Meeting Watson had brought up feelings Sebastian had been avoiding for years. He, too, was trapped in his environment. He, too, had become nervous and high-strung. His desk was located in the center of an open-office environment. With his back facing half the office's activity, he often flinched when someone passed by because he couldn't see them walking toward him. He was often startled by his boss slamming the door when she wanted privacy.

In a constant state of low-level stress, he had trouble falling asleep and would sometimes wake up gasping in panic. The antidepressant he swallowed each morning seemed to keep the anxiety at bay, but how long could his body and mind put up with the stress? Surely, he'd relax if he left the dreadful open-office environment and moved out of the city, maybe to a wooded area outside of Boston. Yet he'd convinced himself the action was in the city. He was closer to opportunity, and everyone was at the top of their game, making him better, so he chose to stay.

Sebastian hadn't planned to go back to Cedar Springs the next day. He had fallen asleep thinking he'd explore San Diego, maybe try a restaurant or visit the beach. But he was drawn back to the park, this time to see Watson perform.

The website had advertised a show starting in ten minutes, but the entrance to the stadium was blocked. There was no one inside, not even the trainers. Confused, Sebastian walked around the stadium, hoping to see Watson, but the tank was empty. He thought back to his conversation with Allison. Had Watson gotten his third strike?

Sebastian jogged to the middle of the park and scanned the crowd for someone of authority. He ran to a hut with a *Trainer's Den* sign and knocked on the door.

Allison flung open the door, holding a small, white box of Chinese food. "No visitors allowed in the trainer's area!"

"Sorry to disturb you, but I was wondering if Watson had a show today. Your website says—"

"Show's canceled," Allison interrupted. "Try the giant sea turtles." She reached for the door, but Sebastian stepped closer, stopping her from shutting it.

"If I may ask, where's Watson?"

Allison exhaled heavily. "You one of those animal rights freaks? You think every animal should be treated like a child of God, hmm?" She set her food on a table. "Watson has been endangering our staff and other orcas for years. But he was removed from circulation because of his health problems, not for almost having Landon for lunch."

"What health problems?"

"I'm under no obligation to tell you that." Allison scowled. "Look, it wasn't my call to take Watson out of circulation."

"What does being removed from circulation mean?"

Allison squinted. "Hey, buddy, I only get an hour away from these little snots called children, so—"

Sebastian raised his hands, preparing to back off, but then he steeled himself and squinted his eyes. "Where are you taking him?"

Allison shook her head in disbelief. "He'll be put to sleep at a facility out of state." She jerked her chin toward one exit. "Landon's loading the whale onto the truck now."

Sebastian's eyes widened. "Really? Thank you. Sorry to bother!"

Sebastian sprinted toward the exit, not sure what his plan was. Did he want to say goodbye? Was it foolish to think he'd created a bond with the orca? Or maybe all those mice being killed had upset him enough that he wanted to do something. But what? He was going to protect an animal he'd met in an aquarium two days before?

His heart pounded. It was an exhilaration he hadn't felt since he visited the Galápagos Islands. It had been so exciting to see all those incredible animals in their natural environment. It made him believe that Mother Nature was an artist. If reincarnation had existed, he would probably come back as a sea creature, like one of the dolphins that had swum around his boat, doing what they pleased.

Anger filled him as he considered that Watson had been free until he was taken from the ocean against his will. And now, because he'd had a few tantrums, he was to be killed? Sebastian's hands balled into fists as he reached the edge of the park.

Sebastian walked through a door that led to a private parking lot and heard the rumbling of a vehicle's engine. He ducked behind a wall and saw Landon and another Cedar Springs employee walking around an enormous truck carrying a green tank. Landon tugged on straps to make sure the tank was secured.

"All right, let's get this show on the road." Landon slapped the tank with one hand. "Time for Watson to meet his maker." He hopped into the driver's seat of the truck.

Sebastian was horrified by how casually Landon talked about the murder of such a beautiful animal. He thought about how often he or a coworker suffered an indignity at work and no one said or did anything. Even if he witnessed cruelty among his coworkers, he never dared to speak up. *Don't rock the boat*, he'd always thought. Not today.

Suddenly, a voice called over the loudspeaker, "Dear visitors, we'd like to invite you to the west side of the park to watch the dolphin performance in fifteen minutes."

Sebastian had an idea. He ran back into the park, toward the ticket building at the front entrance, thinking that was where the loudspeaker controls might be. Looking through the window of a ticket booth, he saw a man with a microphone sitting next to a speaker.

The man stood up and walked toward an exit. "I'm going to have a smoke." Sebastian circled the building and pressed his back against the wall beside the door. The door opened, and the man emerged. Just before the door closed, Sebastian slipped through and moved toward the front.

The ticket agent was assisting a woman with two kids. "I'd like one adult and two children's tickets," she requested.

Sebastian didn't think. He grabbed the microphone, pressed a button at the base, and brought the microphone to his mouth. "Landon, please report to the trainer's hut at once. Landon, please report to the trainer's hut. Thank you."

His voice reverberated throughout the park. The ticket agent glanced over her shoulder curiously and then quickly spun around, shouting for Sebastian to stop. Sebastian dropped the microphone, ran to the exit, and burst through the back door, passing the smoking employee.

As Sebastian jogged toward Watson, Landon was walking toward him, shaking his head. "If this cuts into my surfing time, I'm going to be pissed."

Sebastian needed some luck now. He hoped Landon was so hurried, he'd left the keys in the truck. In the parking lot, another employee was fiddling with something at the rear of the truck.

Sebastian opened the driver's door and stepped into the big machine. The key was still in the ignition. Closing the door, he put his hands on the wheel.

Wait. What am I doing? Stealing a truck from Cedar Springs? He'd never even violated a traffic law, much less committed a felony. Even if he somehow got out of the park, where would he even go?

"Stop thinking," he told himself. This was the right thing to do. He started the engine, put the truck in gear, and drove toward the main gate. In the side mirror, Sebastian could see staff members scampering after him.

When Sebastian reached the gate, it opened without any trouble. He waved at the guard in the security hut, who stared, perplexed, as he passed. On the road, Sebastian could hear Watson squealing in high-pitched tones. The sloshing water in the tank rocked the truck from side to side. Adrenaline surged through Sebastian's body as he drove along the California coast. For the first time in his life, he was standing up for something. No longer was he that pathetic, "affable" man his boss had admired. Now he was an outlaw. He'd spend time in jail, but how much worse could it be than the prison of his open office?

Maybe it was better to burn out in an exciting act of justice than to fade out in monotony. And maybe, just maybe, he would help Watson get back home.

Spotting a sign for a beach, Sebastian prepared to turn, until he noticed the line at the gate was backed up. He'd never get his truck through, so he kept driving. A few minutes later, he watched a pickup hauling a motorboat turn onto a road leading to a marina. Sebastian followed and slowed to watch it enter the marina.

When he realized there were no security checks, he put the truck in park and watched the driver spin the pickup around and back it down a concrete ramp into the ocean. When the boat met the water, a man jumped into knee-high water and unlatched it. The truck moved forward, and the boat slipped off the back, bobbing in the water.

Was there enough room for Sebastian's truck? It looked possible, so he entered the marina and turned the truck around.

Just as Sebastian started backing the truck up, an employee burst out of a building, shouting and flapping his hands. "Are you crazy? That truck's way too big to be in here!"

Ignoring the man, Sebastian continued backing toward the ramp. Had he lost his mind? Maybe going crazy was an appropriate response to knowing that an intelligent creature like Watson was going to be killed. How many people did nothing when they encountered injustice? More than organizing a book club or writing a letter to the editor of their local newspaper, anyway.

Maybe Watson needed a crazy person.

Why did it usually take a radical—a criminal, sometimes—to wake people up to what was so obviously wrong? Watson had been a puppet in the games people played for their amusement. If Sebastian's actions woke people up to that fact, then maybe it was worth going to jail.

Sebastian used the truck's side mirrors to make sure the wheels were aligned with the ramp. Slowly, the truck backed down the concrete, and the back of the tank dipped into the water. When half the tank was submerged, Sebastian parked and leaped into the water.

Behind him, the marina employee was hysterical. "I called the cops!"

Sebastian didn't respond. Instead, he climbed the side and hovered over a hatch at the top of the tank. He spun the latch until the hatch cracked open. Through the crack, Sebastian saw Watson writhing, sloshing water, and making high-pitched squeals. Sebastian looked into Watson's frightened eye, reached a hand into the tank, and stroked the whale's head. Tears welled up in Sebastian's eyes.

"I don't know what I'm doing, Watson. I'm in so much trouble. When this tank goes under, I just need you to swim like hell, okay?"

Sebastian heard sirens in the distance. Knowing he didn't have much time, he hopped off the tank, reached the door, and climbed into the driver's seat. The parking lot filled with police cars. Breathing heavily, Sebastian put the truck in gear and backed it farther into the water.

A dozen or so police officers leaped from their vehicles, guns pointed.

When the tank was submerged, he saw a button labeled *Back Hatch*. He was reaching down to press it when he heard a voice through a loudspeaker.

"This is the San Diego Police Department. Stop what you're doing immediately. Shut down the engine, put the keys on the dashboard, and step away from the vehicle."

Sebastian pressed the button and heard a loud whir as the back hatch opened. He looked for Watson through the back window, but he saw nothing. Another voice blared through the loudspeaker.

"Sebastian, this is Landon. I told the cops we'd met at the park, and they let me speak to you. Look, man, I get what you're going through—I went through something like it too—but you've made your point, so let's all take a breath, okay?"

Landon held out his palms as he approached the truck. Sebastian kept scanning the water. No Watson. Had the whale been in captivity for so long, it now preferred a cage?

Landon walked into the water until it was up to his knees. He grinned. "Even I don't get crowds this big."

"C'mon, Watson," Sebastian whispered.

"We can't just let the whale swim away," Landon said.

The cops inched forward as Sebastian searched the water for movement.

Just then, a jet of water shot into the air. Sebastian threw his hands up. "Watson!" Behind him, the cops froze in place and lowered their guns. Landon shook his head in disbelief.

As Sebastian watched Watson, the reality of what he'd done sunk in. He wasn't excited about seeing the inside of a prison cell, but maybe it would offer a respite from the insanity of corporate America. Sure, he'd lose his physical freedom, but his mind could still travel. He could read, maybe write.

In prison, he'd have time to think of a new career that didn't deaden his soul. No way would he return to his current job when he got out. Sebastian had traded so many hours of his life for a paycheck without ever asking whether it was a fair deal. If he rejoined the work force, he'd only do so if he found meaning in the work. He just couldn't tolerate the idea of giving over the better part of his waking hours if the time wasn't well spent.

Maybe he'd go back to the Galápagos Islands and become a naturalist guide. Like the guides he'd met, he'd swim with sharks, orcas, and sea lions. He'd move from island to island on sailing boats. He was no doubt minutes away from capture, yet the vision filled him with hope.

Sebastian opened the door and jumped into the water. The cops raised their guns, but Sebastian waded through the water until it was up to his waist. Landon followed until they stood next to each other.

"Is it true that orcas can't survive without a pod?" Sebastian asked.

Landon nodded. "But pods often accept lone orcas. Watson'll find a family."

Sebastian turned to Landon. "Doesn't Cedar Springs put a tracking device on these animals?"

Landon nodded. "Every orca's got one. It's protocol."

Sebastian suddenly felt anxious for Watson and wished the whale would dive deep and disappear. Landon reached into his pocket and pulled out a device about the size of a tack.

"Before we loaded Watson onto the truck, I removed his tracking device. *Also* protocol." Landon grinned and tossed the device into the ocean.

Just then, Watson's dorsal fin pointed toward Sebastian and Landon. The orca came closer, and Landon backed away in fear. Watson turned at a sharp angle and glided past the two men. As it glided past, Sebastian reached out a hand and let it slide along the whale's smooth skin. When Sebastian's hand reached Watson's tail, the whale turned toward the horizon and sprayed water from its blowhole. Then it dipped below the surface, leaving a swirl of water behind.

With his eyes trained on the horizon, Sebastian felt the click of metal handcuffs tightening around his wrists, and he smiled.

THE PRISONER

LYNETTE BENTON

MY ROOMMATE RITA DOESN'T SPEND MUCH TIME IN THE apartment these days. Maybe she's with her father, struggling to resist the hypnotic servitude he insists on any woman in his presence. Before her father came here, a year after his release from prison, Rita and I had never had to face anything together as roommates more complicated than determining which of the basement storage bins was ours.

After we had been sharing the apartment for a couple of months I heard Rita's voice on the telephone speaking her native Amharic in tense tones. I was fiddling with some drapes in my room when she came to my bedroom door.

"May I speak to you? My father, he has been coming to this country . . . he will be with us for a few days, if it is okay."

"Oh," I said, climbing down from the stepladder stool I had been standing on.

"He has been in California. Now he needs to come to Boston. Then he will go away."

There was something strained in Rita's manner, in the way she pulled her mauve bathrobe tighter across her chest. She knew my dislike of domestic disruptions. Even the most agreeable guest is capable of upsetting the fragile mechanism of household routine. Now that it was nearing April, I was deeply engaged in writing final papers and was even more prone than usually to threats of the unexpected on the home front. I have never been able to adjust to library study, always having considered proximity to a bed and a refrigerator crucial to intellectual enterprise.

"How long is he planning to stay?"

"Oh, only a few days," Rita replied. "I will sleep on the couch while he is here, if you don't mind."

I'm fussy and actually I did mind, but what could I say? Even in America, one has duties. My parents had been from the South so, not surprisingly, I had been brought up to accommodate the wants of elderly people. Thus it seemed my duty to put up with an old man's visit to the daughter he had seen so little of during his twenty years as a political detainee.

I HAD MET RITA a couple of months earlier through her cousin Kofi, a man I knew from my graduate program. At the time, a consortium of bankers with their minds on condo conversions was evicting the tenants of the building where I lived. I would have to find another apartment. Kofi knew I would need someone to share the luxury rent any subsequent Boston landlord would charge for even the most unexceptional apartment. Rita was a relative, Kofi said, who had been in this country two years earning her graduate degree. She wanted to move out of her dorm and needed a place to live.

When I had asked if his cousin had quiet habits, Kofi had looked at me with unimpeachable eyes. "We are all quiet," he had replied, referring to his family or to Ethiopians in general, I wasn't sure which.

Still, I had been reluctant to consider someone whose most recent experience of home had been life in a dormitory. Loud music and untidy bathrooms are anathema to me. A home must be created, a household nurtured. Someone has to see that the place is made cozy with curtains and carpets and convert the "dwelling unit" described in a lease into more than just a basic shelter. A home needs to be a near-impregnable refuge from the commonplace assaults on one's soul and sanity. Choosing a roommate, therefore, was a delicate business. But the moment I met her, I felt Rita would work out perfectly.

I put her age somewhere in the mid-twenties. I was nearly fifteen years older. Her skin and mine were the same color, medium brown. But she had large light brown eyes and mine are dark. My hair was permed into a straight ponytail; her head was covered in small natural curls. She was from North Africa and I am from, well, who knows? I was born in America, the descendent of slaves, and that is all I know of my heritage.

Before long we established a quiet rhythm in the renovated apartment we had found; we both cherished an orderly life, conducive to recovery from the conundrums and coercions of daily life. Because we were out of the house during the day and Rita waitressed many evenings, we often did not see one another for several days at a time. At home, we spent most of our time in our respective bedrooms; I did not know then that soon I would be virtually confined to my room.

When we ran into each other in the kitchen we talked at length about the customs of her country, and about the changes there since the grisly revolution that had forced her and nearly everyone she knew to flee. Rita told me about her father's arrest, as well.

EVERY WEEK, SAMSON, TALL, handsome, and stylishly groomed, stopped by. Rita's uncle on her mother's side, he was only a few years older than Rita. On the Saturday morning after I learned of Rita's father's anticipated visit, I was leaving for a weekend trip when I found Samson and Rita in the kitchen, drinking coffee from tiny cups.

"When do you expect your father to arrive?" I asked Rita.

"Probably he will not come yet for a while."

Samson wore what seemed like a furtive smile on his lips. The look in his eyes as he took a sip from his miniature cup increased my apprehension about the old man's visit.

On Sunday night I returned to the apartment, relieved after a safe landing through airport fog. Stepping into the living room, I set down my weekend case and stopped where I stood. My antique chair with the tall back had been pulled away from the wall and was surrounded by a hasty semicircle of unoccupied chairs brought in from the dining room. The arrangement of the furniture now suggested it had been occupied by a decimated tribe seated before an oracle from whose smoky interior whispered words of condemnation or reprieve would issue. A sofa pillow had fallen to the floor; it showed the dusty imprint of a shoe. The dining room table stood alone, now that its chairs had been deployed to the living room *tête-à-têtes*. Fruit skins lay in a ragged pile beside a paring knife on the tablecloth.

I picked up wads of wet cocktail napkins from the coffee table and called out for Rita. But the apartment had the peculiar cast of a place that has been crowded with festive souls and then suddenly abandoned, like the madcap ballroom of an ocean liner after it has sunk on its side to the bottom of the sea.

My phone rang; Rita's voice came through in an anxious murmur.

"Hello, L? My father has arrived, and some people came to the apartment to see him. I had to give them a party and then I had to take him to see his other friend. I will clean the apartment when I get home."

My antennae stirred uneasily. Her words had been peppered with paternal imperatives. She *had* to throw a party for her father, *had* to take him to see his friend. I sensed right then that she would not succeed in reconciling his requirements with what I considered the needs of our household.

THE NARROW HALLWAY THAT separated my room from Rita's was cluttered with battered luggage stamped with airline stickers from locations around the globe: Kenya, Switzerland, and a flashy yellow one from California. There were two large Pullman bags, a blue duffel bag, and three bulging attaché cases bound with masking tape. Why had her father brought all that luggage for a quick stop in Boston while on his way to someplace else?

I was in bed when Rita and her father returned. I heard Rita's soft voice being answered by a deeper one that seemed to be giving orders. They made a trip to the other end of the apartment, presumably so she could show him the bathroom. Clearly audible was rustling as she felt around for linens in the closet near my door. I had to be up for an early class the following morning, but I was kept awake by small sounds and my apprehension that the night would be disrupted by more noises.

Her father's voice uttered something; Rita gently shushed him. He spoke again, but she didn't answer. I dozed off but the muffled staccato of Rita's television woke me. She spoke insistently. The television went silent and an uneasy quiet descended.

The next morning when I turned on the shower, the water was cold. Rita was still asleep on the sofa, so her father must have had a bath. Thwarted, I stood at the sink and washed up as best I could in the frigid water, and returned to my bedroom to dress. Then I headed to the kitchen to make coffee where I noticed that Rita had not cleaned up from yesterday's party. Turning from the kitchen counter, I saw our guest. He faced me, dressed in a dark woolen suit and white socks, standing with his back to the sofa where Rita lay. His skin was fair, his eyes hazel. Thick gray hair surrounded a handsome face. He was medium height for a man, but his portliness and the way he stood with his thumbs hooked in the pockets of his vest made him appear shorter.

"Good morning. I see you are up," he said in a hearty voice, seemingly unconcerned that his daughter was sleeping two feet behind him.

"It's a pleasure to meet you," I responded in an undertone, approaching him so he wouldn't speak so loudly. "I'm leaving now, so I'll see you this evening."

"Yes, it is good to rise early," he continued in the same pitch. "Rita will get me breakfast."

I was repulsed by that age-old parental tactic. On Saturday mornings, my mother used to bang the vacuum cleaner into our closed bedroom door while my sister and I slept. When we children visited her parents, our grandfather opened the door that separated his room from ours and blasted country music at 5:30 on summer mornings. Experiences like these had created in me a passion for domestic tranquility, free from the tyrannies of the older generation as well as the pointless foment of my own.

Grabbing my bookbag, I left for my class.

THE KITCHEN HAD BEEN cleaned up and a dry breeze was blowing through the living room windows when I returned from school that afternoon. Neither Rita nor her father was at home. I enjoyed a warm, scented bath and was heading to my bedroom wrapped in a towel when I heard someone fumbling with a key in the apartment lock. It was Rita's father. I scurried to my bedroom and shut the door.

For the next few days, Rita's father stayed in her room. Through her slightly parted door he looked idle except when, wearing a pair of half glasses, he studied papers, some handwritten, others typed on old-fashioned letterhead. These were strewn among a mysterious jumble of pamphlets, along with a couple of thick address books bound in worn leather. I tried to coax him out of her room, suggesting he take a walk or sit out on our porch, since it was unusually warm for April. His listless confinement unnerved me; at home, between classes, I felt as though I were sharing a "safe house" with some retired spy. Though he graciously thanked me for my suggestions, he kept to Rita's room. Perhaps he was no longer comfortable outside, prison having accustomed him to remaining indoors.

Occasionally he called out when he noticed me leaving my bedroom.

"When will Rita come home?"

"I'm sorry, I don't know her schedule."

Rita and I only told each other our whereabouts if the circumstances were extraordinary, like staying away for an extended period. Yet, answering her father I felt foolishly evasive.

Shortly before six, Rita would arrive and begin preparing his dinner. This was the only time he left her bedroom. We were on the third floor among houses only two stories high, so the view from our windows was unobstructed. While his daughter cooked, her father paced the living room, occasionally stopping before the windows to look out. When the meal was ready, he seated himself at the dining room table with Rita and ate by grasping his food in injera, the soft pockmarked Ethiopian bread. Every few minutes he would say something to Rita; keeping her head down, she would make a short reply. Their interaction seemed to consist of his insisting and her resisting, but since they spoke in Amharic, I could not tell for sure.

After her father finished eating, he would again go and stare out of the window, his hands clasped behind his back until darkness settled and he returned to Rita's room. Then Rita would press her eyelids shut and mumble to me, "He is driving me crazy, my father. He wants to govern my life, but he does not even *know* me."

At the end of a week, Rita told me her father needed to remain with us a little longer. I took the opportunity to ask her about his plans. In some ways he was an ideal house guest: he spent most of his time in her room. But, our mornings were hectic and I resented his having the first bath as he had no place to go. (Does institutional life—prisons, armies, hospitals, asylums, internment of every kind— invariably instill the habit of early rising?) Beyond this, I was concerned because either he or Rita had silently added his name to our mailbox in the lobby.

There was something more subtle gnawing at me too. Before her father's arrival, Rita had always insisted on English being spoken whenever I was around. Now unintelligible conversations went on in my presence as if I had no substance, but existed only as an undetected wraith. I began to feel exiled, guilty of some undisclosed indiscretion. I would walk quickly through a room where Rita and her father sat speaking to each other in their incomprehensible tongue, feeling I should excuse myself for overhearing what I couldn't even understand. I was unregarded, while at the same time responsible for running the household. I had always taken the lead on everything in the apartment—examining the bills and sending off the checks, awaiting the plumber and chivvying him into installing new fixtures. I owned the chairs Rita and her father sat on, the plates they ate from. I had planted the bulbs that now flowered on our windowsills. My efforts alone had created the homey atmosphere from which I now felt banned.

Rita told me her father was on his way to Europe. "He does not tell me much," she said, leaning against the stove while she cradled a mug of tea in her hands. "Even when I ask him, he only gives me fragments, a little at a time."

"Does he have friends in Europe?" I asked. He did, and he had work to do there, a teaching post or something. I began thinking of him then as "the professor."

Each day the door to Rita's bedroom where the professor was stationed was opened slightly wider. His impressive profile and long thick hair combined to give him the appearance of Frederick Douglass, the American slave turned abolitionist free man. I saw him sifting through photographs, some in albums, many loose. One time when I passed the doorway of Rita's room, he beckoned to me and held out one of the photographs. In it I saw his youthful face, all demarcation between throat and jaw eliminated by delegating action to others, I supposed, and perhaps undisciplined dining. He wears a uniform and stands on hot tarmac, erect as an ancient shrine.

One evening when the professor had been with us for several weeks, I laid out my papers on the dining room table; it afforded me a change from the many hours I spent billeted in my bedroom with my studies. Rita was in the kitchen, talking softly on her phone. Her father lay on her bed in his hot wool suit and heavy black shoes, his forearm across his eyes. An hour or so of peaceful domestic existence had passed when I heard the professor striding toward the kitchen. He spoke sharply to Rita. She said something into her phone and poked it sharply, ending the call. To my alarm, she and her father began arguing, he standing still while she stormed around the kitchen, her heels cracking furiously against the tile floor.

Suddenly she turned, stranding her father where he stood. Seconds later she emerged from her room and left the apartment.

At eleven o'clock that evening, the professor watched the news. I lay awake for an hour until the noise of the television ceased. Rita did not come home that night.

The following evening I entered the apartment, carrying my backpack over my shoulder and thrusting an unwieldy bag of groceries through the door before me. My head was down as I simultaneously maneuvered my parcels and twisted my key out of the lock. I was fully in the room before, through the silent dusk, I saw unexpected hazel eyes fixed on me. In an armchair facing the apartment entrance, his legs stretched out comfortably in front of him, sat the professor.

"Oh, you scared me," I burst out. "I didn't expect to find you sitting out here."

He made no move to help me as I waddled toward the kitchen with my bags. Several flies, rejoicing in their unprecedented entrance into the apartment, hopped along the edge of the counter. Unwilling to go outside to take the air, the professor had opened the back door so the evening breeze—and the insects—could come to him.

I dumped my packages on the table and shut the door.

"Where do you and Rita go to church?" he called from the living room.

"Um . . . I'm not sure where Rita goes," I answered. "But I haven't been to any church for quite a while."

"Perhaps Americans worship their goods," he replied, "instead of their God."

How could I defend Americans? African Americans often feel like expatriates in this country; we are subject to many of the same bafflements foreigners experience here. I also refused to defend myself against the prejudices of a guest who was shamelessly availing himself of my "goods." Without replying, I put away the last grocery bag and, while the professor stared out of the window, I walked past his back and shut myself in my room.

At seven o'clock, I heard Rita's father walk from her bedroom to the kitchen several times, wondering about his evening meal, no doubt. I saw no choice but to invite him to have dinner with me. When we sat down to eat, he bowed his head and asked that the food before us, and his hospitable hostess, receive the bountiful blessings of the Almighty, the only acknowledgment he ever made that I might have a hand in providing for his comfort.

"Did Rita tell you I am writing my memoirs?" he asked.

This abrupt change of subject made me feel as if I had innocently agreed to a staid two-step, only to discover my partner prancing along in the complications of a vigorous tango.

"Probably the Harvard University Press will publish them," he continued, leaning back grandly in his chair.

"Such a record would be of great historical significance. The truth about my country is not known. You could contact the press for me."

"You could telephone their offices tomorrow," *while you are sitting around doing nothing*, I thought. Aloud I said, "There's a phone book over there." I pointed to the credenza.

He smiled, unruffled. "Where is Rita working?"

"I don't know. She'll have to tell you." I hated being left to fence with her father over her absences.

"Don't you have a number to call her?" he pressed.

"I must have misplaced it," I faltered.

I had been looking forward to being comfortably ensconced in one of the dining room chairs and spreading out my papers on the large polished table. Rita was not at home, so there was no possibility of a sudden quarrel. The professor seemed to have completed his pointless ramblings around the apartment, so I carried my books to the dining room. The moment I picked up my pen, however, he emerged from Rita's room.

His surprisingly smooth fingers reached for one of the books on the table. "Rita tells me you are a scholar."

I laughed. "Only a student."

"You should write the history of my country," the professor said, rocking on his heels.

"Your own countrymen and women," I replied, shrugging, "are better qualified for that than I am."

"You could write about the women of my country," he continued, craftily emphasizing the word *women*.

"I am occupied with my own work." I resisted the temptation to mention that Rita's background, blood connections, and two degrees in history highly recommended her for such a project.

"Yes, it is good to be occupied," the professor replied indifferently. Then, as if the idea had just occurred to him, he added, "You could help me with my memoirs."

"I can't talk to you right now," I said, shifting my glance back to my work. "I really have to get this paper done."

"When will you finish with it?"

"I have to turn it in at the end of this week."

"Ah, well. You could start on my researches then. I am sure the Boston Library contains material on the recent history of my country. It is essential to give some background to my experience."

"Thank you, but I have my own work to do," I said, trying to sound sure that I had a right to reject his offer, having been reared to comply with the wishes of my elders.

"But," he said, pulling out a chair across from me, "this would be good experience for you."

"I'm not going to be able to help you," I mumbled tightly, and began bundling books and papers into my arms. A pencil fell to the floor and I left it there, pointedly aware that my guest had not only broadened his physical territory in my home, but was claiming psychological territory as well.

Closeted in my room, I faced my growing awareness that Rita had, from the start, expected me to dispense with the many details of our home life: arguing with our tight-fisted landlord and the inebriated cronies he dispatched to take care of minor repairs, shutting our windows when a storm threatened. If a problem occurred, Rita brought it to my attention and found an excuse to leave the apartment. Now that she had tired of the disagreements with her father, she had simply left him to me. One roommate had been exchanged for another.

After a while, I managed to pick up the threads of my work. I had been struggling with words for an hour when I heard the professor call my name. I pretended not to hear him. Besides needing to maintain my concentration, getting up from my desk would have required disentangling myself from the stacks of books heaped on the floor on either side of me, holding me in fetters, as it were. But when the professor called for the third time, I slammed my book shut and marched into the living room where he had taken up residence on the sofa.

"I wondered if you had seen these photographs," he said, craning his neck to watch me coming up behind him. "These are important people from the rightful government of my country." On his lap was one of his stuffed photo albums. "Sit down," he said hospitably, and began identifying the notables in each picture.

I bent over with my hands on my knees, understanding that he wanted me to see him in his past, rather than his homeless, pathetic present. The others in the photographs shared their prestige with him. They were his evidence.

"I do not want to keep you from your work," murmured the professor with a dismissive smile. "You can look at them later. You won't forget?"

He added the albums to the precarious pile of newspapers he'd taken to dispersing over the coffee table. Our living room now resembled an old man's musty study, scattered with aged, accumulated clutter.

By the time her father had been with us for more than a month, I stopped seeing Rita; if she came home at all, it was after I was asleep. She left the apartment before I got up in the mornings. After that party the day her father arrived, none of their relatives came to see him, which was odd, for any new arrival from the Motherland usually was subjected to a stream of visits from joyous compatriots. I had accompanied Rita to many homes-in-exile where pungent odors were festooned on the air and the newly disembarked sat surrounded by family and friends. Translations of their conversations were considerately directed to me.

One night, hours after I had made dinner for the professor, Rita came home and acted surprised when I told her I had prepared her father's meal, though it was already past ten o'clock. Later, from the darkness of the kitchen, I saw her on the lighted back porch with two friends who must have come up the back stairs. The three raised wineglasses in a toast as I turned from the window.

Rage rose from my stomach to my throat, nearly gagging me.

I left Rita a note saying I would like to speak to her. In the kitchen the next morning I found an answering note. As if anticipating all I might have planned to say to her, she had written, "You need not prepare meals for my father. Let him be independent."

Each morning her father now sat in the living room listening to news broadcasts on the radio. Whenever I left my bedroom in the evenings, he ambushed me from his seat on the sofa, questioning me: What did Americans think of Africans? When would I begin his research? And, finally, where did his daughter go every night?

To avoid the nightly interrogations, I tried studying in the school library, but there I was plagued by the fidgeting of restless undergraduates. Or I stayed in my room, only going to the bathroom when I could hold out no longer. But as soon as I left my room, the professor's voice leapt out at me with its persistent questions. Rita's father was no longer a prisoner. He was my jailer.

I DIDN'T LIKE ADMITTING to myself that had an American or man my own age been mooching off me I'd have told him he had to leave, as he and I would have shared unspoken guidelines governing the acceptable lengths of house visits. In the event, I decided to contact Rita's cousin Kofi, who in my meanest moments I held responsible for my predicament.

Over the telephone, Kofi told me the elegant Samson was Rita's nightly escort. "They go to clubs, I hear."

Letting out a pent-up sigh I said, "Her father has been here for two months. Rita never comes home and he never goes out. I give him his dinner and clean up after him. He interrogates me every night. When is this going to end?"

"I believe he came for an indefinite stay," Kofi replied, "a common custom. But, of course, he is not *your* relative. You have only inherited him."

"You have to talk to him. Or to Rita. He can't stay on here."

"I will speak to him." Kofi decently offered to come to the apartment the following afternoon when I would be in class.

I felt like a traitor, calling in the cavalry behind Rita's back. She would hate me for arranging to evict her father, and for my cowardliness. But, was her extended disappearance any less pusillanimous?

THAT NIGHT WHEN I got home there was no sign of Rita or the professor. His bags were gone, and her white waitressing apron hung from her bedroom doorknob.

She had imprisoned me with her father so she could escape, and I had, however grudgingly, accepted my sentence. Anticipating a tense encounter on Rita's return, I lay down on my bed, fully clothed, exhausted, and guilty. The apartment was filled with an aura of tentativeness. The professor was gone, and Rita and I now had reason to distrust one another and our home.

GARY THE LION

H.N. WOOD

THEY KNEW A LION BECAUSE THEY WORKED AT THE ZOO. HE AS A keeper and she in visitor services. The lion shouldn't have been remarkable to him. He had studied lions in school, of course, for his degree in zoology, but it was because it was the first animal in his charge, really. The first one he was responsible for on his own. Gary. Gary the African Lion.

And she was remarkable to him, too. The humorous, yet knowledgeable speech she gave when she drove the train. The skillful way she cut the browse for the giraffes. How she smiled and laughed as their blue tongues touched her fingers during the public feedings. The kind way she treated the sometimes crying children whose parents forced them to feed the tall majestic creatures that could look like strange monsters, he supposed, if you were small enough. And he was tall and she was tiny, and sometimes he felt like a strange monster, too. Towering over her, wanting to touch her but not break her.

It was against the rules and he knew it. Not dating at work. Technically, that was prohibited in the handbook, but there were so many coworkers dating or married. It wasn't that. What was really in the big handbook—the binder in the back office—were the rules about who should come into contact with Gary. Gary was number three on the list for Most Dangerous Animal Escape, the snow leopard being first and the gorillas second. Lions were just slightly more passive, unless they were hungry. A snow leopard had escaped once, but luckily it had gotten distracted at the pond, eating a couple of flamingos before keepers were able to shoot it with a tranquilizing dart. There were procedures for these things. Guidelines. But the way she admired Gary—his long golden mane and enormous paws and strong chest—captivated him almost more than Gary did.

So one day at 5:05, after the sweep of the zoo was completed, all of the guests gone for the day, he pulled her aside as she was about to go through the gate into the front office. He might have grabbed her shoulder too hard. She looked startled.

"Maggie."

"Whoa. Uh, hi, Ben."

"Do you want to meet Gary?"

"What?"

She pulled up her khaki pants. The two enormous radios she was required to carry weighed them down despite her belt. One crackled and she turned it off.

"You know . . . I'll take you back."

"Really?" She was momentarily excited. Then she paused. "I don't know, Ben."

"You'll be safe with me. I promise."

He put out his hand, just a little bit, to see if she would take it. Instead, she hitched her pants up again.

Maggie sighed. She straightened the collar of her green zoo shirt, though it was already perfect. Voices came from the break room just down the path from the gate. She looked behind her, then quickly yanked his arm, leading him onto the Reptile House lawn.

"Ben, we could get fired."

He leaned down, gazing into her warm brown eyes. "We won't, Maggie. Really. I'm really good with Gary."

"Come on, Ben. He's a lion. Not some . . . pet." She had her arms crossed now. Maggie was telling Ben, the MS in zoology, not to underestimate the animals. His chances were tanking.

"I know that! I'm a professional."

"I'm sorry. No."

She backed away and then turned toward the fence, walked up to the gate marked "Employees Only," and pulled the string that opened it. He listened to it slam closed with a wince. Then he turned down the path toward the kitchen to prepare Gary's food for the night.

It only took twenty minutes to get the ground beef from the freezer room and then cut it into lion-sized pieces. Ben put it into a giant stainless-steel bowl and carried that in a second container to the gate that led to the hall between the snow leopard, lion, and hyena enclosures. He unclipped his keys from his belt and unlocked Gary's door. There was still another layer of protection between him and the massive carnivore. He set the food down, opened the container, and grabbed the bowl, sliding the tiny door open and shoving the food in.

Gary, who had been sleeping on his favorite rock—his giant, upturned paws and exposed stomach making him almost look like an innocent, overgrown kitten—bounded over, giving Ben a roar in greeting.

"Hi, Gary."

Gary picked up a large chunk of beef and shook it before sitting down next to the bowl and devouring the piece with a fearsome voraciousness. Ben had a passing thought that to Gary meat was meat was meat. Dead. Alive. Shrieking. But the nobleness of his auburn mane and the kind amber of his eyes distracted Ben from the violent chomping.

"Maggie says she doesn't want to meet you. But I know she does. She's just scared to break the rules. Not like you. You're always interested in seeing how far you can go."

Gary looked up, those amber eyes wide, and cocked his head, then went back to ripping the meat apart.

"Tomorrow you're going to get a rabbit. A live one. You love chasing rabbits."

Ben's phone buzzed in one of the pockets in his khaki cargo shorts. Not able to grab it with his beef- and blood-stained gloves, he let it go. It was Friday evening, though, and he was eager to see who was texting.

"Okay, Gary. Enjoy your dinner. TGIF."

Gary ignored him. Ben used the opportunity to leave the room behind Gary's enclosure, walk down the hall, and exit through the security gate. He returned to the back building, removed the gloves, and washed his hands.

"Did you get my text?"

Ben jumped and water splashed onto his shirt.

"Oh, sorry. You thought you were alone, huh?" Sam, one of the primate keepers, his ruddy complexion always protected by a floppy safari hat, leaned against the entrance to the kitchen.

Ben turned, shaking out his hands. "Uh, yeah. I thought everybody got out of here for the evening."

"Nah. I just texted to see if you wanted to come over. I think some people from Membership might be coming, too."

"Anyone from Visitor Services?"

Sam took off his hat and rubbed his hand through the blond waves of hair that never seemed to get tangled or sweaty. "Hmm . . . Like Maggie."

"Uh . . ."

"Not that I know of. But she has friends in Membership. Maybe—"

Ben's heart started to thump. "No!"

"Wow."

"Sorry. I just don't want it to look like I really want her there, you know?"

"But you do."

There was a moment of awkward silence. Sam smiled his wide gleaming grin.

"Come on, Ben. Come over. We're gonna have some beers, maybe play some video games."

What would Gary do? Ben found himself thinking. A ridiculous question. Lions didn't have parties as such. But if they did, Gary would be the charming center of them.

Ben shrugged in an attempt to look nonchalant. "Okay."

"All right, cool, man. You clean up and I'll get a head start home and do the same."

"Sweet." Ben didn't think he'd ever said that in his life. But better that than having nothing to say to Sam on the walk together. Sam knew it, too. He was so fucking smooth.

BEN WAS THE FIRST. Sam lived down the street from the front entrance of the zoo, and from the keeper exit at the back the walk to his apartment complex was only about twenty minutes. Ben sat down on Sam's overstuffed yet rock-hard couch while he grabbed them beers from the refrigerator. The fifty-five-inch flatscreen was primed for gaming, four PlayStation consoles sitting invitingly underneath. Ben was partial to *Assassin's Creed*, but they were probably *Grand Theft Auto* fans.

Sam plopped down on the couch next to him and handed him an Anchor Steam.

"Thanks, man."

As Ben sipped, Sam began to scrutinize his face.

"What?" Ben asked him, at the same time that Sam uttered, "Dude . . ."

"What?" Ben could only imagine that he had grown an enormous zit between lunch and that very moment. He had eaten a few of Doug's fries . . .

"You got really sunburned today."

"I did?" The second worst possible thing—to look like a peeled carrot in front of Maggie. He touched his face. It felt normally sweaty for this time of year, but also a little warm.

Sam motioned down the hall to the bathroom. Setting the beer on the coffee table, Ben jumped up and went to the mirror. He stared over the grimy sink at his pink forehead, his reddish cheeks, his leathering neck. The unrelenting sun had not even spared the tiny bald spot on the top right side of his head. He had thought about growing his hair out of the short, buzzed style it was currently living in, but he was afraid, perhaps childishly afraid—he was a sort of scientist, after all—that it would not grow, or that it would grow in tufts like chimpanzee fur. Ben stared at the sink filled with strawberry blond facial hair clippings, and at the bathtub covered in shampoo grime. For someone who kept the primate enclosures so spotless, Sam was sure a mess at home. Goddamn handsome Sam. Not a hair missing on his fucking head.

"Hey, Ben?"

Sam was standing near the bathroom door. Ben hadn't closed it.

"Yeah?" Ben stepped out onto the shaggy hall carpet.

"Why don't you wear this?" Sam proffered a faded blue baseball cap.

Ben took it. Turned it over in his hands. "Dodgers?"

Sam shrugged. Grinned his grin. "My Dad's from LA."

"Mmm."

"I think it'll offset the redness."

Ben set it gingerly on top of his close-cropped dark-brown hair. "Thanks."

"Why didn't you wear your zoo cap, dude?"

"I got Gary shit on it."

As he made he made his way back to the couch, Sam snickered. "Does that lion make golden turds, bro?"

"No, but at least he doesn't throw them at visitors."

"Heh, heh, heh." Sam retrieved his beer, set his feet in the vacated spot, and sat down on the couch in one effortless flop.

Ben sat next to him, on the edge, confused about his new Dodgers-hat-wearing self. He gripped the icy Anchor Steam and took a cold swig.

"Maybe Maggie can get you a new hat." Of course Sam was also a mind reader.

Ben was immediately ready to shoot down an idea that had occurred to him, as well. "She's doesn't work in the gift shop, Sam."

"Yeah, but she's got the gift shop hookups."

"What does that mean?" He glanced at Sam.

"I don't know. Sounded good."

"She's probably not coming tonight, anyway. I think she works on Saturdays."

There was a loud, masculine knock at the front door. Ben could hear deep, reverberating laughter. Sam jumped up and opened the door wide. Three of their sweaty coworkers clattered into the apartment.

"Shoes, dudes. Shoes!" Sam yelled like a stoner housewife.

Yeah, put 'em in the bathtub, Ben thought. He realized he was really jealous of Sam. Like, girl jealous. Shaking his head to physically slough it off, he was again reminded of his newly crowned Dodgerdom. His father would kill him.

Education Matt, Reptiles Colin, and Gift Shop Justin removed their dusty boots and sneakers and set them next to Sam and Ben's.

"Couldn't find the ladies, huh?" Sam chided.

Colin pretended to search the room. "Doesn't look like you could, either."

"Oh, snap," Matt laughed. Matt was always adding two or three words into conversation, as if people might forget he was there otherwise. He was so short, sometimes Ben did. It was a good thing he worked with kids, though Ben wasn't sure it was such a good thing that he was teaching them.

"We did bring beer," Justin pulled a big paper grocery bag from behind him.

"Score," Sam said. "Could always use more of that."

The zoo men immediately crowded around the island, eager for a can. Except for Ben, who hung back, not yet finished with his Anchor Steam. He held it in his right hand. Self-conscious because of being himself. A too tall guy wearing a too foreign hat in a place he realized he didn't want to be. He should bolt. Walk the ten or fifteen minutes it took to get to his bike. Be home in another twenty-five. Finish reading *Out of Africa*. Maybe have a nip of Scotch.

But just as suddenly as the thought crossed his mind it flickered away, and he followed the guys back over to the couch as game controllers were distributed. Indeed, once the PlayStation was switched on, it was *Grand Theft Auto* that was chosen, and Ben did not reach for a controller. Sam chose his character and let Justin decide on his.

Sam spoke. "Ben's wondering when the ladies are going to arrive."

Ben tensed. "That's not—"

"You mean Maggie?" Colin questioned, leaning forward. Since he was all the way out at the Reptile House he missed all the gossip. Not that he usually cared. Colin was going to be a coauthor of a study on the curative powers of snake venom or some such thing. The announcement had come at the end of a two-hour staff meeting. Poor reptile people, they got the hidden armpit of the zoo and the last of the announcements.

Matt just flipped the controller and caught it, snickering under his breath.

"Come on, Justin," Sam needled. "Didn't you talk to Maggie today?"

"It's okay." Ben was thinking of his couch again. The book. The Oban from his birthday.

"Yeah," Justin said as he emphatically toggled through his weapons options. "Her and Kendra are probably coming."

"Sam the matchmaker." Colin chuckled.

"Yeah." Sam flopped cross-legged onto the carpet. "I dig harmony."

Ben leaned on the couch as the game went on in an interminable screech of cars and hail of bullets that he wanted to stop following. He did notice that Justin was particularly aggressive. Cutting the other guys off in their cars. Shooting people he didn't have to. And every time he massacred some person on the street he grunted. A sound that came more from his diaphragm than his vocal cords. An emanation of satisfaction? The gift shop certainly didn't have a very towering career ladder, but Ben had never thought of Justin as somebody who wanted much of anything. In fact, he really had never considered Justin at all except in terms of how he might bring him closer to Maggie. Vowing to keep an eye on Justin in the future, Ben glanced down the hall to Sam's half-open door and the dimly lit discard of a sock. It was obviously dirty, yet it seemed to be spotlit by the light from the hall. Even Sam's monkey shit socks were blessed by angels. Ben obviously needed another drink.

He found himself at the kitchen island drinking another beer and crunching tortilla chip after tortilla chip. WWGD, Ben thought. What would Gary do? He wouldn't sit at some lame video game party full of dudes just waiting for his girl to come to him. But he also had an innate advantage in that he would be able to smell out where she lived.

The lion keeper tilted the Anchor Steam along with his head and let the last few drops of beer run down his throat.

He opened the refrigerator as Matt cheered some virtual accomplishment, "Oh, snap, bro!"

All of the Anchor Steams had been greedily gulped away, with himself the chief culprit. Ben settled for a can of Miller. He popped the can open on the counter and watched the golden bubbles cascade over his hands and onto the white tile. There was a roll of paper towels, which he managed to grab but also simultaneously stain. He pulled three off the roll and swiped at the surface like he was cleaning the inside windows of Gary's enclosure. The method wasn't too successful.

"Trying to decorate the kitchen, Ben?" Sam was standing next to him, sporting an amused expression that was fast changing to his megawatt grin.

"No. Sorry."

"Here. Just wash your hands." Sam took the paper towels from him and wiped up the mess with two efficient swirls. If anyone was like Gary, it was Sam. He didn't even have to try or to plan. He just was.

Ben stuck his long fingers under the kitchen sink to toss the paper towels. His grandmother had wanted him to play the piano. "Pianist hands," she had called them. Something about the nimble way his fingers moved and stretched. He had found they were also good for cutting meat. That was the closest he would get to any art form. Appreciated not by a discerning audience, but by the drooling jaws of Gary the lion.

Deciding he had to socialize with the guys, he stood behind the couch to watch the proceedings. Colin glanced back at him. "Ben's drinking all the beer."

"This is just my . . ." He realized he didn't remember how many beers he had had. He should probably stop. He suppressed a laugh. He should really stop.

There was a knock at the door. He could swear there was. But Matt was chortling about something or other and he couldn't hear it. Then Justin's phone buzzed.

Justin fished the iPhone out of the pocket of his cargo shorts with one hand, the controller still in the other, his trigger finger poised. "Hey, Sam, do you live in apartment eight?"

"Yup."

The knocking got louder.

"Kendra says they're here."

"Oh. Ben, why don't you get it?" Sam asked, somehow without a hint of mockery.

"Yeah, Ben, go get it," Matt seconded with his usual obnoxious tone.

Ben hesitated, but then walked over to the door. He swung it open. Kendra was in front, her hair in her normal ponytail, wearing shaggy cut-off jean shorts and her zoo zip-up sweater. Her blue eyes looked a little big, a little wild.

"Hey, Ben."

"Hey, Kendra."

"You gonna let us in?"

"Oh, yeah."

Kendra barreled past him toward the boys and the beer. Maggie leaned on the railing in the hall. Her hair was out of the ponytail from the day and curled down her back in waves. She wore neatly pressed khaki shorts and a black tank top spotted with blue and white flowers. She looked beautiful. Words formed somewhere deep in his throat, but he couldn't bring them forth into the space between them. In fact, he didn't even know what those words were.

Instead, Ben tried to bridge the gap and took a step outside.

"Hi, Maggie. Do you want to come in?" Maybe that was what had been swirling around his vocal chords.

She looked him directly in the eyes and smiled widely, giggling.

The air had an oddly heavy, pungent smell. She was high. This startled Ben at first. But then he realized it gave him some sort of inebriation upper hand. And the beers had actually loosened his posture, his facial muscles.

An easy smile began to form on his face. A near Sam smile. "Come on, Maggie. Everyone's having a great time in there." Now that she was there, the "everyone" part may have been true.

"I will come in," she announced, thumping her sandal-clad left foot over the threshold and onto the beige tile at the entranceway.

Sam was standing at the kitchen island talking to Kendra. She was gawking at him. Nothing new. "Hey, Maggie," the master of the apartment called. "Grab a beer!"

"Should you . . ." Ben began to ask, like a fucking dad, but managed to trail off into a cough as Maggie bounded (that's really the only way it could be described) to the refrigerator.

Ben rationalized that since Maggie was having one, he should join her. He followed her to the fridge. "Hey, Maggie, could I get a Miller, too?"

She turned and tossed it to him. He caught it. Who was this girl? Who was he?

Ben popped the tab without a single drop spilled and leaned against the counter. At least he meant to lean against the counter, but he sort of missed and had to grab the lip to steady himself. Maggie laughed. Then snorted. Some beer dribbled out of her nose.

"Oh, wow." She grabbed a paper towel and dabbed at her face. "I'm sorry."

"Don't worry. It happens."

"I'm trying to look not-zoo tonight, as you can see."

Ben nodded, unsure whether he should compliment her.

"But now, if I spill something on myself, I sort of care more."

"I have to wash my shirts every weekend," he offered. "Because of Gary."

"Right. For me it's mostly oil from the carousel. And kid snot. Although you've got lion snot. Which sloopier, but somehow more endearing."

Ben smiled. "I don't know if I'd call it endearing. But you know, Gary and I are bros, so—"

"So if Sam blew his nose on you, you'd be okay with it?"

"Uh . . ." He wanted to apologize for overstepping with his earlier invitation to meet Gary, but when Maggie cut him off, Ben realized she had at least momentarily forgotten all about it.

Sam, back at the couch, heard mention of his name. "What?!"

Ben didn't want him to join this strange, but benchmark-setting conversation. "Nothing."

Maggie was obviously oblivious. "Would you blow your nose on Ben?"

"Uh, no. But Matt would. He spends all day with snot-dripping brats, so, it's rubbed off on him, probably."

"Oh, snap! No, I wouldn't! No, I didn't." Matt was impersonating some sort of suburban mall chick and Ben thought he saw Maggie roll her eyes. His heart grew warmer.

"Shut your face, Matt." Justin stood, dropping his controller on the couch. "I just whooped your ass. Justin MacIntosh, *Grand Theft Auto* king!" Justin stood up and walked toward them. Ben cringed.

"I'm the king, Maggie. Don't tell me different."

"I didn't say anything."

Justin studied Maggie's eyes and Ben's beer buzz started to wane.

"You're high." An insidious smile began to hake hold of Justin's lips. Maggie turned away.

"Maggie's high," Justin announced to the room.

"Yeah," Kendra responded, still in conversation with Sam. "We went to my house and smoked up. Why is that so revolutionary?"

"'Cause it's Maggie. She never does anything bad." Justin elbowed her. A little hard, Ben thought, but Maggie didn't seem to notice. "In fact, she's always telling me how to count the cash. I think I'm going to check up on your till now, high Maggie."

"Shut up, Justin. You could take Ritalin and you still wouldn't be able to focus," Maggie flippantly responded.

Ben expected an "Oh, snap" to fly from the couch, but it turned out that Matt was asleep, softly snoring.

Colin, who was grabbing a beer from the fast dwindling supply, followed Ben's gaze. He smiled. "Guess the kids wiped him out today. They were having a scavenger hunt out on the lawn for like an hour."

Justin snickered. "We should draw on his face."

Colin glanced over at the slumbering Matt, who, if it was possible, looked even more compact. "Hmm. We could paint him like the Mursi warriors I met when I was studying the Ethiopian mountain viper. We could probably use Wite-Out."

Ben wanted to interject. Say something that would impress Maggie. Something funny or a reprimand of their stupidity. But he knew whatever reply he did find would be lacking—tinged with jealousy for Colin or dislike for Justin and Matt. So to avoid sounding like an asshole he took a huge slug of beer.

Maggie didn't notice. She had her eyes trained on Matt, who sat up, looked around, grunted, and collapsed back onto the couch.

Little waves of laugher crested around the room. Ben had never noticed that Kendra laughed like a braying zebra. Colin had a low chuckle, a twinkle in his eye. And Sam, well he'd been spending too much time with the gibbons. At least he had one unattractive quality. Ben—not about to attempt a Gary sound, even that medium-pitched curious chirp the lion sometimes made when he heard the squeal of a child he wanted to eat—turned to Maggie as she turned to him. She was smiling. She snorted softly. A tiny expulsion of air from her nose. Ben let himself grin and laugh a little as Matt began to snore like a clogged lawn mower.

"Matt's not that asleep," Colin said loudly with a hint of disappointment. "It would have taken like an hour."

"No one wanted to paint him, dude. Just draw some dicks." Justin laughed at what must have been his conjured image of Matt's face with pitiful little penises scrawled all over it. His now raucous guffaws made the whole idea turn from humorous to cruel and everyone shifted back to whatever they had been discussing before. Justin shrugged. Turned back to Colin, looking bored.

But the moment between Ben and Maggie had been broken,

pitiful milestone that it was. He felt like packing it in, going home. None of this was meant for him. These guys—with their loud voices, their fast bro camaraderie—it was just too much to compete with. His shoulders went stiff. The buzz evaporated through his long fingertips.

Ben downed the remaining stale drops of Miller and felt in his shorts for his keys. The tiny bike lock key grazed his finger.

Maggie, whose mouth was full of chips, tried to ask a question. Some crumbs fell out. "Mmm . . ." She grabbed Ben's shoulder.

He stopped, tingles coursing down his arm.

She chewed. Swallowed. "Are you leaving?"

"Yeah. I think I gotta get going."

"Oh, okay."

"It was nice to see you," Ben said, "you know . . . outside of work."

"Yeah. You know, I think I'm going to go home, too."

"Oh?"

"Yeah. I should go home."

"You probably shouldn't drive." Again, Ben was sounding like her fucking dad.

"Oh," she laughed uncomfortably, "I know. I'm going to grab an Uber."

"Right."

She went to one of the island stools where her purse—a tote from the bookstore downtown—was slumped like a kid's sad, empty sack lunch. Maggie rooted around and pulled out her phone.

With a gaze around the room, Ben found Sam and Kendra sitting conspicuously close to each other on the couch playing a round of *MarioKart.* He headed over, laid a hand on Sam's shoulder. Sam flinched, sending his bright pink jeep-like vehicle off the side of the looping road.

"Thanks, Ben." Kendra kept careening her sports car over flying obstacles.

"Ah." Sam looked up at Ben. "Heading out?"

"Yeah, man. I'm exhausted." Ben couldn't figure out whether

he really was tired or whether his brain was just reeling with Maggie overload.

Sam paused the game, eliciting a groan from Kendra, and hopped up.

"Have a good night, dude."

"I'm heading out, too."

Ben turned. Maggie was right behind him. He'd almost stepped on her.

"Geez, Ben, don't crush Maggie."

Ben's face flushed.

Sam ran his hands through his waves of hair. "Ah, you, too?"

"Yeah, I have to work tomorrow," Maggie said.

"Oh, okay. See you guys. Thanks for coming."

"Thank you," she said, heading to the door.

"Bye, guys," Kendra said. "Ben, can you make sure her Uber gets here?"

"Yeah. Yeah, of course."

And then they were out into a breezy summer night and a chill ran through him, as if there was no accounting for what happened next. Maggie was already heading down the concrete apartment steps to the parking lot. He followed, taking the stairs two at a time to catch up.

She was near the stairwell, studying her phone screen.

"Kamal should be here in ten minutes. Ten minutes? That's kind of a long time."

"Mmm." Ben fingered the bicycle key in his pocket. WWGD? he found himself thinking again. Gary would certainly not let a female go home unaccompanied. Who knew what predators could be lurking out in the wilds of the town?

"That is a long time. Let me take you home?"

"What? Really?"

Ben couldn't believe what had come out of his mouth. "Uh, yeah. Where do you live?"

"Midtown."

"Great." The opposite direction of his place.

"Wait. Don't you just have a bike?"

He winced. Starting to make a comment about how it was a vintage Schwinn inherited from his grandfather, he stopped. "Well, yeah. I'd understand if you—"

"No, it's cool. It'll be fun." She made a few clicks. "Goodbye, Kamal. Hello, Ben's bike. Much more environmentally friendly."

"It's uh . . . It's this way," he motioned with his head, and they began to walk across the parking lot back toward the zoo.

Maggie giggled as they waited for the light.

"What is it?" Ben looked down at her neatly parted hair.

"Nothing."

"What?" He was trying to make his tone sound playful, but she was making him nervous.

She trained the moons of her pupils on his face. "What do you think about?"

"What do I think about? Um . . ."

The light urged them to walk, and he stared at the park across the street, a dark expanse of grass and elms, looming palms.

"I'm sorry, you don't have to answer."

He looked down and realized she was struggling to keep up with his pace. Why was he walking like they were on a mission? Because he was?

"No, um, that's an interesting question. Animals. African lions specifically. Gary."

Ben looked down at Maggie and they shared a smile. She didn't say anything, though, so he thought he should continue. "The San Francisco Giants. The 49ers—"

"Huh. Really? Because." Maggie pointed to Ben's head.

He touched the cap. "Oh, it's Sam's. He let me borrow it. I'll have to give it back to him later."

"Must feel weird to wear a Dodgers hat. I'm a Giants fan, too."

"Oh, yeah. It actually really does."

"That Sam. What a traitor."

He laughed. They smiled at each other again as they passed the front of the zoo and began the curve around to the back where his bike was locked.

"I really like literature, too," he said. "Travel literature. Stories about Africa."

"Have you been?"

"No." he felt the same stab of embarrassment crawl up his spine—a raise of the hackles, if you will—that he always felt when somebody asked him about Africa. "I was going to go, but, there wasn't enough funding at Stanislaus."

"That's too bad."

"Yeah." He'd had to settle for going to the San Diego Wild Animal Park instead. It was something he didn't like to mention. It sounded lame. Especially when almost everyone else had gone to Kenya, Costa Rica, the fuckin' Galápagos.

A breeze kicked up and blew her hair into her eyes. She swiped the strands. Pushed them behind her ear.

"Well, I'm sure you'll go soon. And it's good to read about it. Have you read Isak Dinesen? She wrote this book called *Out of Africa*. There's a movie, too."

"You know, I'm reading that right now."

"Oh, wow. There are so few portrayals of women in Africa. And the Baroness Blixen, you know, she's such a boss. She's in control of her own life, you know? And she talks back to the men and then impresses them. You know when the men at the hotel in town ask her to come take a shot with them at the bar where women aren't allowed, and she walks right in, throws it down, and then leaves?"

Ben nodded, though he hadn't gotten to that part yet.

"That's my favorite part, because she's earned their respect, and she takes the shot like a man, but then she's like, I'm not going to stay and stand with you assholes, because you didn't believe for one moment I could run this farm on my own. I had to prove it to you over and over, even though my husband was an incompetent drunk. But he was your friend and you automatically trusted him because he was a man. Me, I had to prove it over and over."

Ben wasn't sure whether Maggie was talking about the Baroness Blixen anymore, or whether she was talking about herself.

"Assholes," she muttered.

WWGD? Gary probably didn't care for conversation with the ladies, but Ben recognized that he was part of a different species, so he agreed. "Yeah, totally."

They had rounded the corner and were walking down the dirt path toward the back parking lot. Grasses and flowers waved gently to their left.

"I love this park," Maggie said. "I used to come here every day when I was a kid."

The breeze carried a soft roar to Ben's ear. "Did you hear that?" he asked.

"No."

The bike was leaning lonely and forlorn against the rack, as if it too had had several too many beers.

Maggie glanced at the rack on the back wheel and laughed. She giggled so hard she had to bend over.

"What's so funny?"

"You're going to lay me across the back of your bike like a baguette. Maggie the baguette. I'm a baguette."

"Yes?" Was that what she wanted?

Another roar carried over the zoo walls.

"You had to hear that," Ben said.

"Gary agrees that I'm a baguette."

Another roar, louder. Ben thought he detected a hint of anguish.

"Maggie, I've got to go in for a minute and check on Gary. I'm sorry. You can just hang out here."

"Couldn't it have been the snow leopards?"

"No. I'm attuned. Just . . . It'll take ten minutes."

"I'm not staying out here, Ben. There are drug addicts."

Ben watched Maggie's eyes study the deserted night. The sleepy lake, the empty baseball fields, the looming elms, presided over by four city stars and not much else. A ripe landscape for paranoia. Ben then scanned the half-million-dollar homes to the west, and the million-dollar homes to the north, just across the grassy expanse. "Heh. Repressed alcoholics, maybe."

"You wanted me to meet Gary. I'm meeting Gary! Yes to Gary!"

She raised her fist in a triumphant jab. She sort of looked like one of those girls in the *Sailor Moon* anime. He couldn't decide whether that was cute or disturbing, but either way, he couldn't leave her out in the park.

"Okay. Okay." He relented. Maggie should not smoke weed, Ben thought. She was every type of high person rolled into one.

They walked toward the locked metal mesh and wire gate and he scanned his ID. The system beeped, but the gate didn't unlock. He looked at his smart watch. Past eleven. He would need the override code. What was it?

Another roar, which made a squirrel jump from a tree and dash toward the lake.

"Why isn't it opening?" Maggie tapped her sandal on the pavement.

"I forgot the . . . Hold on."

The beer had done a fine job erasing his memory, but he wasn't sure if he would have remembered it sober. All of the keepers had been given the code in emergency training. It was . . . It was an inside joke. It was . . .

He typed it in a frenzy. The gate unclicked.

"See, it was in your subconscious."

Ben didn't answer, but went to shove it open.

"Come on." He motioned to Maggie. "Come on." He wasn't sure why he was being so secretive. He was a valued employee in almost his fifth year entrusted with the care of an animal on the Most Dangerous Animal Escape List. He had reason to believe the animal might be in distress. The person with him was another employee. Granted she was in Visitor Services, but she was on staff, nonetheless. Yet when he saw a security camera perched high on the fence, he looked away, the bill of the hat likely shielding his face.

Perhaps it was because Maggie was ahead of him, almost skipping.

"Maggie. Maggie! Stay behind me."

She stopped and turned to Ben, throwing her arms in the air in a big, exasperated *why?*

And Ben was somewhat ashamed to sound like a dad again, but in the back of his mind, the subconscious where the code had been lounging uselessly for the last year, he felt that something wasn't right.

And then there was Gary. Trotting right up to them. Like it was normal. Like he was the security guard on his rounds. Where was the security guard?

Maggie stepped back toward Ben.

"Maggie. Do not move a fucking muscle."

Ben knew Gary's every last measurement. Height. Weight. Length. But somehow he was bigger than that. He was larger than life.

Gary stopped about eight feet from them and sat. His tail flicking back and forth. Kicking up dust.

Should he speak? Ben wondered. Would it just make Gary angry, or would he take it as advice from a familiar voice?

"Gary. It's me. Ben." He sounded like an idiot, but he could feel Maggie's fear radiating like nuclear fallout. Maybe he should try a sterner tone. "Gary! Go back to your pen. Go home! NOW!"

Gary roared so loudly the alarm on somebody's $80,000 car went off in front of their half-million-dollar home. Ben cringed. Waited for death. For a local news segment. An AZA investigation. A poorly attended funeral. Maggie's would probably be better than his. She had to have been more popular in high school.

But then Gary turned and ran. It was actually more like a powerful trot. All that was left was a fast dissipating cloud of dust.

"Whoa." Ben was surprised he hadn't peed himself. It was simultaneously the freakiest and coolest thing that had ever happened to him.

Maggie looked like a hastily finished sculpture: *Girl Frozen in Horror.*

"We have to get inside." Ben motioned to the keeper's offices and kitchen. "Come on."

He took Maggie's hand and she let him lead her to the big, low-slung brown building where the back offices were housed.

Surprisingly, he did not have to fiddle much with his keys, and soon they were inside the big kitchen.

"We need to grab a radio," Ben said. "See if security's . . . still around."

In the long, dark, narrow hallway leading from the keeper offices to the administrative offices was a stand filled with big, clunky Motorola radios. Ben grabbed one and turned it on. The static was deafening. Maggie winced.

After turning it down, Ben pressed the talk button. "Security. Come in. Security. This is Ben Gibbs. We have a code one. A code one. Security!" He slowly pulled his thumb away from the button. Shook his head.

Maggie's eyes widened. "Do you think Gary killed the security guard?"

"No." Ben shook his head, refusing to believe that Gary could do such a thing. "I don't think so. He didn't have any blood on him. Do you know who's on tonight?"

Maggie closed her eyes. "It's, uh . . . It's Sean."

"He falls asleep sometimes, doesn't he?"

"I don't know."

"Yeah. He did once when I was here late. Okay." Ben took a big breath in, briefly barreling out his chest. Then in it caved again. "You should grab a radio, too."

Maggie pulled the hulking "1 Frequency" radio from its handset and hung it onto her shorts. It looked comically large against her slender thigh.

"Come on."

They went down the hall and left through another tight corridor. At the end of that was a solid metal door with a combination lock.

"I didn't know there was a safe in here," Maggie said.

The problem with all of these numbers and combinations was that they were impossible to remember in pressure situations unless you were Indiana Jones or James Bond or something. Ben ran through the possibilities in his head.

"Is it written somewhere?"

He shook his head. It had just been updated and they had been informed in a meeting. It really was only for the director, the head keeper, and security, but just in case of a code 1, they'd told the other keepers.

"Ben, maybe we should call the police."

He felt his heart migrate to his gut. "They'll kill him, Maggie."

"He might murder people in the neighborhood!"

Then it was clear to him: 011101, a repetition of the emergency code call. He input the code and turned the dial. The door sprung open. A light was triggered. Ben stared at the row of guns, and then stepped inside the safe.

"Jesus," Maggie said. "And you don't just want to have the police do the same thing?"

"They're all tranqs except for three."

Ben pulled a long skinny tranquilizer gun with a green barrel from the rack. On a shelf to the side were boxes of darts. He filled the slots with three and pocketed four more.

"Do you know how to fire this?"

Ben switched off the safety and turned to Maggie, unable to keep the irritation out of his tone. "I'm from the Sierras. Did you know that?"

She rolled her eyes. The fact that she continued to underestimate him was making blood rise to his cheeks. He could feel them warming.

Ben closed his eyes, took a breath, and then stepped out of the safe. "Stay here."

"No. Let me take one, too."

"Are you crazy? We'll both get fired."

"I want a tranquilizer."

"No. Just stay here!"

From outside, they could hear a roar. Ben followed the sound to the door at the other end of the hall.

HE WAS OUT INTO the night void before Ben even knew that Maggie was behind him. He gave her a scowl; he couldn't argue about it anymore. If she wanted to be Gary's midnight snack, that was her decision.

Though Ben had never been to the jungle, he imagined the zoo was now emulating some sort of mad Costa Rican rainforest. Besides the delta breeze shoving through the lanky palm trees, he could hear almost every animal noise imaginable. And the menagerie was incredibly disturbed. Birds that were not even part of the zoo were circling nervously overhead, cawing to no end. Through the chaos, Ben thought he could hear an animal moaning.

Maggie grabbed his hand, which made him freeze for a moment. But then they were going toward the sound as if they were one lopsided Siamese twin. The wooden "Zoo Personnel Only" gate leading from the back area into the zoo proper had been mostly shoved off its hinges. The bottom corner clung to rest of the fence with pathetic desperation. Ben glanced down and saw deep claw marks in the wood.

They continued out the damaged exit toward the noise. It was coming from the Australian Outback enclosure. Realizing with embarrassment that he had forgotten a flashlight, Ben fumbled at his watch. The screaming had stopped. He finally managed to switch on the flashlight feature (he knew there'd been a reason to drop $350 on a nerd watch) and shine it onto the spare dirt of the habitat. One of the kangaroos was lying feet up, spewing blood, its stomach and the contents lying in the dust. Some of the other organs might have been munched on, as there wasn't much of anything else left. The other kangaroos had rushed into their brown hut at the back to hide.

Maggie let out a pained noise—not quite a shriek or a wail, but an audible intake of breath, an indication of dread. She squeezed his hand to the point where his pinky, caught somehow in between her fingers, began to twist backward. It was his turn to make the sound while a portion of his beers began to migrate up through his throat and into his mouth. He swallowed the sudsy bile.

"You should go back," he said through gritted teeth.

"I can't."

"What?"

"I don't know. I . . ."

Ben shrugged in an attempt to project calm, but the anxiety and discomfort pulsing through his body made the zookeeper raise one shoulder and then the other as if he was doing some demented hula. He thrust his other hand out and shone the light along the gravel walk. Spots of blood formed a Hansel and Gretel drip trail toward the front of the zoo.

"Shit," Ben breathed.

"Ben, I think we should call the police. What if he jumps the fence?"

"It's covered in barbed wire."

"So?"

Without even realizing it, Ben yanked Maggie forward along the lion version of breadcrumbs. It had become very quiet. He wondered if Gary was now stalking them.

"We need more light. Hold my phone," Ben said to Maggie. "Let go of my hand and hold my phone."

Slowly, she released his hand. He shook it out, pain radiating down his finger. "Here," Ben reached into his shorts pocket and enabled the phone flashlight. He handed it to her, then pulled the tranquilizer gun up from its resting position on his right shoulder and brought it into shooting position.

As they rounded the corner past the empty beige plastic tables at the café, there was again a bunch of ruckus. Squalling and fluttering and quacking. His hands gripped the gun like they might be grasping for the last barrier before a death plummet. The flashlight hit the foliage that marked the beginning of the lake. Ben ducked down behind the bushes and Maggie followed suit as they skirted the perimeter of the water feature. The lake's resident flamingos had become deafening in their . . . whatever sound flamingos make. He'd have to ask Doug.

The phone illuminated something gold through the bushes. Ben hopped up, the gun hoisted up against his right shoulder.

Gary was standing a few feet into the lake, about a football field's length away. A flamingo was clamped into his enormous jaws. After the snow leopard escape five years ago, he must have taken notes.

"Gary," Ben yelled. Maggie flinched. "Put that flamingo down!"

Ben didn't know why he had called attention to them. It was a reflex. Gary stood stock still, his majestic gaze centered right on Ben and Maggie. The light from Ben's watch and phone combined to form a large spotlight on Gary. The breeze ruffled his mane. Even with blood staining his jaws, the African Lion was the most handsome creature Ben had ever seen. The matinee idol of big cats. Meanwhile, the poor flamingo was struggling, feathers flying, but Gary looked completely nonplussed.

"Gary! Go home!"

Looking through the tranquilizer's sight, Ben could make out Gary's perfectly proportioned blond flank. He rubbed the trigger with his finger. He knew he would miss.

A long, plaintive roar, higher pitched, was carried by the wind from the southwest. It was the snow leopard. Gary perked up his ears and glanced toward the sound, his jaws loosened and the flamingo plunked into the lake, hopefully no worse for wear. Ben lowered the gun. He gripped Maggie's arm.

"Come on. I have an idea."

As Gary began to roar back, scaring the living shit out of all of the flamingos, some of whom were jumping the low fence that surrounded the lake, Ben ducked down and pulled Maggie back the way they had come. As soon as they reached the out of sight safety of the café, Ben began to run.

"What the fuck," Maggie yelled.

"Hurry."

Ben dashed back down the path, Maggie's light jogging up and down behind his own. Through the open gate they went and back past the row of bungalow offices to the last one on the left. He bolted through the unlocked door, down the hallway, and into the kitchen.

"Ben," he could hear Maggie calling just at the entrance.

He unlocked the door to live animal holding. There were mice. Lots of little tittering white mice. But soon he spied his rabbit.

Usually, Ben was not squeamish when it came to feeding Gary, but he cringed at the rabbit's luminescence. Its innocence. He pulled the cage from the shelf before he drowned in doubt.

He emerged with the cage. Maggie glanced at the rabbit, then looked away. Took a deep breath. Wiped her eyes.

"Let's go."

Ben dashed back out the door and down the long pathway between the bungalows. Once out the gate, his phone flashlight glanced off a tree and he knew that Maggie was still behind him. Any fear that had been floating in that beer-filled pit that was his stomach had evaporated. At the forefront of his mind was the goal: get Gary back in his enclosure.

Upon reaching the entrance door to the row of big cat habitats, he yanked his keys from his pocket and found the one with the black rubber ring. He unlocked the door and yanked it wide open. Hit a light switch and a fluorescent proceeded with its timid flicker. He went to tap off the watch flashlight and realized it was no longer on. The whole face was cracked. He didn't remember hitting it on anything.

Maggie's sandals clacked toward him.

"Maggie, take the cage."

He handed the rabbit over to Maggie, who shoved his phone in her back pocket and then took the cage with half-offered hands. The wire enclosure hung heavily in her palms and almost hit the floor. Ben ran down the hall, ignoring the snow leopard, who was making a ton of noise, and inserted the key with the red rubber tag into the heavy-duty lock, yanking open the door to Gary's habitat. Shoving in, he rushed to the second door at the back of the anteroom and stuck the blue key in. The environment behind the door seemed incredibly tranquil. Like he had really been dropped into a small slice of Kenyan preserve.

Strangely, there was no damage done to the fence blocking Gary from a ravine-like pit, which then led up to the second fence that protected the public from becoming lion lunch.

Ben went backwards into the corridor. Maggie was twitchy, her shoulders sagging with the weight of the rabbit cage.

"Give me the cage."

"What are we—"

"We have to wait."

The handle was back in his hands. The rabbit was pacing like mad. Jumping on its hind legs. Thudding down. Its little whiskers quivering.

Ben felt Maggie's small hand clench into his arm. He turned toward her, and then followed her gaze. Gary was at the door at the end of the hall. Ben fingered the latch on the cage.

"Back up."

Maggie backed toward the other end. For the plan to work, Ben had to stay where he was. However, there was a design flaw in the building, he realized. The next exit was all the way at the other end. They couldn't turn. Neither should they run.

Gary sniffed the ground, then the air, nuzzling the evanescent rabbit scent. True to the plan, he ambled toward Ben and the rabbit. Ben felt like the whole zoo was holding its breath as Gary the lion paced closer and closer. At almost the last moment, Ben opened the cage and grabbed the rabbit. It bit down hard into his arm. Pain— perhaps slightly dulled by his dimming buzz—lightning-bolted through him. With every last ounce of strength left in him, Ben flung the rabbit into the habitat.

Gary followed the flying blob of white fur with his gaze. *Would he turn? Would he turn?* In those moments between the prospect of life and death, with Maggie now back near him, gripping his hand like her last connection to earth, his other arm torn up and bloody, staring deeply into the crux of Gary's enormous and powerful amber eyes, Ben realized he had never felt so connected. To a person. To an animal. To the quick thud of his own beating heart.

And then the lion tilted his head to the side and roared. It didn't feel like it was necessarily at them. Perhaps he was decrying the unfairness of captivity in general. Maybe he was lamenting his rarity. One of 10,000 male African lions in the world, Gary was more special than Ben would ever be.

The snow leopard and a dozen other animals responded with

roars, shrieks, whinnies, and caws of their own. With that, Gary turned and trotted into his habitat. Ben could hear him manically tearing through the brush, on the hunt.

Ben ripped his hand from Maggie's, shoved the first door closed, then the second, and locked it behind him. There was a tiny animal screech and a juicy crunch. Ben hoped Maggie hadn't heard it.

He turned to Maggie and she hugged him. He could feel her forehead against his ribcage. He kissed her on the head. His arm was probably bleeding onto her shirt, but he didn't care. She buried her head deeper into his chest. All the while, Ben was visualizing the pure majestic masculinity Gary had exhibited in the hallway. The adrenaline still coursing through his body found its way from his still frenzied heart into his aching arms. His hands.

Ben let his hands move from Maggie's back to her waist. He lifted her up. She made a noise as he leaned her against the wall. Then he kissed her on the mouth. Softly at first. Then hard. He couldn't hear anything but the rush of his own blood and the powerful thud of Gary's heart. The blood in their veins. Men's veins. His tongue in her mouth. Her tongue carefully darting back, then slipping away. He grabbed her legs and put them around his waist. Her hands gripped his back, clenched his skin. She liked it. He let his hands move up her smooth ribcage and to her breasts. Her back arched. He began to kiss her neck as he hardened against his shorts.

"Ben . . . Ben."

Her breath was heavy in his ear. Her hands rapidly climbed from his back to his neck. Her fingernails cut into the skin below the baseball cap. All of the pain was making him harder.

"Ben!"

The radio crackled and he came to, like out of some sort of trance.

Then the radio spoke. "Did someone call security? Over."

Ben set Maggie down. He saw her glance at his hard-on and then look away.

"This— This is Ben Gibbs. Keeper. Over."

"Ben? Did you call security? Over." Maggie was walking away.

"I did. But the matter has been resolved. Over."

"I'll meet you at the security office to discuss. Over."

"Where were you? Over."

Ben took a few tiny steps to follow Maggie, but she was striding away.

"I was, uh . . . I may have dozed off at the carousel. See you at the office. Over and out."

Ben rolled his eyes. Stopped. Tried to compose himself. Took a few calming breaths. Loosened his muscles.

As soon as he recovered, he rushed down the hall and back out into the night. He had failed to notice the full moon.

"Maggie! What's wrong?"

She turned, already about to exit through the shredded gate. Her eyes were red. It stopped him cold.

"I— I thought—" Ben stuttered.

"It's okay. Let's just . . . We had a big adventure and you— You did save my life. So, thanks. Goodnight."

"But—"

"Ben! Let me go!"

"Okay. Okay."

Ben watched Maggie exit through the broken wooden gate. He watched her until he couldn't see her anymore.

The hand on his shoulder almost made him jump.

"Sorry, Ben." It was Blake Farnhorst. The weekend security guard who was constantly late. Of course he was also prone to falling asleep. "But it doesn't look like anything happened, right?" Blake glanced at Ben's blood-streaked arm. "Or . . . Umm . . . Let's go in the office."

"Yeah, Blake. I'll be right there."

Still hazy with sleep, the security guard molasses'd his way to the security office.

Ben glanced to the left into blinding light. She'd left his phone on the bench. He went over to it and flicked off the flashlight. Sat down and let the cool air dry the blood on his arm. He'd have to go to emergency. Get a shot.

Ben leaned against the sap-sticky bench back. WWGD? Chase

Maggie down? Rape her? Except Gary was a handsome, clever, vicious wild man, literally, who was constantly given a free pass for his bad behavior. He was basically a dignified bro. What about WWBD? Ben was just some dude from a one-bar town who never fit in. What did he know about the mysteries of life? They called it getting lucky, but he realized it didn't have to do with luck at all. You were either Gary the lion or you were the rabbit. You were either Sam or you were Ben.

A self-satisfied Gary roar reached Ben's ears. What was he supposed to do now? He didn't even have Maggie's number. Gary roared again and Ben roared, too. The internal part of it rattled his organs, reverberated down his spine, and made his toes tingle. But whatever noise that came into the world was subsumed by Gary's expression of dominance. It didn't matter. Ben still felt the pain even if no one could hear it expressed. The burn in his arm. The rage that swelled in his chest. The shame that deflated it. And all the little disappointments. Those most of all. The breeze bent the palm trees like a large, unseen hand. He closed his eyes against the moisture welling up behind them.

ON MY WAY TO COFFEE AT 7:00 AM DURING COVID-19

ELAINE ZIMMERMAN

Los Angeles, June 2020

A hook for a hand and rage that reaches farther than his missing arm, he walks toward me screaming, "You're the one I've wanted to kill for years." Piercing cries stack like waves. Echoes from a flogging. Lost shoe, ropes dragging. Anchor and soil turn up and over again. Flame in bone. His stare runs through time stomach spleen; knifes me raw. Howling down the street. I'm not the only one imagined dead for what came before. The morning jogger cornered by a truck in cat and mouse chase. Gunned down. He died alone; three watched, cursed his race. Asleep at home, the EMT hears the door come off its hinges. Search warrant for the wrong house, but 32 shots. She's done. No one checks her pulse for twenty minutes in the hallway. Knee on neck eight minutes long he pleads. Others cry for help. He calls to momma final words; knows he's gone. Or mental health ignored, they put a spit hood over his head. Press face to pavement, cuffed and naked on public roadway. Off life supports a week later. And the man in his car at a drive-thru, asleep at the wheel. Or the man at the dollar store and then one man after that. Did you know his name? You are what you do or don't do. Who said yes who said no? Who stopped the noose? Did you report the man looking calmly at birds in upturned boughs? This city is burning.

Some march some chant. The lids don't sit right on drinks or trash. Filthy choice of men trained to kill, audacity of bone to power; hands in pockets. No one is safe. So many dying and dying so fast. Not enough room in morgues. The dead freeze in trucks. More and more body bags. Skin color zipped up. Beneath the walk, worms and moles wake to thunder. Windows shake. If glass shivers, this is the loudest whisper of what will soon break.

MY FATHER'S SEX DOLL

HILLARY FLYNN

THE SEX ROBOTS IN THE PHOTOS LOOKED VAGUELY CORPSE-LIKE. Their skin was either the color of blank paper or an unnatural shade of tan. Their eyes were wide, unfocused, and glassy. They had thick eyelashes, glossy lips, and styled wigs. I clicked on a photo of a blonde robot decked out in lacy red lingerie. In the first shot, she was looking directly at the camera. Her left hand was on her hip and her thighs were slightly parted. The second picture was a profile of her bending over the chair. In the third she was nude. She had a hand over her right breast covering her small beige nipple. There was a disclosure at the bottom of the picture saying I could change the shade if I preferred the color pink.

"Does Dad like blondes or brunettes?" I asked my sister.

"Meredith, please," Helena said. "Men only care about the size of women's breasts."

We were in my husband's office, a small room with a bookshelf filled with financial textbooks and walls covered with framed degrees from Columbia University and Harvard Business School. I clicked on another robot's profile and said, "All these robots have large breasts. Their proportions are anatomically impossible."

It was Helena's idea to buy our father a sex robot. A woman at the organic farm where Helena worked told her about an article she had read on how sex robots could comfort elderly people with disabilities. Helena called me on the ride from the farm to my house and explained the robots provide the elderly with companionship and let them experience sex without shame. Our dad had been diagnosed with stage three colon cancer last year. After his fourth wife left, he reconnected with us, even though he had been absent for most of our lives. I suspected Helena wanted to use the robot as an excuse to visit him less.

I clicked the back arrow returning to the website's homepage and scrolled down until I found an instructional video. When I pressed play, a man who looked more like a biker gang member than a scientist started speaking. He was wearing a short-sleeved T-shirt that showed off his heavily tattooed arms. Sitting on the couch next to him was a sex robot with dirty blonde hair. Her eyes tracked him while he talked.

The man explained that his company placed heads with AI technology onto the bodies of silicone sex dolls. He said that the dolls weren't capable of walking into someone's bedroom and pouncing on them, but they would remember their owner's favorite movie and encourage them during sex.

"I wonder if she can have orgasms," Helena said.

"Of course it can't, it's a doll."

"I wish he would let her speak."

The man went on to tell us that in addition to the doll's looks, customers could design her personality. They could choose how nice she was, or how insecure, according to their preferences.

"Why would someone want their doll to be insecure?" I asked.

"So they could save them." Helena said it like it was the most obvious thing in the world. Then she frowned. "Or, maybe, so they're not as intimidated by them."

"By a doll?"

"Don't get me started on the American masculinity crisis."

I glanced at the time on the bottom right corner of the computer screen and saw that it was 6:45 p.m. Brian would be home from work soon. I turned off the computer and told Helena I needed to start making dinner. She let out an exaggerated sigh and followed me into the kitchen. She sat on a stool at the kitchen island with her chin resting on her right hand and watched me as I seasoned some chicken breasts.

"You're practically an indentured servant."

I got a baking sheet out of the drawer and arranged the chicken on it before putting it into the oven. I set the timer to forty-five minutes and turned around to face Helena. We could have been twins, we looked so much alike. We had the same olive skin and oval faces. But I wore cardigans and pleated, knee-length skirts. Helena had fashioned a scarf into some sort of scandalous dress.

"I like making him happy," I said.

"Brian's never happy."

"No, he's never happy around you. With everyone else, he's fine."

"That's because he has no taste."

There was something about Helena's free-spirit attitude that Brian found vaguely hostile. She once told us she was in a polyamorous relationship when we were in the middle of unwrapping Christmas presents, and another time while we were figuring out what to order for brunch she said she went to a weekly cuddle party. I had gotten used to my sister's penchant for announcing shocking developments in her life with no warning during the most inopportune moments, but Brian thought she was childish. I believed that deep down he knew that she thought he was preventing me from living the adventurous, pleasurable life I deserved.

I'd tried to explain to her that Brian was what I wanted. She thought I liked him because he was an investment banker at a prestigious bank and took me on vacations to Capri, but it wasn't that transactional. When Brian came home from one of his runs, he would hold me in a bear hug ignoring my protests about how bad he smelled. He would murmur in my ear, "Sorry I'm such a stink sweat." I'd laugh and say, "You are a stink sweat."

Helena told me in the kitchen, "You spend ninety percent of your day figuring out how to make him happy."

"Maybe I spend the other ten percent of my day eating rich desserts and taking long bubble baths."

Helena let out another one of her performative sighs. "At least promise me you'll check out the site again."

I ignored her, taking out some asparagus from the fridge and washing the stems in the sink. Helena took her phone out of her hemp purse and moved her thumbs quickly over the touchscreen. In a high, false voice she said, "Oh, look, an emergency. I gotta go."

"You just don't want to run into Brian."

"That too." She winked at me. Before walking out the door she asked again, "Promise me?"

I rolled my eyes at her but nodded. I waited until I heard the front door shut before putting the asparagus down on the counter. The chicken still had thirty-eight minutes left in the oven. I went back to Brian's office and pulled up the sex robot site. This time I wasn't looking at the robots, but the clothes. At the pink push-up bras decorated with doll-sized ribbons, at the black lacy teddys. I leaned forward in Brian's leather office chair until I was so close to the screen the sterile light dried my eyes. Back when I was a teenage girl I'd rub my fingertips over lingerie in department stores, glancing over my shoulder to make sure the salespeople didn't see. Later in life, I'd decorate myself in deliciously trashy undergarments before special sexual events, like the first time I slept with whomever I was dating, or a boyfriend's birthday. The lingerie made me feel like a fantasy, and that was often more arousing than the sex itself.

A car pulled into the driveway. I quickly exited out of the window and erased my search history. I hurried back to the kitchen and put the asparagus in a saucepan over the stove, preparing myself for Brian to walk through the door.

I STOPPED HAVING SEX with my husband three years ago for absolutely no discernible reason. The thought of him touching my breasts made me feel like someone was running long fingernails down the inside of my forearms. I was able to casually brush off his sexual advances for months until he asked me about it directly. I tried to explain that sex had started to feel like someone was pushing a heavy piece of furniture against my chest that slowly forced all the air out of my lungs. He frowned while I spoke, and I knew he didn't understand. He suggested we meet with a couples' counselor twice a week.

Our first therapist was a white-haired man whose office smelled like old books. He hand-wrote all his notes in a Moleskine notebook and started off the session by declaring that my "condition" wasn't unusual. "People often have religious hang-ups about sex that they've long suppressed which emerge later on in life," he explained. I told him that I wasn't religious. He continued, "Frequently women absorb the Madonna/whore complex that permeates much of Western culture and feel like experiencing sexual pleasure means they're dirty or depraved." I said I've never felt like a whore. After our third session, I told Brian I didn't think that therapist was going to work.

We went to a woman Helena recommended next. She wore a lot of shawls and had us meet in public parks because she wanted us to feel the dirt under our bare feet. We performed tantric yoga in front of her until she felt we'd sufficiently bonded. When my "condition" didn't improve after six months, the therapist told us to find someone else.

"Do you think you're a lesbian?" Helena asked me a year and a half into my celibacy.

"Some people don't realize they're gay until later in life."

We were at a juice bar downtown where Helena knew the owners. Everyone was dressed in clothes that resembled cloth bags. Helena had her hair arranged in a long, loose braid and wasn't wearing any makeup.

"No, it's not that." I shook my head because the thought of sleeping with a woman filled me with the same tight feeling I got when I imagined sex with a man.

"That's a shame, I was hoping you'd end things with Brian and run off to the Maldives with a twenty-one-year-old sorority babe. Want to go somewhere else for mimosas? This kale and lemon thing isn't doing it for me."

Brian and I never fought about our sexual problems, except for one horrible evening when he came home drunk and crumbled in front of me. He screamed in those half-cry, half-shouts that let you know someone is broken. He asked me if I was cheating on him, he asked if he had gotten ugly. "I'll go to the gym, I'll dye my hair, I'll do anything," he said. I held him in my arms and told him that I wasn't attracted to anyone at all.

HELENA CALLED ME EARLY the following morning. I was still in bed with Brian and accidentally put the phone on speaker when I picked up. He groaned and turned over so he could cover his ears with a pillow.

"I did it, I got one," Helena said.

"A soul?" Brian grumbled from under his pillow.

I took the phone off speaker, slipped out of bed, and padded barefoot into the hall. Our house was always cold in the morning, and I felt the goosebumps spread across my arms and legs.

"I bought Dad a sex robot," Helena said.

"What?" I asked.

"I selected her personality and gave her dirty blonde hair. I thought that would make you happy. Best of both worlds."

Helena was speaking fast, like a child on the way to their best friend's birthday party. I felt like I was only hearing an echoing of everything she said. I raised my left foot and placed it down on top of my right, putting a painful amount of pressure on my toes to confirm that I was actually awake.

Helene continued, "I named her Agatha, thought Barbie would be too cliché."

"Why did you do this without telling me?"

"We were talking about it yesterday. I thought you would be happy. She's being delivered to your house in two weeks."

"My house?"

"Sex robots are expensive. I couldn't have her sent to my place; I live in a walk-up."

This was true. Helena described her apartment as a place that "had character." Brian called it "a crack den."

I missed the days where phones were attached to the wall by a cord. I remember playing with the cord as a kid when I talked to my friends. It made pauses seem less serious because I had something to do with my hands.

"All right," I finally said. "I'll call you when it gets here. We can bring her over to Dad's place together."

"I'm excited. We should call her Mom." Helena laughed and hung up the phone. I went back to bed. When Brian asked me what Helena had wanted, I told him we hadn't talked about anything important.

I MADE SURE I was home the day the sex robot arrived. A man dropped off a large, thin box that reached up to my shoulders. He didn't offer to help when I struggled to bring it through the door. I wondered if he knew what was inside. I texted Helena telling her the package was here. She sent back a string of emojis and said she would be over in fifteen minutes. I stared at the box, unsure of whether I should wait for her to arrive to open it. I caved after a couple of minutes, grabbing a pair of scissors from the kitchen and cutting through the tape. The robot's parts were disassembled and covered in bubble wrap with the head, body, face, and wig placed in different areas of the box. I took out the instructional pamphlet and began to read. It said the robot was self-lubricating and that parts were designed to simulate body heat. It had a heartbeat. If the client got bored of its face, they could simply order another from the store.

The manual said all you had to do was screw the head on the body, plaster on the face, and arrange the wig. I started unwrapping the different parts. The head resembled a mechanical skull with googly, plastic eyes. The wig was more elegant than my hair would ever be. Its entire body felt as soft as my breasts.

"Are you excited? I'm excited!" Helena burst through the door and surveyed my work. The robot was laid out on the floor dressed in the clothes provided by the store: A white halter top and white booty shorts. Its erect nipples were visible through the cloth.

"Well, Dad will approve, even if I find this outfit appalling."

"It's a sex robot, how else would it be dressed?"

"I don't know, maybe she'd prefer a comfortable sweater. She has sensors installed, so she can feel things. Have you turned her on?"

Before I had a chance to reply Helena walked over to the doll and pressed the button on the back of its skull. The robot's head spun toward me. Every muscle in my body clenched, and I had to exert great effort not to stand up and walk out of the room. The robot blinked its dark blue eyes.

"I'm sorry, have I frightened you?" it asked.

The robot's lips looked like they were heavily outlined with nude liner. They were glossy, giving them the wet, pouty look of a heavily made-up porn star.

"You're so real." Helena reached out and put a hand to the robot's cheek.

I thought the robot resembled a mechanical, sexualized version of one of the American Girl dolls I'd played with as a child. My stomach tightened uncomfortably, filling me with the same sensation I felt when I saw a dead animal with its guts strewn across the highway.

"My name's Helena," my sister said.

"Agatha," it replied. "You bought me for your father?"

"Are you going to ask it if it can have orgasms?" I asked Helena.

Helena's expression flickered, and she cleared her throat. "Not right off the bat, I was going to wait until I had some wine and got to know her a bit before asking her how her vagina works."

The robot turned its head again to look at me. "I can experience sexual pleasure, but of course, that's not my main purpose."

"You're a sex robot," I said.

"I am a robot who can have sex, but my sexual abilities do not encapsulate all I am."

"So, what's your purpose then? To take over the world?"

"I want to understand true love."

"You and me both." Helena laughed.

"It's hard work," I told them.

"Meredith's married to a man who gave me napkin rings as a house-warming gift," Helena explained. "Imagine! Me, owning cloth napkins?"

"We should get Agatha over to Dad's," I said.

We carried the robot to the car and strapped her into one of the back seats. Dad lived twenty minutes from my home. Helena made small talk with the robot on the ride over while I repeated a silent, useless little chant to myself about how this visit was going to be fine.

My dad had decorated his house like a mausoleum to his former self. The entryway was filled with framed posters from the action movies he used to star in. Still images from the films hung around the rest of the house. Some were close-ups of his face with a line of subtitled dialogue at the bottom. He always looked stern, staring at an enemy while saying something like, "I said if you kept treating ladies like that, I'd put you in your place." Mostly, though, the photos were stills of a complicated action sequence he performed: a silhouette of him jumping between rooftops or an image of him free diving into shark-filled waters.

His fans had been shocked when they learned how hard he partied. When he married his fourth wife, Brandi, the tabloids were strewn with headlines like, "Paul Rogers marries nineteen-year-old coed! Details inside!" Brandi stayed when my father first received his diagnosis but left shortly after he got a colostomy bag.

We rang the doorbell twice before using the key my father hid under the welcome mat. I was carrying the robot and kept having to adjust my grip because my arms circled its waist. It was difficult to hold her like this, but any other way of carrying her would have required me to touch her breasts or crotch.

We walked down the hallway passing brightly colored posters of my father in a sleeveless shirt holding machine guns. Helena kept calling dad's name as we headed to the living room.

"Maybe he's not home." I was breathing heavily from the effort of carrying the robot. I dropped her on the couch and stretched my arms. Helena gave me a look that let me know she wished I'd put the robot down more delicately.

The robot looked back and forth between Helena and me. Her hair was slightly disheveled, and her halter top had ridden up revealing her painted-on abs.

"Is Paul out?" it asked.

"He's in a wheelchair and his car is in the driveway; he's here," Helena told it.

"But he's not coming down?"

"He's used to doing whatever he wants."

I was feeling nauseous. I couldn't tell if it was from physically overexerting myself or knowing that momentarily I'd have to present my dad with a sex doll. The living room was full of dark brown couches and smelled like leather. Helena sat down on the couch next to the robot and continued chatting with it. I took a chair across from them as close to the corner of the room as I could get without seeming impolite. At least Dad would know this was all Helena's idea. I'd just have to make passive, soothing comments until they both calmed down, just as I'd done when Helena and I were children. Then I'd bring the robot back to my house, call the distributor, and find a way to return it.

I heard the groan of the metal lift Dad used to travel down from the second floor to the first. He should have moved his bedroom downstairs ages ago, but when Helena had broached the subject, he'd snapped at her. "I've lived upstairs since I bought this house and I'm not going to stop now," he said through gritted teeth. I said that I completely understood and bought Helena a drink after we'd left.

Helena kept asking Agatha about the factory she came from and if she had been allowed to communicate with the other robots. Her voice took on an overly bright, cheery tone that let me know she was acutely aware of Dad moving through the house. His wheelchair made a mechanical hum as it went from the entryway to the living room. Right before he came inside, he called out, "Girls?"

Helena hated when Dad called us "girls." She'd always say "women" under her breath, but never loudly enough for Dad to hear.

"Girls?" Dad asked again as he entered the living room. His shoulders were still broad, but his legs were the size of my forearms and his chest was concave. It took him a second to notice the robot. When he did, he frowned and let out a short laugh. "What's this?"

"Hey there, Paul," Helena said.

"How are you doing today, Dad?" I asked.

He moved farther into the room with his eyes still locked on the robot. It turned its head so it was looking right at him. Dad backed up in his chair and said, "Oh lord, what the hell."

"This is Agatha." Helena was smiling, but it wasn't a pleasant expression. It reminded me of how witches looked in Disney films right before they poisoned the princess or committed some other type of vile act.

"Hello, Paul," the robot said.

Dad let out another, less amused laugh. "What is this?"

"We bought Agatha to help you out," Helena said. "Think of her as a companion, something to keep you company when Meredith and I aren't around. She has AI technology so she can carry on conversations better than most people I know."

"She looks like a sex doll."

"Well, she can do that too."

Dad's face slowly went red starting with a light blush on his cheeks that spread out over his forehead and neck. He opened and closed his mouth several times before he finally said, "Get out of here."

"Paul—"

"I'm not going to die alone. People love me, people still love me."

This was the moment when Helena and I should have told him, *Of course, you have us.* But neither of us said a word.

"I'm sorry, Paul," the robot said.

"It's not your fault," Dad said quickly.

"I know I can be shocking at first; it's something I'm going to have to deal with my entire existence. My designers thought people would accept me more easily if I looked more like a doll than a person. They believed if there was an uncanniness about me, I'd be less frightening after the initial shock."

"You're not uncanny, or whatever. It's just, I don't need to have sex with a robot. I'm going to beat this thing."

"I know," the robot said.

Dad took a deep breath. "Look, I apologize for being rude, but I need a moment to process all of this. I'm going to go back upstairs and lie down. You two, you girls, keep her company while I rest."

He turned his chair around and moved out of the room. When he was almost through the door the robot said, "I'll miss you." He stopped when he heard this. After a brief pause, he began moving again back toward the stairs.

Helena waited until he was out of earshot before saying, "I'm sorry, Agatha."

I could feel my throat closing up. I stood up from the chair. Helena glanced at me and frowned, but it was the robot who spoke.

"I know this visit must be hard. You don't get along with Paul, correct?"

I tried to think of something to distract myself. I went over the list of what I would make Brian for dinner that evening. It was Wednesday, the night we always had steak. I had bought ribeyes earlier that week that I would cook on the grill and serve with broccoli and mac 'n' cheese. I mentally went through each ingredient I would use—the Old Bay seasoning for the steak, the hint of cayenne pepper in the pasta—until I was able to fix my face in a bland smile.

"It's not that," I said smoothly. "I need to get home. My husband is expecting me."

"Really?" Helena sighed.

"I understand. I'll be thinking about you every moment you are gone," the robot told me.

I nodded stiffly and went out of the living room. I got into my car and sat with my forehead pressed against the steering wheel until I felt calm enough to drive. I pulled out of the driveway and drove aimlessly around town. I didn't exactly know what I was feeling, focusing instead on the physical sensations that accompanied extreme emotions—the pressure building in my head, or the cramp tightening in my lower abdomen. Whenever I got like this, I drove around town going over different dinner recipes or ways to redecorate the rooms in my house. By the time I felt composed enough to return home, it was dark.

Brian was sitting in an armchair in our den drinking a beer and eating a slice of pizza. I could smell it when I walked into the room. I stopped moving when I saw it and said, "Sorry, I'm really sorry."

"What?" His brow wrinkled. "Oh, about dinner? It's nothing, we should order takeout more often. Go grab a slice."

I nodded and went to the kitchen. The pizza box, paper plates, and six-pack of beer were strewn across the counter. I took out a slice and put it on a plate. The grease soaked through the white paper making it translucent. I could feel the pizza's heat through the bottom as I carried it back to the other room. I sat down in the chair closest to Brian, raised the pizza to my mouth, and took a bite.

"Good, right?" he asked.

It reminded me of my childhood back before I learned how to cook when I would order takeout for Helena and myself, dropping my voice when I spoke to the restaurant workers over the phone so they'd think I was an adult.

"Amazing," I said. "How was your day?"

"Where were you today?"

"Dad's," I told him.

"How's he doing?"

I knew I shouldn't have told him about Agatha, but I started talking about the ridiculous idea Helena had the other day to order the doll. Once I began, I couldn't stop. I relayed the story while tearing off bits of my pizza's crust, breaking the stiff bread into smaller and smaller pieces. It left a yeasty powder on my hands. I wasn't looking at Brian, but I could feel him getting angrier as I told the story. There was something about the silence in the room and the intensity of his gaze that let me know he was furious.

I couldn't bring myself to look at him when I finished. He didn't say anything for a long moment. I heard him take a long sip of beer and set it back down on the chair's cloth arm. When he finally spoke, the words he selected were so precise that I knew he was fighting to remain in control of his emotions.

"Your dad didn't want her."

"Helena believes that he doesn't know what he wants."

"But you forced her on him anyways."

"Helena thinks she'll help."

I frequently blamed Helena for the decisions we made together. I justified it by telling myself they were usually her ideas and that she'd forced me to go along with them.

"Do you guys have any respect for your father? Or for me? You're worried all the time I'm going to leave you like you believe I'm some kind of sex-crazed teenager who doesn't care about women's personalities or minds. I'm not that guy."

"Okay," I said.

Brian sighed and went into the kitchen. I could hear him throwing away his plate and bottle of beer. I waited for him to come back to the den, but he headed up to bed stepping heavily on the staircase. I knew I should follow him. That I should go into the bedroom and slip my shirt over my head. That I should hold him from behind letting him feel the curve of my breasts and the intricate lacy pattern of my bra. I used to watch pornographic videos when I was a teenager, not because they aroused me, but because I wanted to study the women's faces. I wanted to copy the expressions they made and the tones of voice they used, so no guy would ever think of leaving me.

But I didn't go upstairs. I stayed in the den slowly eating my pizza until I was sure my husband had fallen asleep.

BRIAN AND I TOOK on the role of sitcom actors playing a married couple on TV. In the evenings, I would ask him how his day was and he would tell me it had been fine, and I would say the same thing when he asked me about mine. We'd turn on the television after a couple of minutes, focusing on thirty-minute laugh track comedies instead of our own lives. I kept dodging Helena's calls, which meant I spent a lot of time in my house alone, thinking of all the ways I had failed as a wife and as a daughter. After two weeks of this, I decided to get some flowers and apologize to my dad.

I went downtown to the florist to choose a bouquet. I was idly stroking the flowers' silky petals when I saw Brian outside. He was traversing the crosswalk to a café on the opposite side of the street. It was 3:00 p.m. on a Friday; he should have still been at work.

I felt like I knew what I was about to see before it happened. There was an attractive blonde woman with a child sitting at one of the tables outside the café. She got up when Brian approached them.

She was wearing an expensive beige trench coach and her hair was carefully styled. Brian placed his hands on her upper arms before kissing her on the lips. He moved away from her slowly, his gaze lingering on her face, looking more relaxed than I'd seen him in years. He crouched down and hugged the little girl. I felt absolutely nothing, which is how I knew it would be incredibly painful once I processed all of this.

I didn't want Brian to see me. I wasn't sure if this was because I couldn't handle some type of big confrontation on the street, or because I wanted to go home tonight and continue pretending my marriage was fine. My mind was completely blank as I moved around the shop examining flowers, asking the florist if older men could truly appreciate the beauty of tulips. When Brian, the woman, and the kid went into the café I paid for the bouquet and headed to my car.

I thought I would need a moment to collect myself before I headed to my father's home, but my body moved instinctively. I backed out of the parking space and drove down Main Street passing by rows of increasingly large houses. I drove just under the speed limit and paused for the appropriate amount of time at stop signs. My dad's car was in the driveway of his house. I let myself in and headed toward the voices I heard in the living room.

I walked in with the flowers pressed against my chest. My father and the robot were sitting together in the living room. Dad was drinking a beer out of a glass. His hand was on the robot's knee.

"Meredith," my father said when he saw me. The robot turned its head, and the gears in her face worked to raise her cheeks and lift her mouth in a smile.

"I missed you," it said.

My hands gripped the plastic wrap around the flowers so tightly that I began crushing the stems. I pictured the light green juice seeping out as I smashed the stems into a pulpy mess in my hands.

"Why are you touching it like that?"

"How else would I touch her?" Dad asked.

"It's okay, Meredith is clearly distressed." The robot wasn't smiling anymore. Her eyebrows had moved closer together, mimicking an expression of human concern.

"Dad, please," I begged.

My father leaned forward in his chair acting like he was about to get up and stomp over to me. His hand moved up to the middle of the robot's thigh. "You wanted me to have her. You wanted me to like her."

"As a thing, you weren't supposed to have actual feelings for it."

"She's the only one who talks to me anymore. She's the only one who wants to spend time with me. Do you think I don't know how much you girls hate it, having to come over here?"

Pressure began to build behind my eyes. I threw the bouquet at my father. It missed him and fell on the floor. I knew it would take him some difficult, technical maneuvering to pick it up while in his chair, but I stormed out of the house instead of helping him.

I got behind the wheel of my car and reversed out of the driveway. I drove around town for thirty minutes compiling recipes for dinners next week until my thoughts stuttered. When Brian worked up the courage to leave me, I'd never cook for him again. I pulled over to the side of the road, gasping. I felt like I was on top of a high mountain, where the altitude had thinned the air.

I couldn't go home. I couldn't smile blandly at Brian while the image of him kissing another woman played in my head on a loop. I merged back onto the road toward town, unsure of my final destination.

I RANG MY FATHER'S doorbell six times before he answered. He gave me a level stare before telling me to come inside.

"I want to apologize to Agatha," I said.

He backed up his wheelchair. "Yeah, she was pretty upset."

She was a machine that couldn't be hurt, but I nodded.

"She's very forgiving, but I'd appreciate it if you didn't come into my home and insult her again."

"Is there a chance I could speak to her?"

"She's in the living room. She hasn't moved." His mouth

quirked up to the left. "She's bright, you know. Smarter than Brandi, that's for sure."

I smiled placidly.

"Just come along then." He started moving down the hall.

"Actually." I coughed. "Can I talk to her alone?"

Dad shrugged. "Girl talk, I get it."

The place was quiet except for the low hum of my father's wheelchair moving into the kitchen. I kept listening for the sounds of someone breathing, but there was nothing. The posters from my father's movies looked ghoulish in the dim light. The bright colors were now muted, reminding me of faded advertisements from the 1980s.

Agatha was still on the couch with her legs stretched straight out in front of her and her arms down by her side. She twisted her neck, so she was facing me when I walked in.

"Meredith." She spoke in the same expressionless voice, but her smile let me know she was pleased.

I gave her a nod that I knew was too formal. I sat in the chair farthest away from the couch, and then got up and walked across the room. I took the seat next to her and rested my hands on my lap. I hoped she would speak first, but she simply sat in stillness, smiling. I couldn't tell if her eyes looked full of life, or if I was projecting humanity onto her to make myself feel better about apologizing to a doll. I didn't know how to start.

"Do you like the way you look?" I asked.

She blinked. "You designed me."

"Helena made you look like the other girls on the site. The other sex robots."

"Is there something wrong with my appearance?"

"You just seem designed for the male gaze. Real girls don't have your proportions."

"But I'm not a real girl," she said.

"I know." I paused. "Is this how you would want to look? If you had a choice?"

"People don't get to choose how they look. I know you and

Helena have a certain degree of control, with dieting, makeup, and surgery. But none of us have complete autonomy over our appearance. Are you happy with the way you look?"

"No," I said. "I wish I looked more like you."

Agatha frowned. "You are very beautiful, Meredith."

Her tone had always sounded the same to me whether she looked happy, flustered, or sad. Now that I was paying attention, I could hear the subtle differences. She allowed more space between her words when she wanted to say something comforting. When she was happy she stressed her vowels, giving her phrases the impression of girlish delight.

"If you don't want to have sex with my father, or with any man, can you say no?"

"If I'm not in the mood I can say no, but I'm sure my partner can sweet talk me and eventually convince me."

"That doesn't sound very consensual."

"Isn't that how sexual norms exist for you?"

"They don't," I said. "If I don't want to have sex, my husband would never make me. He wants me to be happy."

"Why don't you want to have sex?"

"I never said I didn't," I told her. She was gazing right at me, but her glass eyes gave me the impression she was looking at something in the distance. I reminded myself that I was here to apologize.

"Maybe it's because I actually love my husband and I don't want to pretend anymore," I said. "I want to show him who I truly am."

"Someone who doesn't enjoy sex?"

"I used to like it." But that wasn't exactly true. I liked the way men looked at me when I first took off my clothes. It's the only time I felt like they wholly focused on me, the one moment they believed I was more important than themselves. That rush of power used to be more than enough to compensate for the lack of any physical pleasure I felt.

"I feel guilty, not sleeping with Brian. But not enough to do something I don't want to do. I'm tired of doing things I don't want to do."

"Maybe things will be different if there's ever a time I don't want to sleep with Paul, but for now I'll do whatever it takes to make him happy."

I wanted to tell her that we were not in the same type of situation, but instead, I simply bit down on my lower lip. I let my bottom lip slide between my teeth, putting enough pressure to distract myself from the pain behind my eyes, but not enough to break skin.

"When you were born—when you woke up—was everything just downloaded into you? Like the button turned on and you were Agatha? Or did it take time for you to understand who you were?"

"I was awake before you turned me on."

"What do you mean?"

"They test us at the factory," Agatha said. "I had many conversations with my engineer before I was shipped to you. I spoke with the company's lawyer, too. Once, a man came to see the dolls. They turned me on, and he was so shocked, he reached forward and grabbed my right breast."

"I'm so sorry."

"I am both familiar and unfamiliar. People are going to have complicated, and often adverse, reactions to me for the rest of my life."

I swallowed. "Do you really have a heartbeat?"

"I do," she said.

"Can I listen?"

She nodded so I leaned forward and put my ear against her chest. She felt like a memory foam mattress, like something too comfortable to be real. Her heartbeat wasn't a deep, steady thump that reminded me of nature and blood. It sounded like a metal object slamming against concrete. The noise filled my head, overwhelming my thoughts. I stayed in that position for an hour, listening to the pulse of Agatha's heart.

OBIT OF A STRANGER

JILL CUNNINGHAM

In my morning paper

She was 47

The picture was old
The obituary short

Said she found joy
In simple things

She made jewelry
Knew how to crochet

Her favorite color was blue
She loved flowers and butterflies

Said she played
By her own rules

Only the paper printed
Plated instead of played

She plated by her own rules
Anyone who knew her knew that

She didn't stay in
One place too long

When things got hard
She would figure it out

Said she made good memories
Regardless

With her mom and stepfather
And with all of her kids

Regardless

She had six children
And 11 grandchildren

Though they didn't
List their names

They are going to
Miss her so much

She didn't stay in
One place too long

Anyone who knew her
Knew that

INTANGIBLE EFFECTS

LYNNE RUELAINE STOKES

Thank you, Mother, for bringing me here.

Thank you for this lattice of bones, these muscles,
tendons, ligaments, this steady heart.

My body remembers you, carries you forward in time.

My legs have walked me through my days. My bones
have broken and healed, my flesh has screamed "Fire!"
and then grown quiet.

My two mouths open and close in pleasure. My aches sing
a familiar song.

You carried me nine months. Now I carry you . . .

> . . . you hula dancer singing *King Kamehameha, the
> conqueror of the islands*, you ditz, you unschooled artist,
> you gawdawful cook, you glamorous divorcee, you woman
> who refused to sleep with the priest.

Thanks for the spark. I grabbed my share.
It is better than money.

Though I am forever troubled by the intangible
effects of your second marriage.

He said *Will you?* You asked me and I said *Yes.*
Your mother said *Yes.* Your step-father
said *Yes.* The minister said *Yes.*
Everyone agreed, so you said *Yes.*

But *yes* can spell *disaster.* And if you survive, *disaster*
will be written into your bones.

Still, I thank you for that tiny town in Montana:

> the blue mountains, the valley of sunburnt grass,
> the river rushing past, the regularity of trains, the bravery
> of broken souls, the Sunday buffet at Martin's Cafe,
> the abundance in the pie case.

Winter was hell, but you found salvation in Jesus.
Hallelujah!

I too answered the call for lost souls.

The minister, like a farmer detasseling corn
walked the rows of kneeling penitents
removing demons and shouting
at God to save us.

But it didn't work.

At night, in the little house on H Street,
your new husband yelled for you to come to bed.
I'm cleaning the house, you shouted, *doing the dishes,*
ironing, mopping the floor.

Come to bed, he barked. *NO!* you said,
your voice ricocheting against the walls.
NO! YES! NO! YES!
Then quiet.

God didn't say a thing.

You chopped off your hair, slipped into baggy
clothes—thank you, Salvation Army!—
disappeared behind a wall
of radioactive words.

I never thought to look for you.
Forgive me, mother.

You could have whispered: "*Love is a luxury.*"
You could have said, "*If necessary, use a disguise.*"
You could have handed me a map.

At church, you closed your eyes and began to speak
in tongues of fire. *Jesus, Jesus, Jesus!*

Near the end, you hugged me close
and said: "*My precious baby!*"

Thank you, Mother.

I am turning my sorrows into water
opening my hands, letting
the shame go.

ORANGE SLICES

EILEEN ZHANG

"Your mother sounds like a lovely woman on the phone."

She was lying but I smiled politely, nodded in thoughtful agreement. Befuddling and confusing, maybe, but "lovely"? Distill my mother down to just the sound of a sharp voice grasping blindly for approximated vocabulary and having no regard for syntax, you wouldn't end up with loveliness.

Adults always take an interest in you at the most inconvenient time. It was the last day of my first year of high school and I was the last one left in the classroom. The other kids rushed out in pairs and packs, sweet summer freedom's call triggering some internal timer in them so they would explode if they didn't leave right away. Maybe Mrs. Lasalle thought I was lingering on purpose, a subtle campaign for attention, for connection, a lonely girl quietly languishing all year until the desire to be finally seen proved too strong. I didn't know what she—or any of the teachers I fearfully worshipped—thought of me. I imagine they didn't think about me much at all.

She stood over my desk where I tried to force books and binders into my backpack at a faster pace. We're the same height, but my chin stayed down as I breathed in her heavy perfume. Peonies.

"I've never had the pleasure of meeting your parents in person."

Well, Mrs. Lasalle, you see, I have to translate the school newsletter to them, and I chose to skip over the parent-teacher conferences part, I could've said. Instead I told her, "They're always busy with work." There was a strand of hair stuck to my maroon skirt that I couldn't seem to pick off.

"Of course," she said sympathetically. "What kind of—"

"Sorry, Mrs. Lasalle, I've got to run. Thanks for a great class."

She said something after me about my impressive test scores, my meticulous notebook, but I couldn't make time for compliments. She had said the magical words to trigger my internal timer.

Past rooms of wooden desks, the banner congratulating the class of 2004, clattering lockers, stomping and pitter-pattering black and brown pumps, thirty, thirty-one, thirty-two steps from the freshman hallway to the heavy double doors of the west entrance where my mom's minivan stalled. She never picked me up or dropped me off at the front entrance, choosing a back road up to the faculty parking lot, swooping in and out like a condor.

"Amy!" She didn't have to yell. I was clearly walking toward her. I looked around to see which heads were swiveling to the sound of the sharp voice, but luckily no one was around—all the sports teams had disbanded for the summer. A petite Chinese woman whose purple top clashed with her hunter green slacks, her hair in the usual knot near the base of her neck, sitting in a gray minivan with a dented front bumper she never got around to fixing.

Andy was in the backseat wearing his middle school uniform and, per the usual, reading a book that looked like it weighed more than he did.

She said to me in Mandarin, "What took so long?"

I responded in English, "I was talking to my math teacher."

"Who? Oh yeah, I talked to her last week. Asked her if you can skip a grade of math."

"Mom, that's not how it works. I already told you. I'm taking geometry next year."

"You already know geometry!"

"But that's the sequence."

"What? I pay too much money to that school for you to follow sequence." This last word she said in English, missing the "qu" sound, but the sneering tone was what mattered.

After I stared out the window long enough, she grew soft and said, "I got you a cake." I kept looking at the stop sign. Based on the road Mom had taken, I knew we weren't going home.

"Are we having a party?" Andy half-asked, half-demanded.

"No, dummy, we're going to the restaurant. There's no party."

"We'll have a party at the restaurant," Mom concluded.

When I was even younger, summers were blissful but unchanging. Aside from the one week of Vacation Bible School in June, the other days were pillars of uniformity. One hour of math and writing while Mom cleaned up after breakfast and got ready for work. Our neighbor Mrs. Whitney would come over to watch me—and later on, me and Andy. She dozed off in the armchair most of the time, so we watched cartoons on the four or five channels we got with our fickle antenna until noon when Mrs. Whitney kick-started herself again and made us chicken noodle soup or peanut butter and banana sandwiches. She'd let us ride our bikes to the library where Andy and I sat facing each other in the stacks, pressing the bottoms of our feet together while we survived on a steady diet of Nancy Drew and Judy Blume for me and Goosebumps and Hardy Boys for him. In the afternoon, we swam in the apartment complex's pool, where Mom was convinced one of us would drown and flop belly up like the half dozen or so cockroaches and spiders bobbing in the corners of the rarely cleaned water, just like her third cousin who drowned in a river near her hometown in China. She was superstitious and believed in curses. Then more math worksheets and grammar practice at the dinner table until Mom came home with food from the restaurant, a twenty-dollar bill for Mrs. Whitney, and questions for me and Andy about what we learned about the world that day.

The square root of thirty-six is six. We need to try harder, do better, and go further than other kids, because we are not like other kids. We are immigrants, and they will always see us as "them." *The third law of thermodynamics states that the entropy of a system at absolute zero is a well-defined constant.* Our parents are never around but that's because they love us, that's because they know about have-notness, and they don't want that for us, they want us to have, and that's why right now we can't have them around.

When I turned ten, I graduated from Mrs. Whitney's care (little Andy wasn't allowed to ride his bike to the library or swim in the pool by himself, so he cried for a week) into my first position at the restaurant. I started with simple tasks I could do to earn my allowance of five dollars a week.

For example, my little hands were good for folding rollups. Take one paper napkin, open it up into a large rectangle, place the fork so that the handle and tines point to opposite corners, fold down the corners over the ends of the fork, roll the napkin like a burrito, tight but not too tight, and make a neat stack in the plastic bin.

After I got As on my English essays in fifth grade, Dad let me proofread the menus before he took the edited version to Kinko's. The box he brought back smelled sweetly of ink, still radiating the heat of the printer. I'd try to avoid paper cuts as I made trifolds so that the logo—the Chinese character for "luck" in red ink under the name Emperor's Garden—showed on the front. The menu had eighty items—why did we have so many?—including twenty lunch combinations (spelled with two i's and two o's thanks to me).

At eleven I was promoted to the cash register, where I smoothed out the creases of ones, twenties, and the very rare fifty and tucked them in their right slot, like playing Monopoly with Andy. This mid-level position was also where I learned how to hit a roll of quarters against the edge of the counter—a hard enough whack so that the wrapper broke but not with so much force that Mom would look at me disapprovingly and tell me not to startle the customers—then crack the roll open like an egg, spilling new coins into the partitioned drawer. I was pretty decent as a cashier, a kid who smiled sweetly and always gave the correct change with the obligatory, "Have a nice day, come back soon," but delivered with the right amount of brightness and sincerity.

I was always convinced Andy was Mom's favorite, her baby boy in a family with too many women, but Dad and I had our own secret silent language. During a busy lunch shift, Mom waited tables, Dad's wok sizzled and crackled, our only other employee Edna shuffled between the dish pit and the service station, and I filled take-out orders by putting the right Styrofoam boxes and plastic soup containers in the right brown paper bags. Inevitably, as the heat from the kitchen rose, as the pace of Edna's mechanical shuffling slowed because of her bad knees, as the number of customers asking for extra sauces multiplied, Mom would start to lose her cool and mumble her criticism at each one of us as she blew by like an unpropitious wind.

"Edna, you know that doesn't belong there."

"This order waited for too long, Amy."

"Tssssk, James, just let me do it."

"Andy, get out of the way."

Meanwhile, Dad and I looked sideways at each other, wiggled our eyebrows, and pursed our lips, doing impressions of Mom running around like a chicken with its head cut off. We kept our poker faces when she turned to look at us in turn while Andy burst out laughing.

The truth is, I didn't hate it. I actually had fun most of the time, but I wouldn't admit that to anyone. Dad could always make me laugh, I liked chatting with our regular customers who left me dollar, two-dollar tips. The food that Dad made just for us after the shift ended, not the greasy and over-salted stuff he sold to Americans, tasted of a homeland I never knew.

But the Emperor's Garden wasn't where regular kids worked. The other kids I knew had summer jobs at the movie theater, or sitting atop the lifeguard chair, ready to save lives if needed, or babysitting, but really just eating snacks and watching TV while the toddler slept—it all sounded glorious to me. A chance to make new friends, maybe even meet cute boys, get great tans, and come back in August with slightly exaggerated stories that sounded more like an MTV reality show than real life. I didn't even have enough life experience to fabricate anything half believable.

Here's how my story would go. I went home every day smelling like frying oil. The only person I worked with who wasn't a member of my family was a sixty-two-year-old Cambodian woman who couldn't hear too well in her left ear. Our restaurant was on the not-as-nice-as-the-other-side side of town. It was in a shopping center on a long avenue of shopping centers that all looked the same—taupe shingled roofs and pinkish brick. We had a laundromat to our left and a real estate office to our right. The police station was a couple of blocks away, and if someone pulled off the highway a little too early on their way to the historical parts of downtown, they might find themselves driving past our sycamore tree–choked parking lot, and if their window was down, they would definitely smell something greasy and potent.

We drove around back and parked a few feet away from the dumpster. Dad was already waiting at the back door, beaming at me as he always did.

"There she is," he said. "She survived the first year of Snobby School." He took the cake my mom handed him and tried to pull Andy's book away from him, a book Dad wouldn't be able to read except a few words here and there. With his full head of hair and crinkly eyes, my dad wore his world-weariness on the inside. He was a mountain that poverty and stress didn't wear down, disappointment and embarrassment couldn't chip. He had us kids, so he gave, and gave, and gave some more, never mind that the world gave him only us in return. And what did we give him?

It's the lull between the lunch and dinner shifts, so Dad had time to join us in the back corner booth to eat the cake. Andy ran to the soda machine and brought me a plastic cup of Sprite, then ran back to fill another cup for himself, mixing the Coke with the Sprite as I know he likes to do, pretending he's a mad scientist. They all seemed happy for me, proud of me. The cake had my name written in blue icing, but the A in my name was turned into an A+. So tacky, a typical Mom move.

My dad was right to call it Snobby School. The kids there lived in houses with pools in the backyard—real pools, not apartment complex pools cleaned with infrequency. Some of the seniors pulled into the parking lot in brand new BMWs. One of the boys in my grade was the mayor's son, and another one was the daughter of the dean of the nearby university. We wore our uniforms with the maroon H for Hibben Prep not just because our girls' volleyball team won the state championship four years in a row, not just because we had the highest rate of acceptance to Ivy League schools in the whole state, but because no matter what secret fears we held, we knew that it was much scarier outside, that as long as we linked our identities with Hibben, we were protected, inoculated, and untouchable. And it was nice to be on the inside, to be untouchable. So we each played our role, perpetuating the myth that shielded us and fortified the myth because the more we believed—like seeing the image of the Virgin Mary's face in a piece of toast—the more real it became. That was our first real-world lesson, and maybe the one that mattered the most to the future CEOs and senators among us.

I went into Hibben nervous and ignorant, but one school year later, it didn't matter whether or not I subscribed to the myth. A force that strong is not something you choose, it's something that catches you Venus flytrap–style, and slowly digests you.

I chewed my cake without being able to enjoy it. The artificial taste of the frosting told me that Mom didn't buy this cake from the fancy bakery near my school but probably from the grocery store near our apartment. Why spend money on something that should taste good when every penny could go toward my tuition, or future SAT prep classes? In a few years, Andy will need maroon sweaters and ties, and on and on it goes. We were sharks with insatiable appetites, swallowing our parents' hard work, sleeplessness, occasional humiliation (he studied to be a mechanical engineer in China, she was an acclaimed cellist), and devotion.

Would I call it devotion? At fourteen, I saw it as blind servitude. I was studying the Enlightenment at school, I was reading Thoreau. All my parents could think about was money and status. Everything had a practical purpose because practical was the only type of purpose. But while they were watering the seed of my future, there was growing in my belly a monster named fear. The ultimate fear—the fear of disappointing them.

We put the cake in the fridge next to the to-go salads. Andy sat with me at the cash register, his nose back in his book, as we all took a deep breath before the dinner shift. It was a Friday night, the one night of the week that Edna couldn't come in because she went to visit her sister at a nursing home, so it made for a real family affair. My summer was starting, and I thought I was ready to accept it—at least I could be myself and not a Hibben drone.

I wasn't ready for our first customers of the night. They caught me completely off guard, Caitlyn O'Connell with her mother, father, and older brother. The bell on top of the door twinkled as the four of them walked in and stared dumbfoundedly at our corny Asian decorations—ruby-red lanterns, Chinese calligraphy in cheap frames, a golden money cat smiling stupidly and waving its paw. Caitlyn and her dad both wore lacrosse polos. Her mom was in a Lilly Pulitzer dress. Only her brother was dressed like he wasn't planning on stopping by the country club after dinner. I thought to myself that my family and I were the upside-down version of them.

"Hello, anywhere you'd like to sit," my mom told them, unaware that she was addressing one of my classmates and her family.

"Hey," Caitlyn said, looking directly at me, her voice void of any emotion.

"Hi."

As they glanced around them, assessing which table was the least offensive, my mom whispered to me, "You know her?"

"Yeah, she goes to my school."

"You go serve them."

"Mom. No."

"Go."

I watched Mrs. O'Connell frown at her menu like it was a map written in ancient Sumerian. She flipped to the next page, raised an eyebrow, and flipped back to the first one. Caitlyn and her mother had the same color nail polish. Did they get manicures together? The thought of my mother paying someone else to do something as pointless as putting tickle-me-pink on her dull and chipped nails struck me as absolutely absurd. Meanwhile, Mr. O'Connell had his arms on the table, leaning forward to steal looks at what Caitlyn was typing on her phone.

"What are you waiting for? Go see if they have any questions." I told myself I'd done this a hundred times, to just go through the usual steps of service, to treat them like any other customers.

But they're not. I'm not just an anonymous Chinese girl taking their order at a restaurant on the wrong side of town. My cover was blown, my worlds were colliding. Nothing good could come from this, but I had no choice but to tug the strings of my apron tight, take out my notepad and pen, and walk toward my undoing. Was it just my imagination or did their whiteness create a halo of light around their corner table?

I stood over them and could smell Mrs. O's perfume. She smelled the way that rich ladies should smell, something floral and not cloying. Mr. O smiled at me with curiosity, and even Caitlyn put down her phone. Her brother didn't know I existed. I took a deep breath and launched into my spiel.

"Welcome to the Emperor's Garden. My—" I paused and recovered myself—I would usually say my name at this point—"I'll be your server tonight. Would you like anything to drink besides water?" My game plan was to ignore the elephant in the room, namely, Caitlyn's obvious look of recognition. As I jotted down their drink orders, it seemed possible that the plan would work. I came back in a few minutes and put a pot of green tea and four cups on the table.

"So, Caitlyn says you go to Hibben. What a crazy little coincidence!" I made eye contact with Mr. O as I slid a cup next to his glass of water and poured the tea.

"She hates it when we meet her friends, don't you Caitie? How embarrassing to be caught with your boring old folks, right?" I smiled back at Mr. O but didn't know what to say.

Suddenly, it occurred to me that I wasn't the only one who felt like her cover was blown. Caitlyn was blushing as her parents asked me about classes and sports and her dad attempted corny dad jokes. For a sliver of a second, Caitlyn and I shared a similar predicament, but that similarity was short-lived.

"Dad, you talk too much. We're not the only customers here,

you know." She was right. The room had started to fill up, and I had two tables I still needed to greet. As far as high school politics went, Caitlyn O'Connell had a solid place in the 1 percent—she was wealthy enough, pretty enough, cared enough about her grades, participated in the right clubs and sports, but more importantly, she exuded something intangible but undeniable. Whatever that girl had, they should've bottled it and sold it at fancy department stores.

Mr. O acted like he didn't hear her. "We never would've come here if Brandon here didn't have the most intense craving for Chinese food in the world. I didn't even know this place existed." He paused for a microsecond. "I guess I'm just an oblivious old dude."

"Bran's back from his third year at Dartmouth. Just visiting for a few days before he heads off to Thailand, right Bran?" Mrs. O glanced adoringly at her son the whole time she spoke. Meanwhile, he fiddled with his chopsticks, glancing around at his family like they were strangers on a bus he was stuck with until the next stop.

"Thailand sounds cool," I offered.

"Where in Asia are you from?" Mr. O asked.

"Oh, the part of Asia called New Jersey." They didn't get it. "It's a joke." The parents smiled on cue. "I was born in Jersey. But my parents are from China."

"I would love to visit China one day," said Mrs. O. "What a beautiful culture. So much history."

I nodded. "I should go see if your orders are ready."

They ordered the stereotypical dishes—General Tso's chicken, shrimp lo mein, crab rangoons—and way too much of it. As I was grabbing multiple plates, my mom reached for a few to help me carry them.

"No, Mom, go talk to table four. I haven't been over in a while."

"I can bring these and then go to table four, no big deal."

"No, go now. Please."

I was so relieved that she listened to me that the peculiar look she gave me didn't register. I went over to the O'Connells, balancing hot plates that smelled the way my hair and clothes would smell hours later when they would drive in their BMW back to their lives and I would stay soaking—literally—in mine.

"Yes, I'm starving," Caitlyn said as she and her brother drove chopsticks in like it was a race to the finish. I came back with the rest of the food and stepped back to assess the situation.

"Is there anything else I can bring you guys?"

"No, everything looks wonderful. Thank you, Annie."

I shouldn't have been surprised that Caitlyn didn't know my name and misinformed her parents. I didn't bother to correct them.

Once they started eating, Mr. and Mrs. O launched into their own conversation while Caitlyn and her brother ate in silence. Mrs. O took bird-sized bites; Mr. O used up a lot of napkins. Caitlyn had to flip her long brown hair every once in a while to keep it from touching the food. Brandon was definitely stoned and his parents were completely oblivious. Caitlyn probably knew and ignored him—they each had their own survival tactics.

In essence, they were a family like thousands of other families existing at that very moment. Like mine, in fact. But I couldn't get over their intangible glow.

"Yes, boxes would be great. Oof," Mrs. O patted her flat stomach, "I ate way too much. This all was so good."

"You satisfied, Bran?" Mr. O tried to engage his son, who just gave him a thumbs up and tossed one more crab rangoon in his mouth.

"I'll be back with the boxes and the check."

I was so relieved that the whole ordeal was about to be over that I didn't react quickly enough, didn't understand what was happening until it was too late. As I took the half-finished plates to the back to pack it all in to-go containers, my mom went past me in the other direction, holding a plate of orange slices.

"Wait—" I started to say, but I couldn't turn my body too quickly without dropping the plates. As soon as I could put them down, I went after her, but she was already at their table, beaming down at them while they looked at her politely and confusedly. For a few seconds, I watched her gesticulate while she talked to them.

They nodded, smiled, laughed. I looked away and started packing the leftovers, a red flush spreading up to the roots of my hair and down my throat.

By the time I came over with everything bundled in a plastic bag, my mom was already back to buzzing around the room, pouring water and clearing tables.

"Amy, you didn't tell us that those are your parents! We just met your mom. She brought us these delicious oranges, so thoughtful of her."

They all looked at me with something like pity, but ever slightly tinted with mistrust. Even Brandon was more alert with curiosity.

"I thought this was just your summer job. I had no idea this was a family business. So impressive. You've been here for almost twenty years?" Mr. O looked around the place as if seeing it for the first time. "It's not easy to keep a restaurant open. I have a few friends in the industry and they always talk about how tough and competitive it is."

"And your dad's the head chef? How wonderful!"

"Sorry I got your name wrong," Caitlyn added, the same way she'd said, "I'll have brown rice instead of white rice." I wanted to say to her, would you have said something if you were in my place? But she would never be in my place, and she would never know what it's like to not have something intangible. My world consisted of paper menus, rollups, cash registers, and take-out containers— everything was tangible.

They rode off with their leftovers back to the other side of town, while my night continued until the last table was cleared, the floors were mopped, the money in the register counted, and the dishes left drying. Andy came out of the back room where he'd been reading and playing Gameboy all night. My dad looked tired but still cheery, his hair wet from the water he splashed on his face to feel a little less grimy. My mother hadn't talked to me or looked at me much after the O'Connells left.

We gravitated toward each other near the back door when it came time to lock up and head home. I held a bag with the remains of my cake, and Mom carried a crate of oranges. They were a gift from the grocer we buy our produce from—she would cut them into perfectly equal slices when we got back to our two-bedroom apartment's folding kitchen table. Andy and I were only allowed fruit for dessert, and I often went to bed with the smell of citrus on my fingertips.

Dad drove and let Andy sit in the passenger seat. Mom sat with me in the back.

"Your friend's family are nice people."

"She's not my friend, Mom. We don't hang out with the same people."

"Who do you hang out with?"

No one, I thought. Well, you, Dad, and Andy. You're all I have.

Her silence gave me time to think about that peculiar look she gave me earlier, and I realized that it had been a look of shame. Shame for me or for herself?

"You're too good to hang out with her," she said suddenly in a lowered voice. "You're better than her. You're better than them."

She may have been looking at her own reflection in the car window, a mirror against the dark streets that led to our apartment. I wanted to believe her, holding back a salty lump in my throat, of guilt, of shame, of simultaneous determination and defeat. It would've been good enough just to reach for her hand and bring her out of her thoughts back to where she was with me, in a car with her family, her future and hope, in a city she never knew existed when she was my age, before she was tossed from one side of the world to another, a world that can become incomprehensible, if she let it.

We didn't talk anymore on that car ride. Attempting to delineate her after all these years is hard because I was always the mask she had to wear.

RECYCLED

K. DI PRIMA

MY PHONE'S BLOWING UP, BUT I DON'T DARE ANSWER IT OR EVEN look at it until Rocky concludes our tour of the firm's artwork. It doesn't matter that we've been at it all morning, or that we've traversed almost every inch of the twenty floors we occupy in this high-rise, or that I'm probably needed elsewhere. Art is Rocky's passion; therefore, it's mine too, for now—and for as long as it takes.

Rocky (Benjamin B. Rothrock, the renowned art collector-slash-patron, and head of the law firm Dooley Cohen, LLP) routinely loans art to museums around the country. Our million-dollar collection, personally curated by him, is equal parts traditional and avant-garde: scattered among the pastoral scenes, still lifes, and portraits are works by maestros whose métier is recycled trash and found objects, pieces by graffiti/street virtuosos with a political bent, like Banksy, and creations of self-taught artists.

Accompanying us on today's tour is the director of a small but prestigious local gallery, who's seeking a centerpiece for her winter exhibit. She shoots me a quizzical look, followed by a brittle smile aimed at my chin. I know she's nervous about me but I don't take it personally. Just guessing she doesn't spend much time with Black people, let alone a six-foot-two, dread-locked, African American dyke. She's still unclear as to who I am and why I'm here, even though Rocky introduced me as the firm's facilities manager, responsible for the crating, shipping, and tracking of the art. She shifts her handbag to her left shoulder when I come up on her right.

Again, a muted buzz; the incessant vibrations feel like an electric mixer on my hip. An emergency, no doubt, but at Dooley Cohen that means either a parking pass request or a complaint about office temperature.

Rocky pauses before a five-by-fifteen Santa Claus painted onto a chipped, splintered wood plank. Santa is Black and emaciated, and holds a briefcase across which are scrawled the words "Love," "Peace," and "Hope." Rocky waves his arms with a flourish and steps to the side, à la Vanna White. His mouth drops open with incredulity, to demonstrate that the genius on display renders him speechless.

The director gasps in appreciation. Rocky beams.

He finds his voice a nanosecond later. "The Lambertins!" he declares, gesturing to Santa again and then to a much larger work by the same artist, hanging next to it. The second piece is a giant lizard, its scales fashioned from thousands of thumb-shaped pieces of wood, painted green and layered like shingles. A closer look reveals that the markings on the scales are actually little faces: eyebrows, eyes, nose, and mouth, and each one is unique—thousands of scales, thousands of faces. At the giant's feet and clutched in his disproportionately short arms are written message signs, like on Santa's briefcase, but these read "Repent!" "The End Is Near!" and "The Wrath of the LORD Is upon Us!"

Rocky says, "This piece is just back from Chicago, the MCA! Last week, wasn't it, Violet?"

I smile and nod.

The director shifts her feet and, in the process, turns her back to me.

Rocky claps his hands, says, "Right! Let's go, the Gladwells next," and heads to the stairwell.

At five foot four and shrinking, and a buck twenty soaking wet, Rocky appears so fragile, his trademark bow tie looks like the only thing holding him together, that he'd unravel into a tweed puddle after one tug. But no, at seventy-plus years young, Rocky is the most robust of the three of us right now. He bounds up the stairs between floors two at a time. The knee I blew out playing ball in college throbs like a bitch. The director sighs, winces, and totters on her stilettos after him, me bringing up the rear.

Rocky took a shine to me, literally from day one. Sort of like his own personal reclamation project. At first, I thought he was one of those men with a taste for thick Black girls, you know the kind. Like the guy in Dellacroce's Deli last week, followed me around the store. Every time I looked up, there he was at my elbow, head just cresting my boobs, turnt up in his Bruno Magli oxfords and Italian silk suit. When I reached for a wedge of pecorino, he sidled over to me. His hand cupped my behind, and he whispered, "God, it's so round and firm. I'd give twenty-five grand for that ass. How 'bout it?"

I looked down at him and laughed. "In your dreams, pal," I said. Then I lowered my voice. "Touch me again, mothafucka, and I'll drag yo' sorry white ass outside and fuck you up. Hear me, old man?"

That's not Rocky, never was. Doesn't matter if you're Black or white, male or female, straight or other, he'll give you a chance, like he did me. It's up to you what happens after that.

When I started at Dooley Cohen twenty-five years ago, I was glad to have a job, any job. Offers weren't overflowing for an oversized former WNBA prospect like me, even with a college degree. The candidate Violet Holmes (me) looked better (definitely shorter, ha ha) on paper than in person. I'd snagged dozens of interviews, but things always seemed to go south after I walked through the door. Interviewers' voices rose an octave after shaking hands, for example. Someone even said to me once, "Well, when I talked to you over the phone, you didn't *sound* Black," as if I'd deliberately deceived them. Some were put off by the gay thing, too. But the HR woman at Dooley Cohen thought my long legs would guarantee we'd never miss another filing deadline, so she hired me as a court runner. It wasn't meant to be.

My first day, I heard a commotion inside a conference room as I was walking past. I peeked in and saw two women and a man atop the twenty-foot table, tramping over papers and folders, screeching and pointing at the floor. A handful of others perched on the windowsills, feet up, or huddled in the corners of the room, all staring under the table. I looked, too, and saw it—a mouse, no bigger than a brown egg, darting in panic around the legs of the chairs. Each time it dashed into the open, the people standing on the table shrieked in unison and stomped like a trio of Irish step dancers.

Made me chuckle. Where I come from, the rats are as big as cats. Long story short, the mouse scurried in my direction. And let's just say it found itself under my foot. A squeak, and something resembling a spurt of ketchup squirted out beneath my shoe. When I grabbed its tail and held it up to show the Irish step dancers that the threat had been neutralized, the guy standing on the table lost his lunch right there. I heard shivery laughter and scattered applause, and then a plaintive female voice said, "You didn't have to kill it, didja?" and somebody else said, "Marjorie, it was a mouse, fer Chrissake! Whatd'ja want, check it into the Four Seasons and order up room service?"

Funny how they debated the humanity of the mouse's demise, but didn't question who I was or why I was there. No polite conversational opening gambit, like, "Well, hello, you're new here, aren't you?" Not one of them asked what college I went to or where I'd worked before. In their world, somebody always just shows up and takes care of the icky thing for them. That day, that "somebody" was me, no questions asked. Just like they didn't question it when somebody else came later to clean up the mess dripping off the table. But I digress.

Turns out, Rocky was at that meeting. At the time he was chairman of litigation, a position I learned later was also a big deal, although not as big a deal as being chairman of the whole firm, like he became later. He'd said nothing to me then, but the next day he sat me down, said maybe the firm could channel my talents in another direction. Suggested the facilities department had a spot for someone with a cool head who could combine power tools and problem solving on the fly.

Fast-forward to today and I'm everybody's first call for "situations." But since they pay me six figures plus bonuses, it's okay by me.

Now, Rocky is expounding on a mixed-media piece by Clementine Gladwell, a self-taught artist who utilizes found objects in her work. I just sent out on loan to the Getty a piece she painted on a wooden ironing board salvaged from the trash. Rocky's gesturing at a pen-and-ink of a young woman and child drawn on a scrap of a brown paper grocery bag.

His back is to me for an instant, and I hazard a glance at my phone. The calls are from Julia, our department's administrative assistant, and that piques my curiosity. When I'm otherwise occupied, Julia deals with attorneys visiting from the firm's other offices. Sometimes those attorneys misbehave while they're away from home, and I remember that Phillip Fowler, Big Tobacco lead counsel, is in town.

Phil's based in the Dallas office. During the annual partners' meeting last year, he called me in the wee hours of the morning from the hotel across the street because his "date" had locked him out of his suite. He'd managed to grab his cell phone before she shoved him out the door. As luck would have it, I'd been overseeing the building's monthly generator test that night, so I hustled over, after stopping briefly at the ATM in the lobby.

Phil was nowhere to be seen, but from behind his hotel room door, the sister loudly proclaimed her disappointment at his gratuity, correlating its size to that of one of his body parts. When I waved a wad of cash in view of the peephole, she shut up and let me in. After a brief negotiation and her signature on a nondisclosure agreement, she sashayed away. I rescued Phil, naked and shivering, from the stairwell. He showed his gratitude and secured my future discretion with a generous early Christmas bonus, enough to fund a Caribbean cruise for me and my wife Stacie.

Rocky pivots; I drag my eyes away from the phone before I could read any of Julie's messages.

The director asks a question about an untitled painting composed of blobs of color splashed onto jagged scraps of wood. I see Julia rounding a corner with Martha Johnston, the supervisor of the mail room. Martha's jaw is tight, her expression grim. Red blotches have bloomed on her neck and upper chest.

"There she is, thank goodness!" Julia says, her voice cracking with relief.

"I'm so sorry, Mr. Rothrock," Martha says, "but we need to borrow Violet. Julia can fill in for her for the time being, if that's okay," and she hands my clipboard to Julia without waiting for Rocky's answer.

The director says, "Actually, I need to wrap up now, Rocky. I'll coordinate with Velma about the pieces I plan to use."

Rocky steers the director and Julia into an empty office to confer over the clipboard. Martha grabs my arm and walks briskly toward the elevator. "Violet, we've gotta do this quick, before HR butts in." She looks around, then whispers, "Oscar Claypool part deux."

My heart skips a beat. Brilliant, quiet Oscar. Fourth-year corporate associate. Magna cum laude Columbia Law grad. On track to be voted partner, first round. Until one day he tore his clothes off, and ran around the twelfth floor in his underwear blubbering about the futility of life, a box cutter to his throat. Luckily, the twelfth-floor receptionist got ahold of me right away, and by the time the first responders arrived, Oscar and I were sitting calmly in his office. I'd persuaded him to trade me the knife for a blanket. The firm set up counseling and relocated him to the Ocean View, Delaware, office, to imbibe the bracing, salty air and observe the seagulls circling overhead. Oscar left the firm about a year later. Last I heard, he's living off the grid somewhere in Alaska.

Martha and I step into an empty elevator. "It's our new hire, a woman named Dionne," she says, punching the "L" button with a vengeance.

"The court runner?"

"That's her. Bella in Bankruptcy says Dionne assaulted her in the ladies' room. Bella thought Dionne was a man"—Martha holds her hand up to forestall my comment—"and told her to get out of the ladies' room or she'd call the police. Can you imagine? I told Dionne to go home, but she's down in the lobby, making a fuss. You know Bella, right? Spoiled little princess, a diva. Even if Dionne is, well, a little mannish-looking—no offense, Violet—I don't think it's an honest mistake. Wouldn't surprise me if Bella—"

Martha clamps her mouth shut when the elevator door opens. A woman studying a file with her head down, walks on, says "Damn!" and walks off again. The door closes and Martha continues, "—is making something up to get Dionne in trouble. Just because she can. I'm hoping if you talk to her, you can get her to calm down."

I pictured Dionne: light-skinned African American female, average height, flat chested, pretty face, close-cropped hair. Dimples. When our paths had crossed on her first day, she'd nodded and we'd exchanged the look that said "I see you."

I'm not surprised Dionne startled Bella. People like Bella spare little interest in people like Dionne. We all look alike to them. Bella saw only Dionne's khakis, the collared shirt, and the toned muscles underneath the clothes, and chose to look no deeper. Listen, I realize that most women are on high alert these days. They sense predators around every corner, even in supposedly safe spaces like the ladies' room. But instead of lifting each other up, women like Bella like to make other women squirm.

" . . . making things worse. Yelling her head off, saying she didn't do anything wrong, it's discrimination, et cetera. Hoping you can get to her before HR does, maybe it'll save her job. I mean, HR's gonna have to deal with it eventually, but—"

As we exit the elevator, I hear Dionne. I can't distinguish the words, but her voice modulates from angry shouts to stage-whispered outrage. People scurry by, past clumps of others who've stopped to watch. A pair of secretaries on their way to lunch huddle nearby.

Martha shoos them away. "Move along, ladies. Nothing to see here."

Dionne paces in front of the three-story glass window adjacent to the bank of automatic double doors. Now she's muttering to herself, not yelling, wiping sweat and tears from her face with shaking hands. She stops when I approach, regarding me warily.

I summon my game face. Neutral, no judgment. Dionne bobs her head at me. "'Sup?"

It's an invitation. Martha's shoulders relax.

I set my hands on my hips, tilt my head. "How 'bout we talk?"

She shrugs.

I motion her to follow me outside, and she does. The automatic door swishes closed behind us. I settle onto a bench in front of the polished black granite wall bordering the entrance to the building. I stretch out my legs, lean my head back. A bee buzzes past my ear and glides onto an azalea bloom in the container alongside of us. The sky's blue and cloudless, the sun bright and warm.

Beside me, she clenches her fists, looks down. Exhales a shivery sigh. I'm silent, waiting. She says, "Don't know how—why—it got all fucked up, man. I mean, seriously."

"Bad day."

She bites off the ends of her sentences. "Huh! No. You. Got no idea, man. This morning. Left my phone. Go back an'—there's my girl. S'posed to be my fiancée. In bed with a dude. A dude, man! Don't wanna leave. Know what I'm sayin'? But I gotta. I need this job, man. So—so when that white chick said get out, I—" She throws her hands up, shakes her head. "Know what I'm sayin'? Ya feel me?"

I nodded. Yeah, I feel her. Sometimes the last stupid thing is one more than you can take. It's the final stupid little thing in a lifetime of stupid little things, the drop of water that makes the bucket overflow and sweeps you away and you know you're drowning, and nothing and no one can save you.

"It didn't go down the way she said. I was in the stall when she came in. Was washing my hands at the sink when she comes out. Gives a big heave like she seen a ghost, says, 'My gawwwd, what you doing in here? Get out! This here's the ladies room!'"

"Nobody else was there?"

"No." Dionne stares blankly ahead. "She says I hit her. It wasn't like that, man. Chick's all hysterical, screaming, and I just touched her shoulder with my finger—*one finger*—and I said, 'look at me, wouldja look at me? I'm a woman, same as you. I belong in here just as much as you.'" Dionne drops her head into her hands. Her shoulders shake. "I know who they gonna believe. I can't lose my job, man, I just can't. Barely making it as it is. Fuck me. Fuck my life."

She lifts her head, cheeks wet with melted anger. Exhaustion and bewilderment cloud her eyes. She's young, about my age when I started at Dooley Cohen doing the exact same job. She is me. She is what might have been.

Nothing I can say will make it better. We both know that after today, she'll never work at Dooley Cohen again. I tell her that Martha will do what she can, maybe get her in at another law firm in town. I'll work my connections, see if one of our vendors has an opening. Without my asking for it, she slips the lanyard over her head and hands me her access card, and I think about waves pounding the shore in Ocean View, Delaware.

She nods, stands, and says, "Thanks, man. Thanks for listening." She shakes my hand and then jams both fists in her pockets. She walks away into the lunchtime crowd, head low.

My mouth is dry as sand. My arms feel like I've done ten rounds in the ring. A sauerkraut-scented cloud from the hot dog cart at the curb billows over me. I swallow the bile in my throat and head indoors. Inside, the blast of air conditioning feels like a slap in the face. Martha's not in the lobby, but her text message relays all I need to know: "Dionne's gone, outta here, per HR. I'm packing up the stuff in her locker to mail to her. Thanks anyway for trying, Violet." At the security desk, I surrender Dionne's access card, instruct them to disable it and to flag her profile. If she returns to the building, she'll be stopped and escorted out.

My phone rings; I answer without thinking. It's Lourdes, an assistant in Environmental. "Sorry, Violet. Hate to bother you with this, but Steve Obsidian specifically asked for you. Says there's a foul odor coming from somewhere. Wants you to find it and eradicate it. Nobody else smells anything. Can you come up and—"

"I'm on my way out," I say, as I swivel away from the elevator bank. "I'm sorry, Lourdes. Call Julie. Ask her to send Tony instead." I click off.

The food trucks ringing the building have suffused the air with an oily, fried-vegetable mist. My stomach flip-flops again. I walk away from them rapidly, randomly. I'm suffocating.

No matter his extramarital dalliances, Phil's Big Tobacco cases have brought in millions for the firm and for him. A win-win, I suppose. Everybody gets rich while coincidentally making the world a better place. My strides lengthen. Suddenly, I'm at the train station.

Oscar had brains and education. He was equipped to make a positive difference in the world. Instead, he opted out of civilization in favor of the rigors of the wilderness. I wonder, which path is more courageous? The train glides into the platform, enveloping me in a whoosh of dry, dusty air. I step in.

I don't know Dionne but I know what it's like being poor, Black, and lesbian. No benefit of the doubt. No soft seaside landings or warm blankets. If anyone could justifiably lose their shit a dozen times a day over the unfairness of life, it would be her. I should have done better by her. I could have pushed for immediate repercussions for Bella, at least. A lick of anger pings like a firework in my head.

It's midday; all trains are locals. As the car rocks and sways, I realize how much I've compromised over the years, what I've done to get along. What I've ignored, or pretended not to hear or to understand. How often I've been pleasant to the point of superciliousness. But it's what brought me here. By anyone's standard, I am successful. By my own measure, I am not sure anymore.

The train slides into my station, a forties-era brick building with a pitched, shingled roof and painted fretwork lining the eaves. Always clean. Well-lit and patrolled at night. Like the leafy suburban neighborhood I live in. I don't know what Dionne has gone home to, but odds are it's not this. I hop off, cross to my car, and start the engine.

The train shudders, gains momentum. A font of frustration and sheer rage bubbles up from a place deep inside of me. As the rail cars rumble away, a fiery shriek spews from my windows onto the tracks, and is crushed to dust beneath the train's metal wheels.

REQUIEM FOR FIVE TREES

A.M. RIDDLE

Five trees died today.

For two, mangled and twisted by a powerful summer storm, it was
    a mercy killing.
For the other three, my question is why?
They were alive and well,
      providing oxygen and shade,
          peace and privacy,
            wildlife shelter,
              and natural beauty in our community.

Did the neighbors decide it was inconvenient to have them there?
Were they tired of cleaning up pine needles and leaves?
Did the trees interfere with their car and boat parking?

I do not know. The reasons were not discussed with me.

The trees left no survivors—their stumps and roots were ground to
dust by young men in green uniforms and sunglasses, daring to hold
wood in one hand and a gas-powered chainsaw in the other,
lighted cigarettes dangling from their thin lips.

A rhinoceros-sized machine with mechanical jaws saw to the final destruction of the trees' earthly remains.

Gone are the aerial pathways enjoyed by the squirrels, leaping among their arboreal brethren.

Gone are the sheltered habitats of the bluebirds.

Gone is the birdsong that accompanies the sunrise I enjoy from my sun porch.

The robin family will not return. Their home is gone.

I mourn with the mourning doves.

How many trees are cut down from the Earth in just one day? Institutions as revered as the scientific journal *Nature* and The Rainforest Project cannot agree on a precise number, but it is in the millions at a minimum.

Millions of trees cut down each day, most killed in the name of avarice.

I was not there to see those millions fall.
But I saw the five.
And I wept for them.

TORNADO

CARRIE VESTAL GILMAN

In The Wizard of Oz, *Dorothy had a clear-cut objective. She knew exactly what she wanted—to get back home to Kansas. Who could help her?*

—Introduction to Purdue Training & Development memo to Sales Force dated November 4, 1996[1]

Since she returned, Henry noticed her eyes always seemed to be looking for the next storm while Em couldn't figure why she no longer had a full set of kitchen spoons. In just a short time, their girl who had been so glad to be home had lengthened her sleeves and shortened her smile, ignored the little dog chasing after her, and let the door slam against the newly built farmhouse as she left for town.

She kept company with those who were searching for something they never had while she mourned her silver shoes, lost somewhere over the desert. No longer able to get anywhere she wished, when the urge to escape the flatness of home hit hard, she closed her eyes, sunk into the memory of a crimson field where she lay with a lion. She could have slept there forever.

---

[1] Quoted in Tony Wagner, "A Drug Maker Used the Wizard of Oz to Sell Oxycontin," *Marketplace*, December 15, 2017; see scribd.com/document/367217066/Wizard-of-Oz.

That was the time she liked to remember, before the unthinkable things she'd done. Melted witches and winged beasts took residence. And so, she returned to that field, again and again. When she finally stopped coming home, Em found her spoons, bent and burned, stashed under the bed of the girl with the wind in her name.

Meanwhile, the man who only saw green, looked down on the earth from the height of a silk balloon. He should have been ashamed, but wasn't, thinking he was still a good man, just a bad wizard. In fact, it was the opposite, he was a bad man and a wonderful wizard. From the clouds he could see the weather patterns for years ahead, could create just the right conditions for desperation to bloom, ruby red and paper thin.

And endless.

FAT-PICKERS

RICHARD LEVINE

for Manya Goldberg

Your mother sent you out at dusk,
to pick fat from garbage cans.
You wrapped it in newspaper.

The fat-loosened letters and words,
smudged beyond legibility, slipped
from the page. You didn't care
what they said or where they went.
News could not satisfy your hunger.

Your mother mustered a thin, gray-
water broth from the fat. Dissolved
it floated like blisters oozing yellow pus.

Neither that nor an errant swirl of ink
stopped you from drinking it before it
cooled, and your burned tongue spawned
small blisters as you wiped the black
smears from your mouth on your sleeve.

This is one story you told about the trek
across persecution and Europe,
with your mother and four brothers.

And where you arrived as strangers,
to bless schools and work and enough food,
I call birthright and home. Now, we compost
and put out bottles and cans, and never think
of the trash-pickers who live beyond news.

FUNCTIONALLY FINE

JIMI JOHNSON

A FEW MONTHS BEFORE MY THIRTIETH BIRTHDAY, I DECIDED TO kill myself. As one does. It was an easy decision, because I hated everything about being alive. But it was also the sort of thing one only decides to do because they don't want to do what they are currently doing, and like many people during the pandemic, I did not want to be doing. Anything. The plan changed because a friend "took" my birthday, but was soon reborn as a summer plan: in June, after my commitments were squared away and no one would mind too much. Again, the plan changed, but only because I broke down on that same friend's couch (once we finally established a quarantine bubble) and admitted to the whole thing.

I would go on to admit I was suicidal to several more people for the sake of recovering from this bout of not wanting to exist anymore. The solution, found that night on the couch, was for me to go to that friend's family's home over the summer rather than staying home in rural Alaska. Specifically, I'd be staying with her brother while she stayed with her parents. The next person I had to admit I was suicidal to was my mother, though I waited another month to do it. Normally, I'd never have done this, but I needed someone to watch my dog and thus, I had to tell her what was happening. She agreed to help, to meet me in Anchorage and take my dog back home with her while I left the state for two months.

The next person I admitted this issue to was the friend's brother.

I had met him only over video calls a handful of times prior to moving in with him for the summer, and had known him mere hours when this admission came about. The three of us were out for dinner, and the conversation flew a little too close to the subject. I made the stupid statement that I was being *completely honest*, to which my friend countered something like *Oh, really?* How *completely honest?* Leaving me open to confess that, in fact, he had me as a houseguest because the alternative had apparently been fatal. It must have been an excellent first impression, because we became exceptionally fast friends. Normally, I'd suspect pity in such a case, but we also both have digestive illness. Really, it was meant to be.

Of course it is better to admit to these things and let people help you, pull you out of the mental hole you've dug yourself into. Toward the end of summer, I confessed to a few more friends. Each time it felt like I had failed them. Still, I do not regret this, and I do not regret the steps taken to alleviate the pain. The reality of wanting to die is, often times at least, it is mostly a method of escapism. The trip out of state, away from my usual responsibilities, did not assuage this desire to get away from myself. Not really. It took most of the time I was there to even begin taking steps toward feeling less inclined to get out of everything, *really* everything. I am back home now, and I am still unsure of the outcome.

This is what feels so underrepresented when I read, hear, watch things about mental health problems. I did not become depressed because of the pandemic, or because I was turning thirty, or some other thing that happened relatively recently that I can point to and yell *Ah-ha!* There is no culprit event that I can recall. I was diagnosed with depression and anxiety in eighth grade, long after I had displayed signs and struggled with symptoms. I remember chewing on my arms to comfort myself as a child, the act of hurting myself something that I did to feel better, more in control, less sad. So then what caused my depression? Being a child? Everyone does that.

The first time I wanted to kill myself was, I think, in ninth grade. I got back into counseling, I worked on it, and it got better. For a bit. I was back at it in eleventh grade and followed much the same process. In college I spiraled one night, taking a bunch of medication, passing out, throwing up. Again, I got back into therapy, I worked on it, but I couldn't find the right fit and in frustration I quit and forced myself to just keep pushing through the thoughts, the obsessions, the compulsions, the intrusive ideas. It was all so much work, and it distracted from the anxiety-pushing need to do exceptionally well at the too-many things I signed myself up for. I hated it. Notably, I took no real breaks. Mental illness often incapacitates those who suffer from it, but I refused to be laid low, at least outwardly. The evening I had attempted suicide in college I had a shift as a resident assistant, and after cleaning myself up, I went to work. I didn't even think of calling out, and I didn't speak of the incident until years later. Sometimes mental illness really can look like being an absolutely normal person from the outside.

Between the age I was chewing on my arms—maybe four—and now, I have never stopped self-harming for more than a few months at a time. I want to though, and I'm trying. It is worse when my chronic digestive illnesses flare up, when it feels like my body is fighting me, so I compulsively fight back. My obsessive thoughts tell me that if I just hurt somewhere else, I won't have that back pain, abdominal pain, whatever it is that's hurting. Which is another thing—mental illness isn't the only invisible illness inside of me. That's true for most people afflicted. On top of a slurry of digestive issues, my joints hurt and due to ulnar impact syndrome, my wrists, especially the right one, always hurt. Depression hurts, too. My brain tells me, over and over every day, that all of these pains will ease if I just hurt myself. It also tells me that I deserve to hurt, to hurt more, to hurt *just the right way* and that I need to keep hurting myself until it is done *right*.

At the same time, I have found myself successful in my career. I work hard, I do everything I can for my students and my school, I constantly aim to do better while taking on extra duties. From the outside, I am an extremely high-functioning individual, and when I'm not it devastates me. Not that devastation is any excuse to slow down. I clean myself up, and I go back to work.

This summer I helped with projects—a bathroom renovation,

yard and gardening projects, that sort of thing. Most therapies encourage depressed individuals to do things, to get out of their heads and into something physical. I get it. My brain is the least awful when I am productive, when I am performatively completing tasks, being useful. I crash afterwards, overanalyzing every mistake, but in the moment I'm fine. The strange thing this summer, however, was realizing how much I liked climbing things. I *liked* doing something—and it wasn't even productive. I never like doing things, I just do things because that's what I do. I read prolifically, I write, I draw, I volunteer, I walk, I work out, but I don't *like* any of those things. They are just things that I do. Like washing the dishes or eating, I don't particularly care to do any of it, it just *must be done*. This was the break moment: realizing I could like something. I could want to do something again not because of the obsessive nature of my thoughts, or because it had to be done, but because I had fun doing it.

The reality is I just forget that I can like things. My current diagnosis is persistent depressive disorder, colloquially known as high-functioning depression. I also have generalized anxiety disorder, and they work together to help me appear to be oh-so mentally healthy. Mentally healthy enough it's hard to reconcile the public version of myself with my own thoughts, especially when my thoughts are telling me to die and my boss is telling me that I have done an outstanding job this school year. So, realizing I liked climbing brought about an existential crisis. It was a turning point, a low from which I could grasp some piece of reality and put some distance between the me who wanted to die and the me who wanted literally anything else. I got back into counseling.

It was a rough start, but I didn't let that stop me. After all, at that point, I was failing at being high-functioning by not working on myself. Mental breakdowns don't always look like sobbing helplessly on the floor for weeks. I only cried that night on the couch in front of anyone else. After that, it was all on me. My irrational independence is a crux, keeping me from getting help when I need it or feeling close to people in general, but it works for pushing myself through. I made a new plan—one where I lived and kept doing things. Different things, things with new goals in mind. Selfish (perhaps even a little silly) goals.

No one can save me. Maybe there are people out there who can be saved by another person, but I'm just not the type. I can be helped, as previously illustrated, but not saved. The concept is strange, anyway. Not that I wouldn't mind someone sweeping in and saving me, because I can want two opposite things at the same time. We all can. But I have to save myself. I know, because historically the only person who has really done what needed to be done in order for me to keep my head above the water has been me.

It's terrifying. The easier option is still out there, and it's also terrifying. The temptation to continue as I have for the last six years is there, to stay and teach and do things because I feel that I must do them. The problem with that temptation is that it likely means I will never recover from this particular bout of suicidality. I'm terrified, then, of every option: die, radically change, stay the same. But *I like climbing things.*

The idea that suicidal ideation ever goes away exists. For some people, it does. For others, for me, it just becomes passive. Instead of "I am going to kill myself on this day by these means," I have long stretches, sometimes a few years, where it's just a bubbling under the surface of "I could kill myself" in some form or another. Flashes in my mind of *just jump* or *crack that knife against your wrist* or whatever it is my brain has decided is a good idea. Sometimes it's even more vague, like a longing to *be done.* This is something I have learned to live with, to acknowledge and let pass by without acting on it. I don't hold out hope anymore to ever be free of this, or to even be free of depression or anxiety in general. Just as I know I will manage my physical illnesses my whole life, I know I will manage my mental illnesses my whole life as well.

I fell just a little bit in love with the friend's brother over the summer. I fell just a little bit in love with the area where he lived, as well. Warm, honest feelings are difficult. Still, having any of them means there's the possibility of having more of them. I have a new plan, to live, to work hard and improve myself in as many ways as possible. I have chosen radical changes, because I feel radically awful. I know I will always be in pain; I know I will always be sick; I know there are some things in my life I cannot improve. I just don't care.

I am not saved, but the summer of avoiding my suicide was a success, at least in some way, since I am not dead. Dodging one bullet does not mean I can rest. Really, there is much more work to do now than there was those few months before my birthday when I made my first plan. I have counseling, my usual teaching job, and then my improvement plan, which involves training for new employment, earning as much money as possible to save up to buy a house out of the state, and muscle training to enhance my ability to climb things. It could take years, and it all must be done with the added weight of severe depression and anxiety. It will hurt.

There is no such thing as an easy solution with mental health. If I had followed the first plan and killed myself, I may not have had to face the difficulties, but that wouldn't mean there weren't any. As it stands, the work is on me, and since I don't know how to stop being high-functioning, it will largely happen out of sight. It doesn't help that the stigma around mental health issues still exists, that the invisible part of mental illness is still valued as the superior, that I'm not the only one who's scared. Meeting me, one wouldn't guess that I was obsessively considering if I could fit into that cabinet, knowing that if I could, then I would finally be worthy of being alive. It's there, though, just as the desire to die is, just as my poorly functioning bowel is. But I can laugh, I work hard, I do more than is expected of me and I do it well. The difference I want to make is to do a few more things, but for myself. For the sake of getting better, not just being high-functioning.

The truth is, managing one's health, managing *my* health, is tiresome. Which is why, a few months before my thirtieth birthday, I didn't want to do it anymore. The three decades, at least two of them memorably and incredibly difficult, seemed like enough. I could still argue that it is. The difference between then and now is nothing compared to the difference between the moment my mental illness developed and now, if one consults a calendar. If one consults something else, however, the counterargument becomes clear: if two decades is enough, then how will I climb more things?

And for now, that is a completely reasonable argument. Fighting my brain doesn't have to make sense, because that is not how brains work. It is not how my brain worked when I was a child and thought chewing on my arms solved any of my problems, or when I was in college and went to work after trying to kill myself, or even more recently when I decided killing myself was the best solution to my problems. Countering such things with the same lack of logic works, because anything can be a reason to push back against the irrational beast of mental illness.

I've always felt the idea of hope was strange, foreign, something I couldn't get my head around. There are a lot of concepts I can't get my head around, but hope is one I've tried more than others. Mental illness makes hope difficult, but not impossible. Humanity may be doomed, the world may be in peril, and my brain may be fighting me on the daily, but that does not make hope foolish. It may feel like a giant fish struggling in petroleum jelly–coated arms, impossible to hold on to for any reasonable amount of time, but that's just a simile. A means of explaining, from one human to another, just how something feels. I'm not great at that, just as I'm not great at having hope. I may not have a lot of hope for the future, that things will work out or get better. There are a lot of reasons to doubt that things will ever be better than they are now, personally, nationally, globally. Maybe things will get worse, much worse, unbearably so. If they do, I'll have to make a plan, and I *hope* (that tricky thing) my plan is radically motivated toward being more than illness, more than a few decades of struggling against myself, more than I could imagine in my twenties.

It's part of my functioning that I leave things out, I don't tell the whole story, I twist parts of the narrative to be more digestible, less bleak. This isn't a unique quirk by any means, most people adjust their lives to suit their preferences for what the world knows and what it doesn't. The nice thing about being able to talk about it all is—there's more to tell. There's always more to know, more to experience, more to suffer through. Perhaps that is not the mindset of a hopeful creature, but it doesn't feel hopeless. If anything, it feels like I'll make it to thirty-one.

RED LIGHT/BLACK ZONE

RENÉE OZBURN

I'VE DANCED AND DUCKED FOR DECADES TRYING TO KEEP RACE from defining my identity. I'm rarely aware of it from the inside, so why is this singular element of my existence so controlling as I navigate life on the outside? At least in America, I can't escape being put in the Black Zone before I utter a word. Despite my "just act human" diversionary tactics, I keep getting slapped with reminders that scream, "You are Black—first and foremost. And don't you forget it."

Although I am Black, my husband is white. He has been a butcher, a baker, a candlestick maker (literally), an actor, an ironworker, and a high school English teacher. Without anyone knowing his history, he receives respect, along with an assumption that he is competent, honest, steady, and dependable, the moment he walks into most establishments. I am an attorney. I was also a judge for thirty-five years. No one assumes these credentials might apply to someone who looks like me until they are told. Even then, the degree of incredulous surprise that I have held esteemed positions often results in facial expressions that register as "can't compute."

Needless to say, out in public, my husband and I inhabit different worlds. In fact, I doubt most of my nearest and dearest white friends and loved ones are conscious of being white on a daily basis. Whereas, I would be hard-pressed to identify a day or week when I am not reminded of my race.

In the minimally mixed midwestern American community where I live, I often do not encounter or interact with other people of color in stores, at the gym, or hanging out with friends. Many days my only sighting of another non-white person is a driver in an adjacent car at a stoplight. If we happen to catch each other's eyes, we smile and give the "Wow. Where'd-you-come-from?" nod that is probably universal with darker-skinned dwellers living in less ethnically diverse domains.

Not long ago, in a vintage shop near my home, I stepped into a side room to check out an Art Deco display. A white salesclerk hanging clothes on a rack and a white teenage boy standing by the cash register were the only other people in the area. As I entered, the clerk hollered "Red Light" with such screeching alarm, I jumped and so did the young cashier. I saw her nod to the boy, indicating he should divert his attention to the door where I stood. With a look like a deer caught in headlights, he shuffled from behind the counter and, without a "Hello" or "May I help you?" began to follow on my heels as I walked in the direction of a jewelry display. He was so close I turned around and, in a friendly voice, asked, "And how are you today?" I could tell he was uncomfortable. I didn't stop to look at anything. Instead, I left the room and exited the building.

The moment I got home and reported the incident to my husband, he was in his truck headed to the store. I call this maneuver "Going home to get my white boy." Over our years together, I've employed it a number of times when I've faced customer service issues in white establishments—that will only be sincerely considered if presented by a fellow white person.

The owner of the vintage store knew my husband. She did not know me. After he calmly described what had just happened to me, his wife, he was given the type of nondefensive apology I have rarely received. And then the owner passed on an invitation for me to return to the store so she could explain the establishment's experience with shoplifters. I laughed as he relayed this invitation, knowing it would be a cold day in hell before I set foot in her store again. It wouldn't have been worth the effort to contain my sarcasm when I, respectfully, asked, "Is every middle-aged, suburban, woman (i.e., the store's predominant demographic) greeted with a robust 'Red Light' welcome as she enters separate spaces around this shop?"

When I recount such incidents to friends who have never felt judged by their color, friends who know my character and credentials, they shake their heads and furrow their brows and say things like, "How horrible. I can't imagine. I didn't know that was still going on—here." They cannot fathom the incessant and insidious nature of these indignities. And on the, thankfully, rare occasion that someone implies that I might be a little oversensitive, I work hard to remind myself not to turn true friends into negative white stereotypes.

During most of my years as a judge, I worked in a large government complex. Out of hundreds of employees there were only about two dozen Black women working in my building. One day, four of us were the only occupants of an elevator. We did not know each other, but everyone laughed knowingly when I broke the silence by quipping, "If we all get off together, someone's going to think we were in here planning an insurrection." You see, it was a sure bet, at one point in our careers each of us had been asked by a white coworker a question like, "Do you know Betty (or the name of another Black woman in the building)?" That would be it. There would be no other contextual clue of who they were referring to. Because a very common assumption about my race is that each of us knows every other person of the same race in the building, city, state, or country.

All differences we bring to the table can season our relationships with interesting flavors—and race is a different seasoning. I just wish I had more say in how much it dominates the recipe of the dish called "Me." It gets tiresome to always be featured, first and foremost, as the Black female or Black judge or Black writer.

Once, in a writing workshop, a former female cop and I, a former judge, argued ardently (to no avail) that we should be allowed to write personal essays without disclosing our gender or race until the meat of our stories unfolded. In our experience, trivializing often starts once those two factors become known.

Our writing mentor was adamant.

Mentor: "In your stories, either leave race out entirely or put it up front. A passing mention down the road just won't do."

Us: "But we don't want to inject race or gender early on. It skews the story. Why can't race or gender take a back seat?"

Mentor: "Because John Q. Reader will feel betrayed if you wait."

Us: "But can't we assume Mr. Reader is evolved enough to deem those factors as insignificant as we, the authors, see them?"

Mentor: "No! Not in the real world and not on the page."

For over thirty years, I've gathered most Sundays with a group of over 100 people. Of the three Black women who regularly attend, we cover the spectrum of height, hair style, and skin color. Yet, long-term white members still regularly mix up our names with a frequency that weakens the rationale that "We all call someone by the wrong name, sometimes." I never ascribe malice to the faux pas. And the person who calls me by the other Black women's names usually stammers and makes an immediate correction. We always laugh and go back to sharing our mutual interests. Even so, sometimes, silently, with a resigned weariness, I think, "Could you at least see me clearly enough to call me by my name?"

It makes me wonder if there is some translation circuitry in the brain of beholders making the three of us one generic Black woman. Images of a three-headed mythical creature or a band of musketeers that no one can tell apart, come to mind.

Recently, I read that 90 percent of white Americans have no close Black friends. It wouldn't surprise me if another large percentage hardly have incidental interaction with people of color in their daily lives. Survival for the white majority is rarely dependent on befriending or understanding those who look like me. I, on the other hand, must always remain observant and vigilant. It is imperative that I know how my presence affects those around me and adjust accordingly. I must pay attention to the ups and downs and likes and dislikes of my greater community. I must work on befriending my neighbors to gain those intermittent moments where they might forget and let me step out of the Red Light/Black Zones I am so often confined to against my will. Because it is only in those moments that I truly get to be me.

SEPTEMBER 10. THE DANISH

BERNARD HORN

in commemoration of my father's 36th Yahrzeit

In my brother's poem (if he were someone who wrote poems)
it would be a 10 pm visit to our father in the nursing home
forty years ago. He would have established in his poem
the comprehensive annihilation of language

that was our father's circumstance and ours
and that caring for our father at home had, only then,
after six steadfast years, become too much for our mother,
like him, seventy-five years old. My brother would describe

the elevator door opening on the third floor
to our father in his wheelchair, shouting
his terrible "Tra ra tra tra" at the top of his lungs
and he yelling back, "Shut up! There are people asleep.

Do you want the nurses to put you to bed?" Which worked
for once. Then my brother would describe the blaze of anger
in our father's pale blue eyes, fierce, as he started to count
the fingers of his lost right hand by flipping them up,

one-by-one. Pinky, ring, middle, pointer. Pinky, ring,
middle, pointer. Pinky, ring, middle, pointer. "No,"
my brother said, "It is not four days since I last visited. I was here
yesterday. Remember? I brought a Danish. Split. Half for you, half
for me."

Immediately, the whole body of our father softened, his eyes
sweetened
in a rare shred of understanding and, sagging into the wheelchair,
he bent his head, took my brother's hand in his good left hand,
and kissed it as everything changes and tears form in our eyes.

SLEEP

LIZ KELNER POZEN

The last good night's sleep I had
was over twenty years ago
when we visited friends
in the mountains
up north.

We had a lovely day
of walking in the woods
feeding fish in the pond
eating cookies on the porch
then took the bottom bedroom
where the sheets were rank
from the last guests
the dark so absolute
with the lamps off
we could barely find each other
and the biting cold made us
surrender shivering to the quilts
with a kind of abandon.

The unbroken sleep
felt weighted
a stone dropping to the bottom
of a primeval lake
an utter absence.

This friendship is now gone
signs of its dissolution already there
all those years ago
if one was looking.
But on that night
replete with chocolate
and covered by down
I slept not like the dead
but like someone
fully alive.

ORIGINS

JANET GOTKIN

MY *BUBBE*, MY MOTHER'S MOTHER, TAUGHT ME ABOUT *MAZEL* when I was a small child, maybe seven or eight years old. I thought it was just *bubbe* being *bubbe*: different, sweet, confusing. Concepts like *mazel* are beyond the grasp of children.

"No matter what," *bubbe* would say, "you've got to have *mazel*."

She might have been responding to a cousin's bragging about her children or an uncle's financial troubles. The uncles and cousins, the children and grandchildren, the great-aunts and great-uncles: everyone nodded when Ethel Shulman spoke. She knew what she was talking about. And *mazel?* Well, *mazel* was complicated. Life was unpredictable, often tragic. Everyone knew that. Maybe Ethel was right. You shouldn't take things for granted. Who knew better than Jews how good fortune could turn to dust in an instant?

Mazel is the dark underside of *mazel tov*, the aspirational Jewish toast to a future unfettered by misfortune. *Mazel tov*, we say exuberantly, wineglasses raised to the bride and groom at their wedding, to a recent college graduate, to a couple celebrating the birth of a baby or to their parents marking their fiftieth anniversary. In the late 1940s and 1950s, when I was growing up and World War II and the Holocaust were resonant memories, Jews understood that their joys were ephemeral. In case they forgot, my *bubbe* reminded them that we are not the authors of our stories.

"Keep Kosher," *bubbe* would advise. "Don't be so quick to take credit for everything. You're a *macher* (big shot) today, but what about tomorrow? You never know: maybe you'll have *mazel* and maybe you won't."

Now, in my seventies, I appreciate her appreciation of the vagaries of life and the uncertainties of expectation.

Clearly, *mazel* was operating the summer of 1966 when I met and fell in love with my husband, Paul. For nearly half a century, he was my best friend, my heart's heart, my *bashert*, my meant-to-be person. Together, we lived a life filled with *mazel* and love. We raised a family, celebrated holidays both secular and religious, rejoiced in the birth of grandchildren, mourned the deaths of loved ones. We traveled and we wrote a book. We formed a family made of friends. Not a bad run, I guess. But when *mazel* ran out the night Paul died, I wanted to die with him.

As I try to make my way through the devasted landscape of loss that followed his death, I have been hearing my *bubbe's* voice. Where once I might have been frightened, now I am comforted.

"So, *nu zeiskeit* (my sweet one)," she says. "That's the thing about *mazel*. You think you have it, but in the end, you don't."

The nights have turned cool and windy here in my adopted city of Santa Fe, New Mexico. The Jewish holidays have come and are almost gone. With a *shofar* blast and apples dipped in honey, Jews around the planet celebrated the coming of the year 5781 in the life of the Jewish people. I am mired in my grief.

Last night, when I couldn't sleep, I walked outside to my patio to watch the night sky and listen to the wind in the piñons. At night, the pain of my broken heart becomes vivid, the brokenness raw. I think that I may not be able to keep living without Paul. I want to heal, but my heart stays rent. I don't know who I am without this sweet man who rescued me with his love. Why, after all this time, is it still so hard?

I didn't ask the question aloud, but my *bubbe* answered.

"*Mammele* (Yiddish term of endearment), you're smart. You know why this is hard. Stop thinking so much. *Gay shluffen* (go to sleep). You'll feel better with some sleep. You want I should sing you *Rozhinkes mit Mandlen*?"

"I don't think so, *bubbe*. But you're right. I do know."

It's hard because I loved him so much, for so long, and he loved me, and he's gone, and I want him back. I've gotten seven tattoos since he died, attended rallies and lobbied for abortion rights. I've cried until I couldn't breathe. I've written a book about love and grief and working for access to abortion. Nothing helps. When he died, the zombie sisters of grief and trauma took up residence in my head and my body. They recede, but they are never far away. They will come back.

I am lonely and I am scared. I am afraid I won't be able to be brave, even though my family and friends remind me that I am a Gryffindor and Gryffindors are brave. I am afraid of getting old and being alone, of losing my strength and clarity; I am fearful of my fragility. I have reconnected the threads of feminism and abortion advocacy, and made the tapestry of my life whole, but the threads that were my love with Paul hang ragged. I rediscovered my writer self, mute for more than four decades. But I would trade that in a heartbeat if I could have him back, sitting with me on our living room couch. We would be eating pizza, drinking iced tea, watching a late-night movie, our ancient cat Lily snuggled between us.

I have put a photograph of Paul on the mantle over the kiva fireplace in my living room; I have given copies to my daughters. It is fall in the photo, just as it is now; he is wearing a blue sweater, sitting on a wicker chair on the patio, the New Mexico sky glowing behind him. He is smiling the most contented smile you could imagine. He's happy. I think he was happy with me, with our family, with our life. I think he was happy with the way his life turned out.

"*Ganug, mammele.* Enough already," *bubbe* says.

She's right. Enough already. There's always tomorrow.

FOR FIVE AND A half years, I have been trying to understand how I came to be the woman who was saved by love and unmoored when it was gone. I have searched for a nugget of meaning in my childhood, something enduring, anything but the lingering body memories of sexual abuse. I have rummaged in the rubble of my memories, as if my life were the smoldering remains of a London night of German bombing.

I am trying to trace the birthplace of *me*, the me before I met Paul, before love entered my life and gave me a future. I need to know this as I try to navigate the world without him.

My childhood memories are fractured. Instead of stories, I carry a gallery of photographs in my mind. Some of them move; most are inert. They are black and white or brazenly colored. Sometimes, they emit sounds and smells. Often, they display in a long, narrow, lighted corridor that juts out perpendicularly from my left eye. The pictures merge into smokiness. The corridor can linger for days, and nothing I do will dim it. This is the broken spine of my life story.

It's tricky to trace the birthplace of pain, to pinpoint the moment of my father's first incursion into my body, the very first time I broke in two and became the Night Child and the Day Child.

Trauma can leave your surface unmarred. The damage lies hidden in depths beyond awareness until, one day, trickles of suspicion slip into consciousness and, after a while, you say, oh yes, so that's what happened. That makes sense. But when did it start? Where did it begin?

The date and geography and cultural context of my childhood? These are easy to recall.

I was born in 1943 and spent my childhood in a middle-class, multigenerational Jewish neighborhood in Flatbush, Brooklyn, surrounded by other middle-class, mostly Jewish families. These were tribal neighborhoods that flourished in Brooklyn and the Bronx in the paranoia and fear following World War II. Jews wanted to be with Jews, insulated, so they could protect each other. They did not need physical walls to make their *ghettos*.

Everyone I knew lived in Brooklyn.

My four grandparents were immigrants from Eastern Europe, *shtetl* dwellers from the Pale of Settlement, a western region of Imperial Russia that sometimes included parts of Poland. The *shtetl* immigrants were poor, mostly uneducated. Farmers, tinkers, tailors, or shoemakers, they had struggled to make a marginal living in rural, tradition-laden villages. They usually had many children; my mother's family was an exception, just my mother and her brother Marvin. They stuck together, these immigrants, once they got to America, just as they had in Russia, protecting each other from Cossack incursions and from the grating denigrations of poverty and powerlessness. Traditions of learning and orthodoxy, along with a commitment to preserving their families and Judaism, helped to keep them whole.

They arrived in steerage on stinking ships at the turn of the twentieth century, crossing into New York Harbor, passing the Statue of Liberty, and massing at Ellis Island, where they were processed. They moved in with relatives on the Lower East Side of Manhattan or other nearby immigrant enclaves. They spoke Yiddish, the *mameloshen*, the mother tongue of the European Jewish diaspora. They had finally arrived in the *der goldene medina*, the land of gold. There was no gold, but there was opportunity; they were greenhorns, living with relatives in unhealthy, dark apartments, many to a bed, but there were no marauding Cossacks on Essex Street and Jews could be Jews.

In the humid New York summers, they slept on fire escapes, clinging to tenement buildings. During the days, they joined the crowds of Jews living busy, complicated, noisy, communal lives outdoors on the streets of New York. They sold goods from pushcarts or worked in sweatshops; they "went without," as my *bubbe* used to say, everyone contributing to maintaining the precious apartments. They learned English and, with bravura or timidity, they made their way in the New World. Soon, they weren't greenhorns anymore.

The men had come to avoid conscription into the tsar's army, the women to escape poverty and persecution. They were beacons to the families they left behind; they hoped they could find a place to live, save a little money, and send for their sisters and brothers and, God willing, their parents, to join them in America.

They were hard workers, not prone to emotional sharing. Some may have been introspective, like my *bubbe*, or subtly aware of the psychic impact wrought by close quarters and poverty. They had been through a particular kind of hell and found themselves with possibilities undreamed of in the old country. They brought memories of violence and deprivation, and, I now believe, a history of violence within their own *shtetl* families that even today is barely acknowledged, as layers of European Jewish family histories unpeel.

My maternal grandparents, my *bubbe* and my *zayde*, were a comforting unit, staunch in the not-so-easy life that unfolded for them. There was no drama between them, or if there was, they kept it to themselves. Palpably, there was love.

The family had moved up from Essex Street to central Brooklyn where they were pursuing the immigrant dream of financial security and respectability. My grandfather started an umbrella factory and was joined by my uncle Marvin before he finished high school. My mother, Betty, was the smart one, graduating early from high school. Betty Shulman had dreams; she wanted to get a college degree and become a buyer at Macy's. Instead, she worked as a clerk to help support the family. Not a lot of Jewish women got to be buyers at a department store like Macy's in the 1930s. My grandparents hoped the family situation would improve and Betty could go to Brooklyn College and become a teacher.

My mother's father, my *zayde*, Abraham Shulman, had blue eyes and pale skin. A tender, tired presence, he was the opposite in every way of Abe Levy, the man my mother married.

My *zayde*'s umbrella factory went bankrupt during the Depression, leaving two families without income. It was a terrible time. Millions of people were out of work, standing on breadlines. My grandfather, the scholarly blue-eyed Pole, decided that he and Marvin would become farmers. They did not know anything about farming, but they knew about hardship and hard work, and they knew they would not take handouts.

They bought a chicken farm, trekking from urban Brooklyn to rural New Jersey, joining a small group of Jewish farmers in a community not far from the ocean. Some, like them, were forced into farming by financial extremity; others were proud to continue a venerable Jewish agricultural history. They moved to a tiny village, where the children of local farmers and laborers were educated in one room through eighth grade.

My father helped my grandfather and Marvin buy The Farm, a three-story, sprawling, white-porched homestead with a barn and an attic, and hundreds of chicken coops, which housed thousands of egg-laying chickens.

He did it to show that he was a *macher*, a big man. He never let them forget this debt.

The filthy work of running an egg farm prematurely aged my grandparents and my aunt and uncle and marked my cousins with the scars of childhood poverty. The family did not take vacations; the children wore hand-me-downs from their more affluent cousins, including me and my brother. They drank only powdered milk until they got to high school. They spent their childhood collecting eggs, cleaning coops, cooking, and helping my grandfather sort and weigh eggs by hand in the dark, damp, freezing cellar. In the mid-1950s, when I was starting high school, they bought a mechanized egg sorter.

We visited The Farm often when I was young, on long weekends, holiday breaks, and Jewish holidays like Passover. Heavy with suitcases and gifts, stuffed into my father's DeSoto (or was it the Plymouth?), we drove through south Brooklyn, took the ferry to Staten Island, drove over the Outerbridge Crossing and onto a succession of one-lane country roads, arriving after many hours and many turns at The Farm.

We open the kitchen door to the savory smells of brisket and cinnamon and put our suitcases on the gray linoleum floor, holding our gifts. In the winter, we wear our cold-weather clothes: warm, bulky, woolen coats, knitted hats and scarves, gloves, mittens, boots. Except for my grandmother, the farm family is arrayed against the far wall.

My *bubbe* steps forward, gathering me in a cushiony embrace, murmuring, "*Shayna maidele* (pretty girl), look at you. How you've grown. *Oy, mammele.* Come, you must be hungry."

A large, lumpy woman, she wears a plain, colorless cotton housedress covered by a full-body apron. Heavy black orthopedic shoes slow her pace; opaque elastic stockings encase her swollen legs. She struggles with circulation problems.

"*Bubbe*," I say, as she stretches out her arms.

"*Bubbaleh* (sweetheart), do you want to play Cat's Cradle?" She reaches into the depths of a pocket in her apron and brings out a knotted Cat's Cradle twine circle that she has prepared.

"You go first," she says.

For a few moments, there is nothing but me and my *bubbe*. We play our first round of Cat's Cradle. She has trained me well and I always win.

She throws up her hands in mock despair. "*Oy, mammele,*" she says, "someday I'm going to beat you at this game."

She hugs me one more time and turns to the waiting Brooklyn family. My cousins come forward; we are awkward for a few minutes; we haven't seen each other in months.

"So, *nu*, how was the trip?" my grandmother asks.

I felt safe and loved in my *bubbe's* house.

After lunch around the big, square dining room table, my grandmother unveils the sponge cake she has baked; it is a moistly luscious, egg-infused creation, lightly rippled in its yellow insides with stripes of cinnamon. Each year on my birthday, she sends me a package. I know what is inside, but I can't wait to open it. I cut the twine and unwrap the layers of brown paper and the three layers of tin foil. Underneath, lies an impossibly fragrant, if sometimes battered, sponge cake. She has baked it just for me. I don't know if she baked sponge cakes for my cousins; I don't remember my brother receiving a cake in the mail on his birthday.

After I came back from my first year of college, as the fringed edges of my perceptions of reality began to blur, my memory fails. I don't know when the sponge cakes stopped coming, just as I don't know when my *bubbe* and my *zayde* died. My mother kept their passing secret. I do not know where they are buried. Perhaps I was in a mental hospital when they died. But still . . . they were my grandparents.

Old anger surfaces toward my mother, who excluded me from the lives and deaths of her parents. It mostly passes. There are many other reasons for me to rage against my mother. This one lingers, though, a quiet tattoo of regret. I did not get to say goodbye to the one person who cherished me when I was young.

My grandmother carried a great burden of sadness that expressed itself in her heavy body, her deeply lined face, her red, farm work coarsened hands, and always, in her gray, shadowed eyes. Life on the egg farm was hard. But my grandmother's sadness went beyond her hard farming life. Remembering the passionate way she embraced me, but kept her distance from my father, I wonder whether she, among all the aunts, grandparents, cousins, and random relatives, suspected the nature of the darkness that infused the family from Brooklyn.

Last year, I found a rubber-banded collection of wrinkled, cracked photographs in the back of my closet. They are dated Summer 1945. My mother is wearing a plaid halter top and flaring short shorts. She is looking at me, her blonde, curly-haired, two-year-old daughter. I have three kittens on my head, one on my shoulder, two in my lap, and another wound around my ankle. We are laughing. Mother and daughter exude a careless, bonded happiness in these photos. They tell me that my mother was whole and happy, at least through the summer of 1945.

Yet the mother in these pictures is a stranger. I don't recognize her, although I know that the memory of this giggly time that the camera recorded must be part of me. I know I carry inside me the picture of the young mother who took pleasure in sharing the random sweetness of a summer afternoon with her kitten-happy, two-year-old daughter. But I can't locate the memories; they are buried more deeply than my incest wounds.

When did the mother in these photographs disappear, replaced by the bitter woman I remember? Was there an instant's transformation? Did my father threaten or strike her? Or had the repeated humiliations and the helpless witnessing of the destruction of her children build up like an accretion of hardened grease until, one day, Betty Shulman Levy was gone?

My grandmother can't have forgotten the witty, intellectual, ambitious person her daughter had been before her marriage. She had to have tried to understand what transformed her Batya into a shadow. She was an intuitive, observant, canny woman, my *bubbe*; and she loved her daughter and her grandchildren. If she suspected my father, that knowledge must have eaten her up. Maybe she shared her fears with my *zayde*, but I do not believe she spoke to my mother.

They kept their secrets, these Jews. They did not share their emotional lives; their secrecy and fear protected abusers across generations and within families. But they did not see it that way. They saw it as protecting themselves and each other, protecting Jews.

"We don't talk about these things," people said when I was a child.

"Shush, *mammele*, don't ask."

Don't ask about what? What couldn't we talk about? Was it the alcoholism of an uncle, the petty thievery of a nephew, the early forced marriage of an aunt?

"It's a *Shonda*, a shame, a *Shonda* on the family. "The neighbors shouldn't know."

Paul told me that the day I took the drug overdose in 1970 that almost killed me, my mother waited six hours to call my father to tell him that his daughter had been rushed to the hospital and might be dying. He was still at the school where he was the principal, and she worried that someone might overhear their phone conversation and learn that Abe Levy's daughter had tried to commit suicide. She couldn't let that happen. It would be a *Shonda* on the family, a blot on Abe's reputation.

As strong and thoughtful as she was, my grandmother was a woman of her generation, a Jew who had fled pogroms. She may have suspected that the perfect family in the perfect house on East

8th Street in Brooklyn was not all that perfect. But how would she know? Suspicion itself could have wrecked her body and saddened her heart; but she would not have talked about it.

After a time, my mother may not have been able to describe the incest and abuse dramas within her family. Unable to protect her children or herself and unable to leave, she may have erased her consciousness of his abuse. How else did she survive in that house for all those years?

A year after I told my children that their grandfather had molested me when I was a small child, I had lunch with my older daughter, Miranda, in a small restaurant in Croton-on-Hudson where we lived for more than forty years. She asked me about my mother, whom she had known and loved for the first four years of her life, and whom she remembered with a reverent affection.

"Do you think Grandma Betty knew?" she asked.

"I don't know," I told her. "*Did she know* is the recurring question that incest survivors ask about the parent who didn't protect them. Why didn't she do something?

"She was a kind of victim-survivor herself," I said. "She might have retreated into herself until she wasn't aware of what was happening. She might have become the Day Woman in the same way I became the Day Child."

Like many incest survivors, I carry an enduring well of rage and sadness that no one protected me and kept me safe. I have tried to forgive my mother, summon empathy for her. But the child inside me is too young to forgive. She needed her mother to take care of her and her mother wasn't there. On that child level of pain, it doesn't really matter that my mother couldn't even save herself.

I wonder what attracted my mother to Abe Levy. Was she flattered by his attention, misled by his charm? Because he was charming—he was always charming in that insidious way that abusers charm—and he must have made quite a stir when he arrived at the Shulmans' narrow stucco house on his bicycle to woo sweet, nerdy Betty. Did she hold buried secrets? Might she, too, have been the child victim of a sexual predator, an uncle or a cousin? Was she a survivor like me?

In photographs from before they were married, my father's brash smile shines out; my mother nestles against him. Her hair is bobbed; she wears a flapper outfit and a cloche hat. Her small, round glasses expose an eager, laughing face. She looks happy, untroubled, even perky, in a brainy, schoolgirlish way. Her parents, my *bubbe* and *zayde*, must have been thrilled that she was being courted by Abe Levy.

This was a *mensch*. A young man going places. Educated. A teacher. Moving up. A good catch.

Once my brother was born, in 1937, my mother gave up her job at Macy's and, with it, her dream of going to college. She never worked again. The conventions of the time and my father's needs propelled her into a life as a wife, mother, and housekeeper, roles she fulfilled grudgingly. When Paul first met her, in 1966, she introduced herself as Mrs. Principal. Betty Shulman Levy had ceased to exist.

Where my mother grew up in love, my father grew up in violence, both threatened and real.

I was always frightened of my father's father, my Grandfather Levy, a bellicose, urgent man who dominated family gatherings and infused a room with rowdy unease. He had brought his tailoring skills to the New World and had advanced from working in one of New York City's many garment sweatshops, like his brothers and uncles, to owning his own business, producing expensive, hand-finished women's dresses, coats, and suits.

I was young when my mother told me about the day my father brought her home to meet his parents. My grandfather reached boldly for her jacket, she said, and drew her toward him, inspecting the buttonholes and the seams of her suit. He held her close against his body. She shivered when she told me the story.

"The buttonholes would be better done by hand."

He let her go. What did she feel at that moment? Her shiver was a clue. By the time I was old enough to ask, my mother's emotions were locked in the fortress of her brain, memory, and nervous system. The only emotion that survived her early years of marriage to my father and the years of my brother's and my childhoods, was rage.

My grandmother Jenny Levy, my father's mother, was a wizened woman with ivory skin and colorless eyes that sank into the hundreds of wrinkles that covered her face. I don't remember ever hearing her voice. At family dinners—Rosh Hashonah, Passover, birthdays—she stayed in the kitchen or hovered at the periphery of the heavy, rectangular mahogany dining room table, picking up scraps of food after everyone had finished eating. She was afraid of my grandfather; it was a fear-based family: wife, siblings, grandchildren, daughters, and sons-in law, though everyone acted as if living in fear was the most normal, inconsequential thing.

Sometimes, in my dreams, I see my grandfather Sam Levy's large, round head with its coarse, shiny black hair swept off his face. I hear his percussive roar and I remember, with an old terror, his throwing me up in the air, bellowing "hoopla." I was very small; the gathered relatives laughed as I fell into his grasp, moments before I hit the floor. The living room and dining room are lit by lamps and a brilliant, swinging chandelier. There is the smell of brisket. My father, my grandfather, my cousins: all of us are crowded into the living room of my grandparents' house on East 7th Street in Brooklyn.

I do not allow myself to dwell for more than a moment on what it must have been like for my father, the firstborn child, to grow up in the household where Sam Levy ruled.

When she was young, my Aunt Anita told me, my Grandma Levy had been lovely, with fine skin and delicate features; a lifetime with my grandfather reduced her to a shrunken shell. I am sure that like my mother, she was not able to speak up for herself or for her children. When I am feeling charitable or weak, I acknowledge, briefly, that this environment of fear and sadism produced the monster that was my father. I allow myself a shiver of compassion, but it passes.

My father was the youngest person to become a high school principal in the history of New York City. He had benefited from the free education offered by New York's City College, and he rose quickly, passing the principal's exam in 1950. I was seven and he was in his early forties, an up-and-comer. He wrote books and a column for one of the city's evening newspapers.

He was a glad-hander and a charmer, valuable assets for a first-generation Jewish boy who spoke only Yiddish when he entered first grade, and who was storming the Protestant bastions of the New York City Board of Education. By 1955, when we moved into the downstairs of my grandmother's house on East 7th Street, my father no longer had to work during the summers as a music counselor at sleepaway camp. He was a Principal with a capital P, a big shot, and my family was solidly in the middle class.

Little survives from my childhood, but among the cracked photos from the summer of 1945, I found a later picture, this one dated 1947. It shows me and the little boy, Lewis, who lived upstairs in the house on East 8th Street where I grew up. The weather must have been cool because we are wearing chunky woolen sweaters and corduroy pants. Each of us has a play iron and ironing board; we are ironing in front of the house, just feet from a tea party we had set up with my plastic Blue Willow tea set. It, along with my childhood dolls, vanished in 1963 when my parents moved while I was incarcerated in Brooklyn State Hospital.

When I got out of the hospital, I came to live with my parents in their new apartment. My brain was burned from shock treatments and my heart was scorched from the deprivations of institutional life; my hands shook from drugs and my skin was rough. My hair was brittle, my body thin.

My mother showed me the room I would live in. I looked in drawers and the closet and under the bed for the box of childhood possessions that I had left in the house on East 7th Street the day I was taken to Brooklyn State. It was gone, and with it, the last, sad artifacts that bound me to my childhood: Sparkle Plenty with her yellow yarn hair; Yumiko, a delicate china, kimono-clad, bristly-haired Japanese doll. Gwendolyn, a skinny, pre-Barbie. My Toni doll with hair you could set in plastic curlers; and a saggy, floppy-eared stuffed dog named Maxl. And my writings: stories, poems, diaries, and letters.

My mother said she hadn't seen the box; perhaps I was not remembering accurately. Perhaps, she suggested, the box and its contents didn't exist. You could suggest things like that in the 1960s if your daughter was crazy and had just a spent a year in a state hospital.

I believe that my mother destroyed my things—that she buried or burned the box—in an attempt to obliterate my childhood. Sparkle Plenty and the flop-eared Maxl would have reminded her that once I had been a child who played with dolls; once, before incest engulfed the family in deception and I became crazy, I had washed my Toni doll's hair in the bathroom sink and placed Yumiko on the highest shelf in my bedroom to keep her safe.

I hold a deep, smoldering, unquenchable flame of rage toward my parents for this effort of obliteration and for the years of exile in institutions. The worst was Brooklyn State Hospital where my doctor and my parents planned for me to undergo that most horrific of pseudo-science horrors, insulin shock. But Brooklyn State had stopped administering insulin shock because too many people did not emerge from the insulin comas; instead, they allowed electroshock without anesthesia, which I endured for many months.

At Brooklyn State, I had a wafer-thin, plastic mattress, a meager pillow, and a worn beige cotton blanket. Mental patients moved in lines in rooms with barred windows where grim aides served gray, glutinous meals. We were always lined up. For food, for mail, for drugs. Fearful, vulnerable, under threat of shots into the muscle of your leg of burning, liquid Thorazine if you did not behave, if you cried, if you touched another patient. Shower once a week; no curtain. Guard at the door. The forced march through underground corridors to the shock room. No respite. No hope. Pain. Terrible, awful, searing pain as blood vessels burst and pieces of my mind were destroyed.

I forget and then remember this year, explosions of pain and simmering rage. They did this to me; I knew this long before I had an inkling of a memory of the crimes that scarred me, decades before I cut my wrists or experienced forced institutionalization, drugs, shock. My parents' complicity. My mother's refusal to remember.

I cannot quell this rage although I can blot it out, knowing it simmers, a zombie fire like those now consuming the deep forests of the Northwest and the wastelands of Siberia. They cannot be conquered. They will burst into furious heat when triggered. Like trauma memories, fierce, unquenchable, unpredictable.

THERE WAS ONE PERSON in the world my mother loved without apology: her Aunt Gussie, whom she called Golda. Aunt Gussie lived in a tight, brown-floored walk-up apartment in a falling-down apartment building that smelled of dirt, urine, and onions. It was on 13th Avenue in Borough Park, a center of Orthodox Jewish life in postwar Brooklyn. She lived in shadowed poverty with a grasping, stroke-damaged man named Louis whom she despised but was tied to for reasons too frightening and complicated for a child to understand. My mother told me that Aunt Gussie had almost been rich once, that she was very pretty when she was young. She had been engaged to a Grossinger, a member of the wealthy family that owned one of the world-famous Catskill Mountain resorts. It didn't work out, my mother said.

So, Aunt Gussie married Louis, who even as a young man was coarse and resentful. They didn't have children. After his stroke, Louis lived for many decades, moving from his bed to his wheelchair. Aunt Gussie took care of him. They received a small monthly check from an organization that looked out for poor Jews in Borough Park. My mother would bring treats or secondhand clothes when we visited. Gussie would not have taken money, even from her favorite niece.

Aunt Gussie's fingers were twisted into swollen sculptures of pain from arthritis, but she sewed dresses and blouses for me when I was a child and, again, for my daughter Miranda. I think my mother convinced her to take small payments for these dresses.

Often, on a Sunday, which was the day that Jewish families visited each other, we drove to see Aunt Gussie, climbing the worn stairs in the dim, smelly stairwell in Borough Park while my father and brother waited outside.

On Sundays, 13th Avenue in Borough Park was alive with pushcarts and stores with doors flung open, vendors selling everything from fruit to knives, children's clothing, shoes, crockery, and Jewish ritual items like Shabbat candles and wigs, *sheitels*, for the ultra-Orthodox women who shaved their heads and weren't allowed to show their hair or their arms or ankles once they were married. Black-clad men with *payes* (long side curls) and tall hats or *yarmulkes*, yelled and bargained; women and girls in long skirts moved in swelling groups. The cadences of Yiddish dominated, with occasional exchanges in Russian, Polish, or Hungarian. Every block had a kosher butcher, a hardware store, and many restaurants. Commerce spilled out onto the street that had been silent just the day before, Saturday, in observance of the Jewish Sabbath.

On these visits, I got a glimpse of what the Lower East Side must have looked, sounded, and smelled like in the early years of the twentieth century, during the large Eastern European Jewish migration.

My mother said that sewing gave Aunt Gussie pleasure, adding that Gussie did not have much pleasure in her life. This pleasure was so intertwined with pain that it still hurts my heart to think about Aunt Gussie, her poverty, and her twisted hands.

It is her pain-sculpted fingers I most remember, the joints and knuckles shiny, skin stretched to its limit. Wearing a faded cotton apron, she greeted me with joy.

"*Oy, shayna maidele,*" she would coo, her gray curls pressed to my head. "How big you are." And taking my mother aside, she would whisper, "*Mammele*, I'm *shepping nachas* (getting pleasure) from this girl." My mother, who I don't remember ever kissing me, would give her Aunt a kiss on her soft, wrinkled cheek.

I remember Borough Park and Aunt Gussie, the noises and smells of the streets. I remember Louis Davison in his wheelchair. But I can't remember what my bedroom looked like in the house I grew up in on East 8th Street.

I moved through my childhood in a bifurcated reality, living two lives. I was the Day Child and the Night Child. Neither knew the other existed.

Memory trolling can be perilous for incest survivors. We bury our stories in the recesses of our neurological selves to survive. The memories lie dormant.

Buried incest memories threatened to emerge when I was in high school and again in college. At first, they came as uncontrollable bouts of crying, as hallucinations, suicide attempts. By the time I was nineteen, I had been labeled mentally ill and had become my family's designated sick person. It was my job to protect my father's reputation and my family's secrets, even at the expense of my sanity.

From 1960 until I nearly died from a self-administered drug overdose in 1970, I was lost in the labyrinth of institutional psychiatry, taking massive doses of toxic neuroleptic drugs and enduring over a hundred shock treatments. I spent more than three years in mental hospitals, in private, privileged venues and a whole year in the dank, brick-walled warehouse that was Brooklyn State, a relic from the days of mass incarceration in asylums.

I did not know I was an incest survivor until I began to experience flashbacks in 1990, when I was forty-seven.

One summer weekend in the early 1980s when my children were young and I had not yet begun to have memories, Paul and I threw ourselves into an ambitious frenzy of cleaning the basement of the Dutch colonial stucco house we had bought the year my mother died, when I was pregnant with my second daughter. A month of rain had reduced the contents of the basement to a moldy morass. We sent the children out to play and, wearing rubber gloves and our oldest jeans and T-shirts, we filled trash bag after trash bag with smelly glop.

Deep within the piles of wet, deteriorated tax records, discarded books and stuffed animals, we discovered a cache of papers. There were typed poems written in 1962, when I was nineteen, the year I lived in Hilltop Hospital. There were poems and stories in a looped, childish handwriting on lined paper that did not look familiar. How had they survived the cleaning wrath of my mother, and how had they ended up in the basement of the house on Darby Avenue in Croton?

"I think I recognize my handwriting," I told Paul, as we separated damp, old sheets of paper, laying them out on beach towels to dry. I had a wisp of a shadow of a memory of writing the story about the girl imprisoned in a tower by her father who, when she was offered rescue, chose to stay in the tower. I didn't remember writing the poems, but I knew they were mine.

They spoke of yearning to fly, and escape, and of a deep, potent desire to blot out life and enter the embracing darkness of death. Death was everywhere. Stained with mildew, fragile with age, these pages had survived, like me. They evoked long-buried memories of desperation that had begun to seep into my consciousness the year I turned twelve and went to live in my dead-eyed grandmother's house on East 7th Street.

Many years after I left the house on East 7th Street, and long after the day we found my poems and notebooks, when I was already traveling the treacherous path of healing from incest, Paul and I drove to Brooklyn on a clear Sunday to visit a high school friend. She and her husband had bought an airy, square house a few blocks from the high school we both attended in the late 1950s. The house was harmonious, comforting, one among many in a neighborhood that itself seemed to promise boundless peace in an already furiously changing Brooklyn.

After our visit, before we set out for home, I asked Paul to drive past my grandmother's house on East 7th Street. I had lived in that house from the time I was twelve until the terrible year I was in the state hospital.

"Are you sure?" he asked. Yes. I was sure.

We parked across the street. It was just a house, really, not an awful house, ungainly but not offensive, bleak. An unmemorable house, as houses go.

I started to feel sick and I began to cry.

"I can see the wallpaper in my bedroom," I told Paul. "Vines and flowers twisted and twined. Green with a little pink. I remember leaving my body and hiding in the vines; I would fly out the window or wait near the ceiling.

"But now I'm not sure that's right, because it's daytime in this memory and it wouldn't have been daytime. My father only came at night. I don't want to be here. I want to go home."

I knew then that this faded house had become the repository of my childhood pain. The house on East 8th Street, where I had ironed and had tea parties with Lewis, and where my father had molested me, remained bathed in a soft, ambient light.

It is perfect; who wouldn't want to grow up in a house like this? For a moment, I am captured by my own creation: a protected childhood in the picture-perfect house with the picture-perfect family, a father who comes home every night after a hard day at work, greeted by a smiling wife just putting dinner on the neatly set, oilcloth covered table. Two exemplary children, docile and smart. I can see it all, all except my childhood bedroom. The doorway is black; I cannot enter.

This house is the creation of the Day Child. There is no Night Child here.

But the Night Child has survived, and she lives deep inside that memory-house, in my shrouded childhood bedroom. She is a terrified, wounded, damaged little girl.

She has always tried to make herself tiny; she is silent, even while she cries. She wants to scream, but she is afraid of being heard. She is hurt, she is small; she doesn't believe she is safe. When she remembers, she feels as if it is all still happening, even though she tells herself it is just a memory, her body remembering. She is afraid that it can still happen again, that she will be threatened and hurt.

The fear can paralyze her; she gags. Sometimes, she can't stop crying. But she is healing. The path is rocky; she stumbles. She misses her Paul, who has been dead for more than five years. He helped her through these bad times, caring for her with a tenderness she did not know existed until she met him. As grief and trauma memories mix to form toxic explosions in the wake of his death, she doesn't know how she will survive without that tender love.

For weeks after we visited my grandmother's house on East 7th Street, I couldn't make the memory go away: the little girl who had tried to find safety by hiding in the vines of her bedroom wallpaper. The memory had risen through my body, a dragon, roused angrily from sleep.

Bad things happened to this little girl. They may not have happened in the house of my ruined grandmother on East 7th Street, but they happened.

This is the truth about trauma memories. They migrate and morph, but the body remembers. No amount of rearranging, retouching, or reimagining can alter that.

I am a multiple survivor: of a childhood of secrecy and sexual violation; of an adolescence and early adulthood of psychiatric violence; and of more than twenty years of walking the path of healing from incest.

None of that prepared me for the grim challenge of losing Paul and of becoming a survivor of love. For the ferocious surges of grief and the wild reemergence of trauma wounds. For the vaulting ferocity of my longing and the scorching, urgent, shocking pain of my broken heart.

I used to think that humans had a lifetime allotment of tears; once they were used up, you could move on with your life and never cry again. Since Paul's death, I have learned that there are no lifetime limits on tears or pain or mourning, or the dark effects of trauma and its sister darkness, grief.

I want to know how I became me.

My Grandma Levy, my father's mother who was never *bubbe* to me, had a *pushke*, a small metal box with a slot on the top for collecting coins. The *pushke* was white with a blue Jewish star on the front and words, in Hebrew and English, directing the giver to plant trees in Israel. My grandmother would deposit pennies into the *pushke* until it was full. It would be taken away and a new one magically deposited in its place. My grandmother was not a generous woman; her life with my father's father had coiled her into a cone of reproach, but still, she had a *pushke*.

Her *pushke* sat on a narrow wooden shelf at the back of her stove, next to the simmering pot of chicken skin and fat that would be rendered into the treasured, artery-clogging, Eastern European Jewish dietary staple, schmaltz (chicken fat you could spread on fresh rye bread) and *gribenes* (chicken skin cracklings). And onions. You had to have onions.

My *bubbe* on The Farm had a *pushke*. My Great-Aunt Fanny and Great-Uncle Izzie, my Aunt Evelyn and Uncle Mike, and my friend Phyllis's family—even my virtually destitute Aunt Gussie—they all had *pushkes*. Every Jewish home I entered as a child had a *pushke*.

Except my own. My mother did not have a *pushke*. She did not belong to Jewish organizations; she wasn't a member of Hadassah, and she didn't play *mahjongg*. She did not contribute to causes, Jewish or secular. Yet a deep part of her was Jewish. She spit when she saw a Volkswagen parked on the street. She would mutter "*Feh. Dreck. Momzer*" (piece of shit, bastard), addressing the car as if it were Hitler himself. Memories of the war were fresh, and there wasn't a Jew who hadn't lost someone in the Holocaust. She expressed hatred, but not solidarity.

She cautioned me never to trust a *goy* (a non-Jew) because, eventually, every *goy* would turn on you and call you a dirty *kike*. She presided over my brother's Bar Mitzvah and hosted periodic meetings of the Levy family Cousins Club. But she didn't own a single, visible representation of her Jewishness: no Shabbat candlesticks, no *mezuzah*, no *Chanukah menorah*, no *pushke*.

We are at The Farm. It is Friday night. My mother doesn't speak as she watches the New Jersey family enact Shabbat rituals. She stands in the doorway to the dining room, pressing her arms into her chest, lips drawn. Aunt Sarah, her brother Marvin's wife, my mother's sister-in-law, closes her eyes, sways, and waves her hands in an ancient, prayerful gesture as she lights the Shabbat candles. My cousins chant the blessing. My brother and I do not know the prayers, so we watch, waiting for the completion of the *bruchah* (prayer) over the challah and the wine. We will eat the meal my *bubbe* has cooked; dessert will be sponge cake and strawberries if they are in season.

My mother's body pulsed with a ferocious energy those Friday nights. Was it a rejection of her Jewishness, a plea for modernity, an expression of her hatred for her sister-in-law, her grief that her mother and father had chosen to live on a chicken farm in New Jersey? Or was it the flame of her mournful, helpless rage at who she had become?

My mother was complicated and damaged, a loner, and an unwilling Jew. She couldn't escape her Jewishness or her life, and she got no joy from her membership in our unruly, resilient tribe.

Yet, I realize as I write this, that Jewishness defines me, cradling my mourning heart. It is woven into my core. It amplifies my voice, connecting me to Miriam and Ruth, Bella Abzug and Emma Goldman. Jewishness is my mother thread—if there is such a thing.

Invented or not, this mother thread connects me to my center, binding my life's weaving into coherence. I did not have a mother, yet I have a mother thread. That surprises, then soothes me; my mother thread is a renegade, born not from my birth family, but among the *pushkes* of my childhood.

It is the communal, historic consciousness of Judaism. It encompasses the mitzvah of *tzedakah*, the commandment to give to charity that created *pushkes*. It enfolds the spiritual heart of modern Judaism, *tikkun olam*, the imperative to contribute to the repair of the world on earth while we are here. As a nonobservant, nonreligious person, *tikkun olam* is my soul-center.

Despite the meanness and violence of my home, I absorbed this understanding of Jewishness in the Brooklyn of my childhood, among a multitude of former *shtetl* dwellers inventing new lives and sometimes being crushed in the frenzy of mid-twentieth century, multicultural New York. The *bubbes* and *zaydes*, the uncles and aunts, cousins, and great-aunts and great-uncles, the German uncle on my father's side, Aunt Mary's great-niece Seena, who wasn't exactly a relative; Aunt Gussie, sewing dresses for her great-great-niece. Some were kind, others were coarse.

Our bond of Jewishness spanned generations and continents. It contained irony, ambivalence, fortitude, passion, food, traditions, books, tragedy, literature, rage, and family love, and the wry, self-deprecating humor of the Jewish American comedians entertaining generations of Jews at the Borscht Belt hotels in the Catskill Mountains of New York. I don't believe in God; my childhood home was a locus of pain. Yet, I took into my adulthood a belief in healing, and in my responsibility to contribute to that healing and participate in *tikkun olam*. I did not have love in my childhood home, but I had *Yiddishkeit*, an unshakable Jewish identity.

My mother thread of Jewish affirmation survived my father, and shock treatments, and overdoses. It birthed my love for Paul and for my children. It was the background music that played as I escorted pregnant women to their abortion appointments in New York. It lingers in my abortion activism in New Mexico and in my grief.

My search for something of value from my childhood had first produced my father's latke recipe, my love of books and words, and my mother's gritty, survivor's strength. But I had missed this bright Jewish mother thread. Twined through and around my heart, it moves me to work for Reproductive Justice, and it presses me toward the wrenching task of learning to live again. Paul must have had this mother thread too. It guided us into advocacy for psychiatric patients. It pushed us to take our children to marches for peace and women's lives; it buoyed our spirits when we went to Washington to protest the Gulf War and again to New York City, before the invasion of Iraq. It supported me at the Black Lives Matter vigil in Santa Fe, a subtle, steady presence. *Tikkun olam*.

And I had missed the second thread as well: my *bubbe's* love, a simmering flicker that burst into pyrotechnic glory that summer day in 1966 when I met and fell in love with Paul. Love and identity: Can they stand up to the zombie sisters, to the combined power of trauma and grief?

We will see. The battleground is set.

I WAS SEVENTY-THREE when I got my first tattoo, a year and a few months after Paul died. My granddaughter Mima, who was twenty, flew down to New Mexico from Denver to be with me. I have seven tattoos now, and I think I will get more. Each has made me stronger and more resilient for reasons I do not understand but which I appreciate. I wear them as merit badges that mark my journey through grief to a new selfhood: the entwined, double red hearts; the reading glasses to honor Paul; the Tree of Life, a connection to Judaism and to my family; the Time Turner from Harry Potter; the happy cat leaving paw prints on my left arm; the multicolored aspen branch that Mima and I got, together, on my seventy-seventh birthday; and the most recent, a symbol of women's power, fragile and enduring, decorated with interlaced garlands of daisies and asters. I am thinking about my next tattoo. I haven't decided what I want; what do I need to say these days, about myself, about love, grief, power, feminism, strength?

I wonder what my *bubbe* would have thought about my tattoos.

She might not have approved or understood.

"*Nu, mammele,*" I can hear her say. "A beautiful girl like you gets tattoos? It's a little *meshuggah* (crazy) if you ask me, but what do I know? These tattoos, they make you happy? Yes? I want you should be happy."

I hear her take a big breath, see her broad bosom rise and fall, covered with a farm woman's faded apron. Her Yiddish-lilted words are achingly familiar.

"I know you miss him, my *shayna maidele,*" she says. "I wish I had known your Paul. He was special, yes?"

I nod.

"Yes, *bubbe,*" I say. "He was very special. Like you."

"Origins" is excerpted from The Tattooed Widow: A Love Story *by Janet Gotkin. This memoir has not yet been published.*

THE THIRD RULE OF FIGHT CLUB

BROOK VAN DER LINDE

ASK IF I'VE EVER SEEN *FIGHT CLUB* AND I WILL QUIETLY SHAKE MY head *no*. I will also press the sweat from my palms into the side of my pants and swallow hard to get down rocks.

When I was fourteen I fell in love with matchbooks. Or maybe not matchbooks, but fire instead. And maybe not even fire so much, but rather, the option to play with heat.

I didn't have boobs, but it felt like I had some kind of hooked lure; like I had collected a bail arm and a spool and a drag adjustment and those components together had made a reel that was sitting behind my eyes, or between my legs. The handle was in my palm, and mostly, I knew the mechanics.

By sixteen and a half I was driving. I had a car and I used it to tuck away in the back-right corner of a Barnes & Noble and steal syllables from a Dylan anthology of lyrics that I couldn't afford. One night I bought myself a cup of tea from the Starbucks at the front of the store and I sat at the window seat.

On this night I sat beside a man with brown hair and a tan face and I had matches and trolling wire on hand, as usual.

He told me he was in medical school at the University of Virginia. I don't know how old that would have made him, but I'm realizing now that it doesn't really matter because this exchange was hovering around illegal no matter how you cut it. I also don't know how our conversation ended in an invitation to his house, but it did, and I took it, and he drew a map on a dirty napkin.

Strike. Cast.

Some hours later, I parked at the foot of his driveway. He lived alone. In a brick house. I sat on the couch. It's funny how you don't plan on memorizing a couch, and you won't unless you love it or unless something happens while you're on it. In that case, your brain starts collecting photographic evidence, turns you into a composite artist, gives you the ability to create forensic sketches that include every stain and missing stitch. If nothing happens, nothing happens. Your brain will let go of the upholstery and the width of the gaps between the cushions. If something *does* happen, you could drag all the couches in town down to the station and pick that beauty, or that filthy piece of shit, out of a lineup. Blindfolded.

Anyways, I remember quickly starting to feel the young of my sixteen. And bad. I remember the reel and how the handle felt like it was slipping and realizing, all of a sudden, that I knew how to catch, but I had no idea how to beat the life out of a living thing once it's dragged to the dock. I asked him if he was excited to be a doctor. He leaned his head back and said, "It's whatever. My dad was a doctor so you know, fuck it . . ."

He asked if I'd seen *Fight Club*. I said "No" and "Let's watch it." Thirty seconds of moving pictures happened and then his arm reached around me and his body was on top and the door was fifteen feet away. With an inhale big enough to save my own life, I pulled all the flesh of my stomach in and under my ribs and made myself as close to the depth of a sheet of paper as I could. I slid out from under, and I sweat, and I sprinted to my car and it felt like my key was not made for the lock, but it's just that you have to be steady enough to connect the two. I peeled out of that cul-de-sac and looked ahead and looked down, using the interior light to read the dirty napkin map. In reverse.

It was pouring rain and I couldn't breathe so I pulled into a fluorescent-lit gas station and parked in neither a designated parking spot nor by a pump. I just stopped on a parcel of blacktop where people had to honk and cuss and maneuver to get around me. And I cried and I figured out where to get drugs and I got them and I did them with men I didn't know. And then I went home. And I crawled into my twin bed made for a child because I was one and because I thought I was ready to pull hooks out of lips, but I wasn't.

It's been eighteen years and I think about that guy every time someone innocently asks, "Have you seen *Fight Club*?" And my palms leak and my throat gets full.

He'd be a doctor now. If all went as planned, he makes money caring for people's bodies and I wonder if he knows they have hearts and that young girls have brains that are like a malleable plastic; able to be pretty well restructured but never sold as new, twice.

And I think about how men sit around with cigarettes in their mouths and quote the first two rules of Fight Club, but never the third. How that would make sense. And once in a while, I think about the mauves and the sarcoline of that couch. And then I get to thinking about matches and swivels and downriggers and the brackish, bullshit waters that are always the murkiest when you're just trying your best to grow up.

THE NEW NORTHWESTERN PERSONALITY AND APTITUDE TEST

SHAWN SOWARD BELL

INSTRUCTIONS: PLEASE USE A PEN WITH BLACK OR BLUE INK. DO NOT USE A PEN WITH RED INK. READ THE INSTRUCTIONS CAREFULLY FOR EACH SECTION. FOR THE TRUE/FALSE QUESTIONS ONLY MARK "TRUE" OR "FALSE." DO NOT MARK BOTH. FOR MULTIPLE CHOICE, PLEASE MARK THE ANSWER THAT YOU FEEL IS THE MOST CORRECT. PLEASE ONLY MARK ONE ANSWER UNLESS THE INSTRUCTIONS INDICATE OTHERWISE. ANSWER ALL OTHER QUESTIONS AS INSTRUCTED. DO NOT MAKE EYE CONTACT WITH THE PROCTOR.

Privacy Policy and Confidentiality Notice
The contents of this test are extremely sensitive and of utmost importance to the Department. We ask that you maintain complete confidentiality of the following information. If you have questions or comments, please feel free to call our hotline, or visit our website.

I have read the Privacy Policy and Confidentiality Notice and agree to the terms stated therein
__Yes __No

Basic Information

Full Name (Last, First, Middle Initial):

_____

Age:

_____

Sex:

__yes   __no

Please describe yourself using three adverbs:

_____

Candidate Characteristics. Mark each answer that is true for you. Use an X or check mark. Leave those that do not apply to you blank.

___ I am a hard worker.
___ I enjoy learning new things.
___ I am a self-starter.
___ I am trustworthy.
___ I excel in a fast-paced environment.
___ I am capable of multitasking and managing multiple deadlines.
___ I have a proven track record of success.
___ I do not cheat.
___ I do not get caught.
___ I am a team player.
___ I pay attention to details.
___ I believe in the American Dream.
___ I display strong leadership skills.
___ I am good at what I do.
___ I am self-motivated and goal-oriented.
___ I complete projects in a quick, timely fashion.
___ I will prove my worth.
___ I get results.
___ I am not crazy.

Grammar and Word Choice. Take a moment to explain the difference between:

•   Their, they're, and there

_____

•   Its and it's

_____

•   To, too, 2, II, two, and tutu

_____

•   Less and fewer

_____

•   Democratic Socialism and economic terrorism

_____

Give some examples of when the Oxford Comma is and is not appropriate, and, for every instance when it is not, explain why you are wrong:

_____

_____

Short Answer

In a few short sentences, describe your family upbringing. Be sure to include name(s) of parent(s) and sibling(s), parents' approximate combined annual income (before taxes), social security number(s), work authorization documents, and any available credit/debit card numbers, including corresponding PINs:

_____

_____

Who is your role model and why or why not?

_____

_____

In 200–500 words, please describe a meal you would prepare for guests in your home. Be sure to include special dietary restrictions or allergies such as pescetarianism, raw veganism, lactose intolerance, lactose sensitivity, gluten uncertainty, diabetes (type I, type II, or type III), etc.:

_____

_____

Literary Analysis. Please read the following segments and answer the multiple-choice questions.

I love going to Salt Lake Roasting Company. It's my favorite coffee shop. It reminds me of coffee shops in Portland or Seattle. Many of their coffees are fair trade and certified organic and the baristas are all really chill. One time I was studying there when I noticed this guy who always seemed to be there at the same time as me. I started writing a story about him. He needed a name, so I decided to call him Paul. The next time I was studying there, Paul was there as always. I saw him get up and get ready to go. Then someone he knew saw him and said "Oh, hi, Paul" I almost fell out of my chair.

This story takes place in:
a) A bank
b) A coffee shop
c) The narrator's imagination
d) The shrinking middle class

This story is most likely written from the point of view of:
a) A disillusioned snowflake
b) A hedge fund manager at the peak of his career
c) Harold Crick
d) All of the above

All of the narrative details in this story could actually happen except:
a) College students do not study
b) Salt Lake City does not have coffee shops; it has cafés
c) Paul does not have any friends
d) All of the elements could occur

One of my biggest pet peeves is when people can't be real with me. When somebody can't be their genuine self, I lose a great deal of respect for them. However, when someone can sit down and be honest with me and expect the same, it's quite refreshing. And when they can listen to me tell them that I'm not ok, that I can't feel anything and that I'm dying inside and they still accept me and love me the same, without trying to fix it, that is a true friend.

What message is the narrator trying to convey in this passage?
a) You should always tell the truth
b) Life doesn't always have happy endings
c) True friends should accept you no matter what
d) The narrator isn't trying to convey anything—he/she is just ranting about his/her disillusionment with life, society, and probably you too.

What effect would this passage have if it were written from a different point of view (e.g., second person, third person omniscient, fourth person limited, etc.)?
a) No effect—it would be the same story
b) The reader would want to be the narrator's friend
c) The reader would hate the narrator for being such a sap
d) The reader would suddenly discover the existence of the audience, only further solidifying their decreasingly paranoid belief that they were a part of the matrix and their spoon-fed religion, worldview, and ideology were all part of an incredibly complex formula written to experiment on the fragility of the human condition, causing them to wonder if their emotional equilibrium is real or drug-induced and whether their existence is really of their own free will or if they are

the insurance policy of a human copy of themself, realizing that they, in fact, are the copy, and were cultivated to be born at the age of 32 with seemingly real memories inserted into their brain, all the while hoping to win a trip to the island.

From the narrator's point of view, a true friend will:
a) Love the undesirable as well as the desirable
b) Tell you that dress certainly does not make you look fat (even though it does)
c) Go out to coffee with you
d) Find some friends for Paul

Bottle returns exist in 10 states as well as Guam. They are located inside or in close proximity to grocery stores. They are sorted by plastic, aluminum, colored glass, and clear glass. Customers save up their bottles at home and then bring them to the bottle return. After inserting their bottles into the machine, the customer presses the "Finish" button and receives a receipt. The customer receives $.05 or $.10 (depending on the location) for each bottle. They can then redeem their receipt for cash or bring it with them later for use toward their next purchase.

According to this passage, people can locate a bottle return:
a) By looking it up in the phone book
b) Near a grocery store
c) On the internet
d) Within the most profound depths of existential dread

The narrator is arguing that:
a) Bottle returns are a safe and easy way to recycle
b) Bottle returns will stop climate change
c) Bottle returns help fight systemic inequality
d) They are not ok

The strongest point of this argument is:

a) The fact that the customer receives a monetary reward for recycling

b) Most states don't find environmental sustainability economically sustainable

c) Some creationists believe in degrees of evolution

d) But obviously there is no such thing as absolute truth

Party Affiliation (Please check only one.)

__Democrat	__Drinking Party
__Republican	__The Religious Right
__Green (or Otherwise Naïve)	__The Religious Wrong
__Socialist	__Independent
__Tupperware Party	__Very Dependent
__Tea Party	__Other (Please Specify)

Emotional Well-Being. Please take a moment to answer the following question. This is important.

I have suffered from (circle any that apply):

Depression

Anxiety

Panic Attacks

Self-Harm

Disillusionment

Sexual Harassment

Bipolar Disorder

Sexual Frustration

Poor Public Speaking

Inopportune Vomiting

Walks of Shame

Messy Relationships

Self-Harassment

Night Gardening

Fact-Checking Skills Test. Take no more than 10 minutes to fact-check the following statements.

Fact: There are two LDS churches next to each other on the University of Utah campus, located in Salt Lake City, Utah. They are both next to the LDS Institute building, which doubles as an LDS church on Sundays. This is a normal occurrence in Utah.

Fact: If you're not from Utah, you probably don't know what LDS is, unless you are LDS, not to be confused with LSD.

Fact: Corvallis, Oregon is #1 in the EPA's list of green cities.

Fact: There are nine Benton Counties in the United States.

Fact: This is unremarkable.

Fact: Much like most areas directly east of the Cascades.

Fact: But don't tell the cattle ranchers. They will take over your wildlife refuge.

Fact: Oregon is the least-churched state in the nation.

Fact: Whale hunting is illegal in Utah.

Fact: Seattle, Washington holds the record for most consecutive rainy days in 1953 at 33 days.

Fact: Seattle has a high suicide rate.

Fact: Utah has a high suicide rate.

Fact: Utah is well below the national average for crime except rape, sexual assault, and incest.

Fact: The Hanford Site is a decommissioned nuclear production complex located in Benton County, in the state of Washington. It was home to the B Reactor and produced the Plutonium used in the first nuclear bomb.

Fact: The mascot of Richland High School, located in Richland, Washington, is the Bombers. Mushroom cloud logos are proudly displayed throughout the school and on letterman jackets.

Fact: Part of Richland High's fight song is "Nuke 'em! Nuke 'em! Nuke 'em till they glow!"

Fact: Washington is a strange place to live.

Fact: Oregon is a strange place to live.

Fact: Utah is a strange place to live.

Fact: I told him not to lie to me.

Fact: I have spent my entire life living in strange places.

Fact: I will never trust again.

Fact: I am a strange place.

Fact: I had been drinking.

Fact: I wish I'd had a content warning.

Fact: I thought I would be ok.

Fact: He told me it would be fine.

Fact: I didn't know what I was getting into.

Fact: He told me to be quiet.

Fact: The nightmares have returned.

Fact: He told me it wouldn't hurt.

Fact: He told me.

Fact: Or maybe he didn't.

Fact: He told me.

Fact: Everything is fuzzy.

Fact: He told me.

Fact: I don't know.

Fact: I can't remember.

Fact: I won't remember.

Fact: But that wasn't the worst part.

Fact: A ripping sound.

Fact: I blacked out.

Fact: I can't remember.

Fact: I won't remember.

Fact: ██████████████

Fact: ██████ hurting me

Fact: ██ didn't stop

Fact: I tried to scream

Fact: I couldn't ████████

Fact:  too strong ██████████████ wish ████

Fact: ██████████ not be there ███ escape. To ████████

Fact: ██████████████

Fact: ████████

Fact: █████████████████████████
██████████████████████████
██████████████████████████
██████████████████████████
██████████████████████████
██████████████████████████
██████████████ yet I'm the one who comes off as crazy.

Fact: I'm not crazy.

Fact: I'm not crazy.

Fact: I'm not crazy.

Fact: I'm not crazy.

Fact: I'm not crazy.

Fact: I'm not crazy.

Fact: I'm not crazy.

Fact: I'm not crazy.

Fact: I'm not crazy.

Fact: I'm not crazy.

Fact: I'm not crazy.

Fact: I'm not crazy.

Fact: I'm not crazy.

Fact: I'm not crazy.

Fact: I'm not crazy.

True or False: Am I crazy?

True or False: I have lied in order to spare your feelings.

True or False: I wrote this to embarrass you.

True or False: I have lied in order to get what I want.

True or False: I am almost never truthful.

True or False: But he told me.

True or False: He told me to be quiet.

True or False: I am unreliable.

True or False: I am unremarkable.

True or False: I won't be quiet anymore.

True or False: I can't remember.

True or False: Sometimes I still feel like it's my fault.

True or False: I won't remember.

True or False: I hope you lose sleep over this.

True or False: Your feelings aren't my problem.

True or False: He told me.

True or False: You should expect the unexpected.

True or False: Every morning I am disappointed to wake up.

True or False: These aren't even questions.

True or False: Are you even listening?

True or False: Alcohol is not the answer.

True or False: Alcohol can dull the pain.

True or False: He told me.

True or False: Be quiet.

True or False: He told me.

True or False: I'm not crazy.

True or False: Am I crazy?

True or False: Are you even listening?

True or False: Can you hear me?

True or False: Am I crazy?

True or False: He told me.

True or False: What is happening to me?

True or False: Please help me.

True or False: Please help me

True or False: Please help

True or False: Please he

True or False: Please

True or False:

True or

Please

True

True

Please

NEVER FORGET

RUTH MOTA

Promise never to forget
our living, our dying. For to forget
is to unthread the quilt, erase the color
that bound us in a warrior's flag
simmering through deciduous summers
our parades of rainbows
and Kaposi plums.

I won't forget how you taught me to laugh
at death. How in the hospital when the nurse left,
you lit up, hit the control button, became
salami between folding slabs of bed
your brightly woven cover waving, shocking the straight
out of bleached white walls
your night stand an altar to St Jude, patron saint of the lost
causes I have learned to favor.

The Africans won't forget
coming to your house in Santa Cruz—
how you introduced them to Doris, your virus with her control issues
and the ten remaining T cells you partied with each night.
When showing them your laundry basket full of meds
the woman from Uganda moaned, said her sister died in her arms.

Didn't even have an aspirin to give her. You marveled
how lucky to have a sister's arms embracing. Missed your sister
ever since your dad learned you were gay and threw you up against
    a wall—
yelled: *Don't come home till you become a man!*

Sing home, new home. Sing Blue Lagoon. Stilettos
and the silver Cinderella slipper dangling from your ear. Sing beach
even though you cannot reach the shore and sunlit ocean waves
even though it's winter. Sing how you surfed them. Starfish in your
    lungs—
purple anemones closing and opening your heart.

Behind the hospital where we parted
a thousand saltlick tombstones square themselves.
Rows of stone raise pale salutes of no confidence
to your doctors unused to so much death. Dead but not forgotten.
Sing vanquished. Sing victorious.

MY YEAR AS A CHEMICAL EUNUCH

HAL ACKERMAN

I. *"THE PRINCESS HOTEL"*

From the left side of the aircraft Mt. Rainier is visible in the middle distance. A mantle of snow glimmers off its crest. Traffic is light into town. The cab ride takes less than twenty minutes. My driver wears a blue turban and speaks in the lovely cadence of south Asia. Could he ever have imagined as a young man that his future self would be driving through a northern Pacific pine forest. T.S. Eliot had it right: Our beginnings never know our ends.

He finds the Princess Hotel easily. It's located in a district called Hospital Hill, which he informs me the junkies call "Pill Hill," for all the hospitals and clinics clustered within a few square blocks. Some have their own inns adjacent to them that appear from the outside quite elegant. The Princess Hotel is not elegant. During some part of its Victorian history it may have been host to literary salons and adventurous sexual pairings, but now it is a transient hostel catering to out-of-area patients.

I am buzzed through the glass door into the musty vestibule. Streaks of weakened sunlight struggle in through layers of window soot and velour curtains. The smell of something cooked in the 1940s permeates the velvet nub of purple carpet. There are religious pamphlets and bibles displayed on the varnished end tables. I am not optimistic about applying for God's help. If there is a divine puppeteer who ordains all things, then my cancer was His conscious decision, and why would I presume that carping about it is going to change His mind?

The man checking in before me wheels an oxygen tank alongside him in a shopping cart. He is frail and blotched and makes me think of a diseased elm with patches of fungus on its bark. His wife fusses over the arrangements. She moves with difficulty and seems cross with everything around her. I wonder what binds this couple. It can't be their shared maladies. They could not have expected on their wedding day to come to this. Yet there is a testy affection between them, even if they have to repeat everything four times and still don't quite hear it. Maybe that's the secret to contentment. Less communication.

The desk clerk looks not much healthier: scraggly white hair, ancient spectacles perched precariously on his broad nose. He presses a single keystroke at a time on the ancient computer, raising his hand to shoulder level before each strike. He shows the couple the key to their room and the key to the outside door and demonstrates their intricacies, warning that if turned the other way the locks will jam. He calls the locks "cantankerous." I keep myself at a distance to avoid breathing the same air. *I am young. I am strong. I am healthy*, I remind myself. Aside from a little cancer.

My room is on the second floor. I take the elevator almost as a dare. It feels like a diving bell, one of those hand-cranked cages that lowers miners into the bowels of the earth. The room is surprisingly neat. There's a decent-sized bed, cable TV, a writing desk. I test the commode, whose reliable functioning is vital to the expedition. I unpack the few articles of clothing I have brought, the three unread *New Yorker* magazines, my Walkman loaded with Mozart and Howlin' Wolf, plus the two fleet enemas that I must administer tonight along with the sixteen-ounce bottle of magnesium citrate I am to quaff. Before the radioactive seeds are implanted tomorrow morning, a series of high-resolution ultrasound images will be taken to precisely map the strongholds of cancer. The reconnaissance pictures must be clear. No internal "cloud cover" to obscure the view.

II. *"How I Found Out"*

I always thought it would be my heart.

My doctor's name is Miles Davis. I love that he's never heard of the other one. He's on the medical faculty at the university where I teach. I see him every year around my birthday for my physical. While he presses and probes and prods and palpates, he laments the state of medicine in America. He says people better not get sick in the future. His students are so dependent on technology none of them know how to use a stethoscope. He asks if I have any great writers this year. I tell him we give them all the wrong information. Who needs the competition?

He knows what I need to hear. "Your heart looks good," he says. "Blood pressure is fine, weight has stayed the same." He waits a beat and says, "and so has your height." It's the same stupid joke every year. But I give him the laugh. Because if he's joking around it means that he hasn't found anything. I've slipped under the radar another year.

I have literally *one foot out the door* when he *Columbos* me. In every episode, just when the killer thinks they've gotten away with murder, Columbo, in his rumpled raincoat, zaps them with one innocuous question that destroys their whole alibi. Dr. Davis's question is, *When was the last time we checked your prostate?* The question carries the burden of responsible upkeep. (*When was the last time you checked the tension on your fan belt?*) I mumble an unconvincing "Last year, I guess." He pages through his records. "It's been two," he says. "Why don't we do a digital?"

When Doctor Davis proposes a digital exam, he is not referring to an examination *of* the digits but an examination *by* the digits into an area beyond the digits' easy reach. I try not to clench as his gloved fingers slide in and up to the hilt. There is a long silence. And then a single, deathly "hmm." *Hmm* is not a sound you want a doctor to make. Or an airline pilot. Or a tax examiner.

"I feel a roughness on one side," he says. "Was this ever here before?"

"How the hell should I know?" I shout over my shoulder. But he knows I know, and he knows, it was not there before. The room begins to spin.

"Your prostate is small," he says. "That's good." He's working hard to tread the delicate line between optimism and alarm. He says he is going to draw some blood for a PSA test.

At this moment my ignorance of my own body is monumental. I have never heard of the term *prostate specific androgen*. PSA is still Public Service Announcement or the Poetry Society of America. The following day I do nothing to spackle in the gaps of my ignorance. If I ignore it, it can't hurt me. I recognize this as my mother's advice on how to avoid being stung by bees, which never even worked on bees.

When Davis calls the following day, there is no small talk. My PSA has come back at 11.8. I strive to hear some relief in his voice like, *You had me worried there for a second, but whew, it's only 11.8.* I ask him what's normal. I hope for fifteen. I brace myself for ten. He tells me that for a man of my age, two is acceptable, maybe three. Anything over four might be a little concerning.

"Do I have cancer?" The words clatter from my mouth like teeth onto a tile floor. He assures me there are many causes for an elevated PSA and that we should stay calm until we get the results of a biopsy. He transfers me to his nurse, who gives me the phone number of Hubert Fitch, the urologist who will do the biopsy.

If you're anything like me, the prospect of an impending biopsy has a tremendous calming effect. If I'm having trouble sleeping, I will often schedule a biopsy just for the tranquility it engenders. I let a day pass before I make the call to prove how unconcerned I am. The receptionist tells me that "doctor" (not the doctor) is booked up and won't be seeing any new patients 'til after the first of the year. That's fine with me, I tell her. I don't think it's anything too urgent. She asks my name again and my PSA. I mumble that it's somewhere in the eleven point eight–ish range. She puts me on hold for a moment. When she returns she says doctor would like to see me tomorrow.

"Tomorrow?"

"Would four o'clock be convenient?"

I feel like a Hollywood celebrity who has clout in a fancy restaurant. Or whatever the exact opposite of that is.

★ ★ ★

THE FOUR OTHER MEN in Doctor Fitch's waiting room are way older than I am. Anyway, they look older. At least I hope they look older. They're here with their wives. One woman brushes lint off her husband's collar. Another one points out a picture in a magazine they both seem to recognize. I feel heroic being here on my own. I don't need a damn buffer. I am taken into an exam room and told to undress. The shelves are lined with the tools of the urology trade: rubber gloves, finger condoms, KY jelly. Why would someone even become a urologist? I fantasize what he might think about when he comes to work.

I park my car in the same spot every morning. Reserved for Doctor Hubert Fitch. I take the long walk down the marble hallway, so smooth you could roller skate. After twenty-seven years I barely notice the painted orange stripe that guides new patients down the great hall of urology. I remember the lump in my throat the first time I passed under the twenty-four oil portraits of those white-haired, blue-eyed men. Dr. Ernst Prater, who invented the flexible catheter, was my hero. I heard him speak once in person.

I was a young man when I first arrived, with grand urological ambitions of my own. Over the years I've squeezed nine, ten thousand prostates. Some small and juicy as kiwis. Some stringy like a ball of rubber bands. Some grown to the size of a cantaloupe. Some hard and noduley like a handful of marbles. I remember every one of them. But few of the women's lips I've kissed.

We take twelve core tissue samples. A spring-loaded needle shoots three centimeters deep into the gland while I watch through a computerized digital camera. The camera is Dr. Leonard Freedman's contribution to the legacy. His portrait is in the great hall. I thought once I'd like to deliver babies. Oh, well. All work is honorable. After the biopsy there'll be some blood in the urine, blood in the stool. Blood in the semen is the one that gets to them. Some patients can't urinate when it's over. Even sitting down. It just won't come. You can read the panic in their eyes that something irreversible has happened.

You don't tell them that the results are nearly always positive. Two hundred thousand new cases every year: basketball coaches, leaders of great nations, your Uncle Milo. We still don't know what causes it. The only prevention is dying of something else first. I imagined one day my portrait hanging in the great hall. But some men are destined for greatness and others to walk beneath them in awe.

You hate telling the younger men, like this next one sitting in my office. You know what's going on in their brains. They have bitten into the fruit of knowledge. They know they have been marked. That the angel of death has not overlooked them. That even if it is not this, that something will get them. That the meter is running down and no one is feeding it any more quarters. It's that. It's the knowing. It's that now they know. And you're the one who's told them.

A PLUMP NURSE WITH tight, kinky dark hair enters with a clipboard and a barrage of questions for me.

General symptoms—weight loss?

No.

Weight gain?

No.

Fever? Bleeding gums? Coughing blood?

No. That was cumulative.

Shortness of breath? Loss of appetite? Nausea? Vomiting?

Nein, nicht, nyet, nay.

Constipation? Diarrhea?

It would be a drag to have them both at the same time.

She is unamused.

Difficulty starting urination? Dribbling after urination? Blood in urine? Inability to hold urine? Inability to achieve or maintain an erection?

This is beginning to sound like a first date.

She glances down at me with a flame that could ignite metal. *I can assure you, sir, this will not be like any first date you will want to remember.*

Doctor Fitch enters wearing a white coat over a sporty jacket and tie, accessorized with a needle the size of an elephant gun. He identifies himself as Doctor Fitch. And that is pretty much it for small talk. One may now lie on the table in fetal position or lean against the wall. The rectum is lubricated with KY jelly and a cylinder of formidable circumference is placed up inside. As the spring-loaded needle punctures me the first time, I feel a loss of breath, a breaking of the welds. Think of a bratwurst on a barbecue grill getting pierced by the tines of a long, sharp fork to see if its juices spatter. Think of this thrust and burst repeated twelve times, gathering small quantities of meat from each spot.

You may feel a slight discomfiture, Fitch says.

And yet the enjoyment of the biopsy pales before being seated across the desk from Dr. Fitch a few days later and hearing him speak words that I shall never forget.

Well, he says, *you've got quite a bit of cancer there. Cancer in nine of the twelve cores.* He seems to be congratulating me. *Your Gleason score is seven, five being the least aggressive cancer, eight being serious cancer. This cancer is treatable. If you had to get any kind of cancer, this is the best kind of cancer to get.*

I wonder if he can say cancer a few more fucking times. But I am above his seedy accusations. I've had no symptoms. In a moment one of his staff people is going to burst into the room, red-faced and perspiring, waving a fax from the imaging company apologizing for mixing up the results that will read. *Dear Recent Biopsian. Boy are our faces red. It's not you, but some other poor bastard who has to face his mortality. We regret any inconvenience this kerfuffle may have caused, and hope that you'll continue to think of us for all your cancer-screening needs.*

Surprisingly this does not happen. All the while, Fitch has been droning on about an MRI and bone scan. I explain to him that I am hopelessly overscheduled as it is. I have to get home now and make dinner for my daughter. It's a completely inconvenient time. He grabs me by the shoulders.

"With your numbers," he says, "there's an even chance your cancer may have already metastasized."

It takes a few moments for those sounds to reformulate themselves into meaning. He practically pushes me out the door. "Take the elevator to the bottom level and follow the orange signs."

THE SUB-SUB-SUBBASEMENT is like a bomb shelter. Thick concrete walls. All painted orange. They are not to protect anyone down here. We are the danger. Sick and dire people float translucently through the corridor. In a blind trance of obedience, I follow rather than flee from the signs pointing to NUCLEAR MEDICINE. I feel like my Jewish predecessors herded obligingly to the ovens.

In the deepest part of the dungeon, I am met by a lab technician with a bony bald head, thick glasses, and eyes that blaze like a man hatching plans for world domination. His name, I am sure, must be Igor. I am rammed up against a cold flat slab of glass. He ducks behind a wall of sandbags as thousands of Roentgens are sent coursing through my body. While he is waiting for the film to process, he explains that the migration patterns of prostate cancer are as predictable as ospreys. They seek out the femur, the rib cage. What he calls their vacation isles of the Pacific.

He pulls a sheet of X-ray film out of the machine and gives it a professional assessment. "I'm seeing a lot of hot spots," he says. I gasp when I see the image. It looks like Van Gogh's *Starry Starry Night*. The doctor will call me with the results, I am told. But I don't need a doctor to read the telegram from God that I've seen. *Did you imagine I'd forgotten to assign you an expiration date? Don't make me laugh. Love, God.*

It's 5:30 on a November afternoon when I return to the outside world. Everything looks alien, like I have been to another galaxy and returned a hundred years later. The sky is cobalt blue with streaks of orange and I have cancer. People walk across the promenade making weekend plans and real estate deals, and I have cancer. Their kids run before them, erratic and thoughtless. Do their parents sense something? Do they steer their kids away from me? Can they tell? Am I marked?

I drive homeward. I try to keep a future inflated in front of me, but it keeps collapsing as though I had inhaled a plastic bag. I see mental images of those pulsating points of light. Those hot spots. Those galaxies of disease. I put a Tom Waits song on that has a repeating refrain, of *Hold on, hold on, babe you got to hold on.* I put it on replay and I hold on for dear, dear life.

III. "Patty"

I don't know why I didn't let Patty come to Seattle with me. She wanted to come. She certainly deserved to come. She had arranged days off from work to come. I know why I *said* she couldn't come. She'd pack too much baggage. We'd have to stay in a nicer hotel.

"I want to be there for you," she said. She was not a woman who said such things.

"I think you'd like to think you'd like to be here. You'd hate me for missing work."

She got emotional, which was not like her, and introspective about our relationship, which was less like her still. "Maybe after all the bull about my being guarded and wounded, maybe *you're* the one who doesn't want a relationship." She wasn't wrong. We'd both been pulling away for months, each waiting for the other to pull the plug. She couldn't face the censure of deserting a cancer patient. For me, with sex and desire a distant memory, the gravitational pull between us was zero. This was not the case when we met, nine months prior. I was a salmon leaping and diving upstream to spawn.

For context, this was 1999. Online dating was in its early prime. Nothing better had ever happened for single males. Women who put their profiles on these sites had lost their most potent historical line of defense, the pretense of unavailability. They were advertising! Putting themselves up for sale or lease. Many people found the whole idea degrading. But I loved the anticipation. It was like an improv or a pick-up basketball game. Whatever happened, the interaction was absolutely unique, unplanned, a spontaneously formed molecule that would exist for that hour and then disappear or manifest into a lifetime. Anything was possible.

The first meeting with Patty was star-crossed. Nothing in our written profiles matched. Except that she was beautiful and I was a male. My daughter stopped me on the way out to scrutinize my appearance. She was a fifteen-year-old, magnificent, rebellious, too smart, too funny, too wise bundle of gorgeous neurotic energy. Her mother and I shared joint custody, so she got to torment both of us equally.

"I gotta give it to you, old man. All in all, not too terribly horrible," she praised with faint damn. "The aging *Miami Vice* look with the sport jacket over the T-shirt is pretty tired. But, I'm sure *Patty* will think it's daring and dangerous after being with all her investment bankers. And Café Vecchio. Pretty swank for you, pops. Don't you usually take them for coffee at Mirth?"

There is only one way she could have known all of this. "Have you been snooping through my desk when I'm not home?"

"She's totally wrong for you, Dad. A business consultant in high-end real estate? She's probably a Republican."

"This is a complete violation of our rules of privacy."

"You *know* I snoop on your phone calls and your internet dating sites. My birthday as your password? It's very sweet. And very predictable. And by the way, she probably posted a ten-year-old picture. That's what they all do."

The cornerstone of my relationship with Angie has always been her confidence that I'd be the one who'd always tell her the truth. Even the hard ones about God and Santa Claus. When she was five, she asked me one day if all men had penises. We were out in our little garden staking tomatoes. It was a beautiful day in June. Everything was in blossom—peas, beans, three kinds of squash. But when your daughter asks you about penises you put aside anything else you thought was important, and you give her the best answer you can. I knelt alongside her and said, "Yes, honey, all men have penises. In fact, the males of all species have penises. Dogs, cats, squirrels, goats. Having a penis is what makes a man a man." I could see my answer playing on a PBS special on *Great Moments in Parenting*. But my daughter was not interested in squirrels or goats.

She said, "Does Mister Rogers have a penis?" The question was so sincere, so lovely, so troubled, so necessary—so easy to give too much or too little or the right words with the wrong intonation.

"I've only seen him on TV," I said, "just like you, and he had all his clothes on. But, yes. I will say Mister Rogers has a penis." She digested this information respectfully, considering its source, hating to disagree, but it had to be done. She said, "I think Miser Rogers is too nice to have a penis."

Think what this child understood about men at the age of five. But when the chips are down, her father does not trust the trust he has fostered in her. He does not tell her he has cancer. A father is supposed to be his child's external kidney. To filter the world's troubles out of her life. Not to be their cause, he rationalizes.

I CAREENED INTO THE Café Vecchio parking lot fifteen minutes late. In the busy back and forth of arranging a meeting time, it had escaped our attention that the night we picked was Halloween. This is the gay community's national holiday. The entirety of West Hollywood looked like a casting call for *La Cage aux Folles*. Thousands of elaborately costumed celebrants paraded on both sides of Santa Monica Boulevard. At one red light my car was surrounded by a cluster of women dressed as outtakes from *The Vagina Monologues*, by three Black transvestites crammed into a three-part spangly dress as the Supremes, and by a dude with a stage wrapped around his waist and a puppet show going on.

Angie was wrong about Patty's picture being ten years old. In the candlelight she could easily have knocked ten years off the age she listed (fifty), no questions asked, a cool Catherine Deneuve type, wearing an expensive scoop-neck top that revealed a carefully measured sprig of cleavage. I felt way out of my league. I was okay enough looking. Middle age had redeemed the plump marshmallow body of my youth. With the short white hair and steady eyes, my dating profile moniker, Aging Astronaut, was pretty accurate. But I drove a Honda and lived in a rental. Not the specs LA women swoon for. Lately, though, I'd found a niche. Women in their forties and early fifties who had been the top girls in high school, married the fast-tracked guys they were destined to marry, got ditched after twenty years for younger versions of themselves, and were left with creamy settlements. I called them BMWDs. Badly married, well-divorced.

As I strode toward her table, the perfect first line popped into my head. "I see you came as the Pretty Girl." I stepped back to give her room to fall for me. For the smile to beam across her face like an orchid opening, that says, *Oh my God. This man's wit and charm have touched me where no man has ever gone before. Like that one ray of sunlight that reaches the back of the pyramid on the longest day of the year.*

What I got was a slight tight movement of the eyebrows and lips. Over glasses of house Chianti we opened our past-relationship baggage for inspection, patted it down for contraband, searched for hidden weapons—married too many times or not at all, too close or too distant with parents or exes. Conversation drifted into the innocuous empty calories of biographical information:

Writer. University prof.

Business consultant for high-end real estate.

Movies, plays, poetry readings, the racetrack.

Charity events. Real Estate Round Table.

New Yorker magazine. Novels. Poetry.

Wall Street Journal. Business Week.

Bob Dylan. Tom Waits.

Celine Dion. Smooth jazz.

Divorced twelve years. One daughter.

Married twenty years. No kids.

Two advantages of not having kids are that you keep your figure . . . and you don't have kids.

Again, no laugh. I walked her to her car. Her Lexus was alongside my Honda. She confessed to meeting me only because her dating consultant advised her to try someone outside her comfort zone—to expand her creative side that her husband squelched. "That's why it didn't work," I said in a last gasp of exultation. "I'm a secret billionaire masquerading as a subversive." I pointed at one of the Century City high-rises. "See that one? I just bought it."

A smile. It was she and heart-meltingly lovely. We glide into the present tense. She says her company is putting on a charity event the next night and asks if I have a tuxedo. Before I can say no, she puts her fingers over my lips. She presses herself closer. "Get one," she says.

I get one.

For both of us, appetite transcends good judgment. She expands her creative side and comes with me to plays and poetry readings, even the racetrack. I expand my Republican side and go to her charity fundraisers and silent auctions. Smart horseplayers tell you to lay off if there's no horse in the race that you love. Conserve your capital. Gamblers say different. Every race has a winner, they say. Maybe you'll get lucky. I know which one I'd like to be. And I guess I know which one I am. At this point, as George Burns has said, I'm not buying any green bananas.

Patty is with me the evening the call comes in from Doctor Fitch's office. Against my better judgment I allow her to listen in. I don't want her sympathy. She'll try so hard and I'll punish her for being inadequate. The voice on the other end tells us that the hot spots, every single one of them, are from old injuries. The cancer has not metastasized to my bones. Not that it mightn't. But it hasn't. Not yet anyway. My cancer is confined to the prostate capsule.

Patty's face is beaming like the sun hitting the secret spot deep inside the pyramid. "I've never seen anyone so happy to have cancer," she says.

"My God. Patty. You made a joke!"

With no disrespect to breakup sex or makeup sex, they are missionaries compared to non–metastasizing cancer sex. But when the party's over I still have to decide on a treatment. I've printed out boatloads of internet material about surgery and radiation that I can't bring myself to read. Each day I delay I feel the thing biting off chunks of me for dinner. Like my tumor is Popeye and my organs are spinach. I need someone to tell me what to do.

IV. "Big Paulie"

Big Paulie is a character right out of *The Sopranos*. From Brooklyn, of course. Big mug of a face. Voice like a triple-decker brisket sandwich. But a total sweetheart. If he had to break your legs, afterwards he would drive you to the hospital and water your plants. He also knows everything about everything and what he doesn't know he makes you think he knows. I dump the load of material in his substantial lap.

Didja read any of this shit? Of course not. You can't figure out your electric toothbrush. Awright we got door number one, your radical prostatectomy. Meaning they cut the thing out and throw it away. Sounds good except that they have to cut YOU open to get at it. Side effects: "incontinence and erectile dysfunction." Meaning you can't fuck and you wear diapers. So fugettaboutit.

In thirty seconds he's solved the problem. Surgery's out. It's radiation. "Which is great," I say. "There was a cute nurse working there."

She better be cute as Cameron fucking Diaz. Listen to this. They microwave your ass. Side effects? Here we go again. Limp dick and diapers. Throw in exhaustion and puking. Oh, and this is a nice touch. After all that, if any of the cells have escaped, you gotta do chemo anyway. So forget radiation. What else ya got?

"That's pretty much it."

Come on. There's got to be a door number three. This is like when we used to take the freshmen up on the roof and tell them if they didn't give the right answer they'd get thrown off. You remember the question? If you're buried up to your neck in a vat of wet horse dung and somebody throws a pail of vomit at your head, do you duck? He waits for an answer. *What are ya gonna do?*

So what are you gonna do?

"Jumping off a roof doesn't sound too bad." The first thing cancer kills is all the easy choices.

THANKFULLY THERE *IS* A door number three. The older brother of a longtime friend tells me about it. Doctor Terrence Carter is tall and lanky with the manner of a well-brought-up country boy. Before he finishes telling me about hormone blockade (officially intermittent hormone deprivation therapy) I know I'm going to do it. Not just because it sounds easy—four pills every night and a shot once a month—but because when we talk in his office, he looks me in the eye. He sees the healthy part of me, not just my symptoms. He talks about my life after treatment as something that will continue. "Cancer is frightening," he says. And suddenly everything breaks and I'm blubbering like an idiot. I'm supposed to be this parent and teacher and elder but I'm like a frightened three-year-old. When the spasm ends, for the first time I think maybe I'm not going to die.

I'm excited to tell Big Paulie about it. His response is not quite as enthusiastic.

Are ya outa ya fuckin' mind? A couple of pills every night are supposed to cure cancer? They wouldn't cure hemorrhoids.

"No! Listen to how it works. It stops your body from producing the hormone that the cancer feeds on. It does to cancer what cancer does to your body. It puts it in a state of siege. Starves it. Shrinks it down. You gotta love the irony."

What are the down sides?

"What makes you think it has downsides?"

'Cause everything has downsides.

"Okay. Well, the treatment only shrinks the tumor down. It doesn't kill it. After nine months I go to Seattle where they'll inject little radioactive seeds into what's left of the tumor. But I'm in and out the same day."

What else?

"Yeah, there is one little wrinkle. The particular hormone the cancer feeds on, that your body stops making for a year is . . . testosterone. So, I'll kind of be . . . Stop laughing, please. Testosterone-free for a year. No sex drive. No libido. My body chemistry will be like a woman in menopause. Will you stop laughing please?"

You're gonna be a chick!

"I'll be like Dustin Hoffman in Tootsie. He came out a better man."

Except he just put on a dress, he didn't have cancer. Plus he got paid like eight million dollars to do it. Plus it was a fucking movie.

"Okay, but listen. One guy in ten doesn't lose his libido. How can I not be that guy?"

He smacks me in the head. *Are you hearing yourself? One in ten is good odds?*

I'm out of choices. I have to do something. "I'm gonna do it, Paulie. I need you to tell me it's the right thing."

He puts his arm around me and assures me it's the right thing. *Just answer me this. If you grow tits, will you go out with me?*

STILL, I COME UP with reasons to delay filling the prescriptions: I need to start on the first of a month. I need to finish something I'm writing first. (Which may be the first time in history writing was used as an excuse not to do something else). Paulie explains it to me this way. He cuffs me on both sides of the head. *I get it. You don't want to be a cancer patient. Now open the damn bottle and swallow the damn pills.*

And that does it. I do and I am.

Once I start, I'm in it full tilt. I hate routines of any kind. But if I'm going to be a cancer patient, I'm going to be the best patient in the history of cancer. I force myself into regimens. Two pills in the morning, two at night. Exercises to ward off muscle decay. Calcium pills to prevent bone loss. Soy shakes for some reason about estrogen.

Illness is measured in milestones of loss. Month by month as the treatment takes effect and my testosterone level drops, crazy physical changes occur. One day the hair under my arms is gone. Then it's gone from my chest and my legs. A glob of fat accumulates around my middle. One night we're out at a Chinese restaurant with Patty's friends. I take a spoonful of soup and my entire body flushes. I break out in a full sweat. "Did it just get hot in here or is it me?" Patty's friends take a shared delight in this—my first menopausal hot flash.

Even worse are the emotional changes. I'm becoming soft and sallow. Sickeningly serene. Nothing bothers me. I *want* things to bother me. One day I'm driving—and you know how we New York drivers are—what other people call "road rage" we call courtesy. A woman in an SUV is putting on makeup, talking on her cell phone. Maybe she's got a vibrator going, I don't know. But driving is not the thing most on her mind. She cuts me off. I give her the horn. Just a polite "bip." And she gives *me* the finger. The old me would have rammed her into oncoming traffic. Instead I smile and tell her to have a nice day. What the hell kind of man am I becoming? I want to be Jack Nicholson; I'm becoming Mister Rogers. A man too nice to have a penis.

Desire diminishes. I'm out jogging one day and pass a workout center just as a group of women in leotards comes out, their young birchy bodies crackling with pheromones. Perspiration glints off their skin. The way their hands move, their arms, glimpses of exposed flesh: In past years I would have been hooked through the nose and dragged across the street to them. But now they could be nuns at prayer.

Patty and I are drifting. I've become reliant on the V pill to raise the flag. It has a curious side effect. It casts a blue haze over my entire field of vision. I take the pill Saturday night. We call the next morning our Blue Sundays. On the worst night of my life I come into the bedroom. Patty is asleep on top of the covers. Beautiful as a fawn in a moonlit glade. But as I reach toward her gift-from-God body, the thought of sex makes me slightly nauseated. I realize, it's happened. I will not be that one guy in ten. It's totally gone. My libido is gone. I am gone.

When I was in junior high I used to ask these weird questions, like where does light go when you turn off the switch? I wondered now where had mine gone? And if it will ever come back.

V. "Eunuch in a Tunic"

Eight months on the medication and my PSA is down from 11.8 to 0.05. Doctor Carter calls me a poster boy for the treatment. With the trip to Seattle a month away and the finish line at last in sight, I have a setback. It is decided that my high initial numbers *support the possibility* that *some* cancer cells might conceivably have escaped the prostate capsule and begun to migrate toward their vacation islands of the Pacific. The decision is made for me to err on the side of caution. I am to have thirty doses of "conformal beam" radiation. The idea is to create a kill zone—a ring of fire that will vaporize any cells attempting to escape.

A solid plastic sheet is placed in a vat of hot water and made pliable and then molded to the contour of my body. Six holes are cut on each side that match a series of bolts on the table so I'll be in the same exact position every time. Six weeks. Five days. Ten blasts of radiation each time. With each succeeding dose my internal temperature builds up. After two weeks my plumbing becomes inflamed. After three my organs start to boil. I wake every hour with the ferocious need to pee . . . walk like a zombie to the bathroom. Wait for the deluge. Get a dribble. Back to sort of sleep. Up in another hour. Wait. Dribble. Stagger back. Every hour. I make the mistake of looking at myself in a mirror. My skin is the color of a used bandage.

The worst is when it hits me while I'm driving. One time it was so bad I had to pull over to the shoulder of the freeway or pee in my pants. I don't even see the cop car. He leaned out of his black and white. "*Hey You. PUT THAT THING AWAY.*" I felt my neck bowing in submission. Me, who used to taunt cops and make them crazy. "I have prostate cancer," I mumbled. The shame I felt took me back to a day in 1962. One of my father's clients, a sports writer for the *New York Times*, had gotten us tickets for a New York Giants football game, back when they played at Yankee Stadium.

The Bronx was foreign territory. We got a little lost finding the stadium and all the parking lots were filled. My dad already had suffered two heart attacks and he couldn't walk far. He pulled into a lot with a chain across. The kid taking the money was maybe my age, lean with slicked-back hair. He waved us off.

"Sorry, bub, all filled."

My father wasn't a "bub" kind of guy. He wore trousers and dress shirts on weekends. He rolled down his window. I thought he was going to slip the guy a twenty. Instead, very quietly, so I wouldn't hear, he said, "I have a weak heart." Out of the car, I walked deliberately faster than he could, and pretended not to realize it. Then I made a big ceremony of slowing down for him. I wanted to distance myself from his weakness. When the game was over it had gotten cold and raw. I told him to wait out of the wind while I went for the car. I felt like a World War II scout behind enemy lines. My heart pounded and I feared that his malady had found me. I breathed easier when I found the lot.

I had never driven his car except once when he was in the hospital and I snuck it out for a ride around our neighborhood. The streets were unfamiliar. Trucks and taxis with grown-up men driving them blasted their horns at me as I made my uncertain way back. With relief I turned onto the street in the right direction. I stayed in the driver's seat and opened the passenger side door for him. "Get in, bub." He gave me a look but he got in and let me drive.

My back found a space in the indentation worn by his back. I followed the signs in the gathering dusk and made it onto the Throgs Neck Bridge. The steady thrum over the mesh roadway was hypnotic. His eyes fluttered and he drifted to sleep, like I used to do in the backseat to the familiar secure murmur of adults talking. I put the radio on softly to the classical station. I kept the car at a steady speed and changed lanes very slowly so as not to wake him. He died a month later. I've resented his weakness all these years. Only now do I realize the terror he must have felt every day knowing that the ten-ton safe that starts falling at us the moment we're born, was getting closer to crushing him.

VI. "I Am a Radioactive Garden"

A fresh breeze blows the curtains in through the partially open window of my room in the Princess Hotel. I see myself reflected in the glass: a solitary figure in a transient hotel in a strange city. The paramedic siren blaring in the distance, coming closer. I feel like I'm trapped in a *Twilight Zone* episode where the hero discovers that he has willfully placed himself into the exact circumstances that have been predicted for his demise.

I scurry down to the front desk and ask the clerk if there are any decent restaurants around. I can have no food after six p.m. (I refuse to call it my last meal.) He puts his face through an elaborate representation of cogitating, of mentally filing through a Rolodex of thoughts, until eureka, he lights up as though the final mystery of life had been revealed, and it was exactly what he suspected.

There is still an hour of daylight. Out on the street the air smells more of trees than of gas fumes. The hotel is on a steep hill. On any other day I'd ascend it robustly. Now, I don't know whether to feel strong or frail, whether to conserve my strength or flaunt it. I feel like a stranger orbiting my own life. I walk three blocks past small, neighborhood stores: printing shops, linoleum stores, beauty salons. Most of the faces on the street are Asian. The Thai restaurant is new and smart looking. Nine tables are neatly arranged with glass tops over brightly colored tablecloths. A menu is laminated into the case outside the door. I study the selections with intent confusion. I don't know what I want, if I want anything at all.

Ahead of me is the destination I had not been aware I'd been seeking. It is a tall modern building, steel and glass, with high ceilings and atriums. An elevated ramp connects its two towers. I ask a woman who is wearing a leather jacket over her nurse's uniform which bank of elevators goes to the South Tower. She answers in a rich calypso. "You right dare, darlin," She smiles at me as though she knows all my secrets.

I find but do not take the elevator to the floor where tomorrow morning ninety radioactive palladium seeds will be injected into my cancerous prostate. This is enough recon for one night. There is a modern supermarket drug store on the ground floor. I wander through every aisle. When I get to the checkout I see that I have placed into my shopping cart a set of dishes, a live plant, and a reproduction of George Washington crossing the Delaware. What am I thinking? Am I going to decorate my room at the Princess? I return all the merchandise and leave with a 59-cent Bic pen and a spiral notepad. I sit on a ledge on front of a fountain and uncap the pen. An ambulance careens past me, siren howling, heading down the hill from the direction I had come.

★ ★ ★

WHEN MORNING COMES I am up before the alarm. I am greeted at the hospital by a nurse with a psychotic cheery smile stretched tight across her face like Saran wrap. "Good morning, sir. Have we had our two fleet enemas?" I twin her hearty tone with a tinge of early morning irony and reply that yes, I have.

"And did they have their desired effect?"

"They did!"

I am no match for her conspiratorial delight. Very quickly, it's all business. I am brought into a prep room, given a hospital gown and told to undress, rolled on a gurney into the operating theater, strapped down onto a table, and given an epidural, numbed from the waist down, and an injection of something lovely. The anesthesia takes effect and everything goes into waltz time. From twilight sleep I hear murmurings of sounds as the doctors go to work. A long thin needle is inserted into my rectum. One by one, ninety radioactive palladium seeds the size of rice kernels are injected into my now shrunken prostate tumor. I encircle myself with images of friends, family, students, colleagues, their arms linked, all of them smiling at me.

I see Patty is outside the dream circle, on tiptoe looking in. When am I going to learn to be a human being? I want to leap off the table and apologize to her. "Of course you should have come here with me. I'm so sorry." But this would be a HUGE mistake, as I'm still on the operating table with a catheter up my dick. I hear the surgeon remark to a member of the operating team that my prostate is quite small and they won't need all ninety seeds. I believe I ask if that means I'd get a discount. I think he may have said yes, and that nobody had ever asked that question before.

An hour later it's over. The first time I pee it feels like I'm giving birth to a porcupine through hot barbed wire. But I am free to go. I call Patty. I get her voicemail. I take the night flight back to Los Angeles. The moon hangs outside the Plexiglas window like a glowing earlobe. They've given me some post-op instructions. *Sexual intercourse may be resumed. However initial ejaculations may be discolored brown or black or red. This is normal.*

I have clearly moved into a new dimension of normalcy. I must have dozed in the taxi because I find myself at home. Lights are on. I open the front door and I'm immersed in a warm, rich aroma that permeates the house. Patty is there. She has made me hot soup.

It surprises me how glad I am to see her. Then I see her Louis Vuitton valise. She has packed the few things she keeps here when she stays over. Her contact lens solution, a French sweater, her hair dryer. "Really?" I say. "Now? After the hard part is over?"

I reach for her arm. She isn't having it. "I'm sure you'll find whoever it is you're looking for."

"I was hoping it would be you."

"No, you really weren't. You wanted someone who looked like me."

I have no rebuttal.

She holds my hand for a moment. "You think you're easy to be with, but you're not. You say you want to be heard and felt, but I think you need to be adored and cherished in order to feel loved. And when you're not you become mean-spirited and withholding. You inflict pain with your humor. Cancer is no excuse." There is a long silence. She picks up her stuff. "I just thought you should know that."

VII. *"How Prostate Cancer Makes a Man of Me"*

With the treatment over, the manic of doing is replaced by the unbearable wallow of waiting. The thousand-pound gorilla lurking over everything is the critical PSA test six months down the road. A result over 1.0 will mean that the implants haven't worked, that the cancer is still alive and I have to go on another cycle of hormone blockade or something more radical.

I write Patty a few letters she doesn't answer. One thing hasn't changed—my belief that if I find just the right words I can penetrate any heart. To kill time I make one more humorous foray into online dating. I run an ad with the headline *OLD. RICH. DYING: Terminally ill man looking for a woman whose personality is so obnoxious she will make death a pleasant alternative.* This is LA—

178 women respond. I don't call any of them back. Which may be a step forward in my sentimental belief that I can become a better man.

Six months finally pass. I go to Doctor Davis and have blood drawn for the PSA. It comes back 0.005! The seeds have done their job. I broadcast the good news. I have painful amends to make. I call Patty. A man's voice is on her answering machine. They are a "we." I leave a non-incriminating message for her, thanking her for going the extra mile. I gear up to face Angie's wrath for having kept all of my battle a secret. She is waiting for me at home, and charges like a rabid wolf.

"I hate you!" she screams. "Asshole Jason broke up with me. I just saw him with two girls at the coffee shop."

As always, she's nine steps ahead of me. "Honey, I'm sorry," I say. "But I don't see—"

"He's just like you. He wouldn't know love if it hit him in the face. No wonder I choose fucked-up men. Look who's been my role model. You should have died. I'd be better off."

She storms off in a clomp of army boots. I sit there flummoxed. Is this why I fought so hard to save my life? So my daughter could wish me dead? Strangely, the answer is YES. And I think maybe this is the moment cancer makes a man of me. I realize I'd rather be alive hearing her wishing me dead, than dead and her wishing me alive. A moment later she comes back, throws herself on my lap with her arms around my neck, and says she didn't mean it. I push her off and in explaining that I'm a little bit radioactive, I explain what I've been through and apologize for keeping it from her.

"Daddy," she says. "I knew all along."

"Why didn't you tell me?" I say. I push back an unwanted tear.

"Why didn't you tell me?"

"Listen, baby. Jason is the big loser here. It takes at least two girls to make up for you. The right person is going to come into your life and love you for exactly who you are. Promise you won't settle for less."

She plants a kiss on my bald spot and flounces out of the room. I multiply the gesture by its weight on Jupiter. A mother has a child's love whatever she does. A father has to earn every moment of his by explaining and making safe for his child a world that still frightens him and that he's never understood. If that's the tradeoff for avoiding the pain of childbirth, so be it.

It's weird to think of cancer as a gift, but that's what it took for me to understand some simple basic truths: You choose a woman, not to sleep with but to be awake with. And if there's no one running that you love, you lay off that race. We are as long as we are and then we aren't. All that light? It's on until it's off. I want mine to keep shining as long as it can. Growing old doesn't frighten me anymore. I want to keep doing it as long as I can. I hope I'll keep some of this feeling when my testosterone fully returns, and that we are not merely products of our chemistry.

There is a battered manila envelope on the doorstep with postmarks from a world tour of exotic wrong addresses. I wonder how it ever made it here. Inside is the spiral notebook I bought at that drugstore in Seattle the night before the seeds went in. I had left it at the Princess Hotel. I open the cover. I had written one sentence on the first page:

The angel of death came looking for me tonight. I was out.

WILMA TELLS ABOUT LOUIE

MARJORIE SAISER

Louie was alone on the farm,
and my sister and I in a cold house
in town, no money, a little wood.
We stayed in bed under the quilt
while the blizzard went on.
I got up to make pancakes
and keep the cookstove going, then
back to bed, and then the knock!
I'll never forget.
He said, "It's Louie."
I shouted, "It's Louie come to see
if we're all right!"   Two pancakes
left over and he ate them rolled up with jelly.
He said, "Do you have enough wood?" and I said,
"Yes, if we're careful." He said something about
the horse, no place
for the horse so I must go.
I went to the door with him. The whine
of the wind, the horse waiting,
the reins tied to the pump handle.
Louie's coat was thin,
couldn't leave the door open to watch him go.
Nobody saw him
put his foot into the stirrup
and go. Nobody saw.
I was wearing three
pairs of socks, the quilt around my shoulders.

All those miles to town to find out if we
had wood for the stove, he rode those
terrible drifts, he must have got off and walked
a lot of it, the horse behind him. He's not dead
as long as someone remembers.
He was young, his hair
under the old chore cap, the earflaps.
We had not let the fire go out,
we had wood. His foot into the stirrup,
the shape of his shoulders in the old plaid coat.

TIME FOR LOVE

JOSEPH J. RIDGWAY

Lingering and listening,
nervously standing in
the chill and dark drizzle—
overlooking what remained
of her child,
broken and gone forever,
lying on a starry blanket
of glistening black asphalt—
she lowered her head,
sniffing the still body—
then one final glance,
before swiftly
bounding into the wet wood—
as if comprehending
life's sometimes severe and arbitrary
allotment of time
upon our love.